RETRACING THE PLATONIC TEXT

SPEP Studies
in Historical Philosophy

General Editors David Kolb
John McCumber

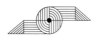

RETRACING THE PLATONIC TEXT

Edited by

John Russon
and John Sallis

Northwestern University Press
Evanston, Illinois

Northwestern University Press
Evanston, Illinois 60208-4210

Copyright © 2000 by Northwestern University Press.
Published 2000. All rights reserved.

Printed in the United States of America

ISBN 0-8101-1702-0 (cloth)
ISBN 0-8101-1703-7 (paper)

Library of Congress Cataloging-in-Publication Data

Retracing the Platonic text / edited by John Russon and John Sallis.
    p. cm. — (SPEP studies in historical philosophy)
    Includes bibliographical references.
    ISBN 0–8101-1702–0 (cloth : alk. paper) — ISBN 0–8101-1703–7 (pbk. : alk.
paper)
    1. Plato—Literary style.   2. Plato—Criticism, Textual.   3. Dialogues,
Greek—History and criticism.   4. Dialogues, Greek—Criticism, Textual.
5. Philosophy, Ancient.   I. Russon, John Edward, 1960— .   II. Sallis, John,
1938— .   III. Series.
PA4291.R48 2000
184—dc21   99–058613

Contents

Acknowledgments

The essays in this volume were initially presented at the conference "Retracing the Platonic Text," held in March 1997 at Pennsylvania State University. The editors would like to thank the participants in this conference, which included, in addition to the authors of these essays, Patricia Fagan, Gary Knoppers, David Krell, David Morris, Dennis Schmidt, Anna Vaughn, Peter Warnek, and Jason Wirth. For their support in arranging this conference, we would like to thank John Stuhr, Nancy Fedrow, and the Research and Graduate Studies Office of Pennsylvania State University. Finally, we would like to thank John McCumber and Northwestern University Press for their help in bringing this volume to publication.

John Russon
John Sallis

Just Reading: The Nature of the Platonic Text

John Russon

> You who are seated on the throne and who hold the tablets of
> writing in your hand, read [*neme*] the list so that we can see if any
> of those who swore the oath are absent.
>
> —*Sophocles*

In Book I of the *Republic*, Cephalus passes on (*paradidōmi*) his *logos* to
Polemarchus (331d), just as Cephalus himself had his wealth passed
on to him (*parelabes*, 330a–b) and as the night relay riders pass on
(*diadidōsousin*) the torch to each other (328a). Socrates himself claims
to be speaking to Cephalus because he likes to learn (*punthanesthai*)
what insight the old have to pass on, based on their experience of life's
road (328d–e). The dominant theme here is inheritance. Inheritance is a
matter of the distributing (*nemein*) of wealth. The *logos* that is the *Republic*
is passed on to us. This, our inheritance, comes to us as a demand that
we read (*nemein*) it.[1] The Platonic writings are an odd passing on, an
odd tradition, such that both the passing on and the receiving can be
described by the same verb: *nemein*. There is an odd reciprocity to this
inheritance, this writing/reading, such that it is difficult to determine
what is cause and what effect, what is original and what image.

This *nemein* that is simultaneously the giving and the receiving of
writing, like its derivative, *nomos*, "law," invokes the notion of *dikē*, "justice."
In Greek culture, *dikē* is fundamentally an issue of apportioning (*nemein*),
of rendering what is due according to *timē*, "honorableness," especially
in the context of the *dais*, "feast."[2] Anaximander has described for us the

workings of *dikē:* "According to necessity: for they give justice and pay retribution [*didonai dikēn kai tisin*] to each other for their injustices [*tēs adikias*] according to the order of time."[3] *Dikē* is the thrust and counterthrust of injustice and retribution, of *hubris,* "outrage," and *nemesis* (another variant of *nemein*), "vengeance," of reciprocal action and reaction. In sum, *nemein* seems to mean distribution within the context of justice, a matter both of handing down and of carrying on, of reciprocation.[4]

Let us now look back at Book 1 of the *Republic,* that "feast of reason" with which we began. Book 1, and the *Republic* as a whole, is an argument about *dikē,* "justice." It takes the form of a series of arguments, each of which portrays itself as complete, but is subsequently revealed to be less complete than it portrays itself.[5] Cephalus, first, shuts down the question of *dikē* almost as quickly as it is raised: He offers a definition of justice (ironically, he defines it as "paying back," that is, as *nemesis*) and considers the issue closed. Socrates, however, does not accept this closure, but shows, by his challenge, that there is more to the question, that the question of *dikē* has not been given its proper due, its proper share of discourse. Polemarchus's inheritance of the argument is equally his acceptance of the need to do justice to justice, to go beyond the putative closure of Cephalus's answer into a renewed questioning. Book 1 as a whole has often been portrayed as a self-contained Platonic dialogue on justice, similar in structure, for example, to the *Gorgias,* which is, as far as we know, complete as it stands; indeed, Socrates portrays himself here, as in the closing of his discussion with Callicles in the *Gorgias,* as having satisfactorily closed the argument. Yet Book 2 of the *Republic* begins with the recognition—this time put upon Socrates rather than Cephalus[6]—that the closure is inconclusive and that the question must be reopened. It seems that the reader—the philosopher—must play the role of *nemesis* if the argument about *dikē* is justly to be given its portion, to inherit its due. Cephalus's argument is exceeded by the whole argument of Book 1. The whole argument of Book 1, in turn, is exceeded by the argument that is the *Republic* as a whole, an argument that again portrays itself as complete as it stands. Surely the lesson is that it is as agents of *nemesis* that we must read—*nemein*—this document, this putatively complete argument: We as inheritors, as *klēronomoi,* have had distributed to us by tradition this torch that has been passed on to us by the old.[7] This marks the inseparability of philosophy and reading, at least in the Platonic context. A Platonic text cannot be read without thought, for only a philosophically challenging reading can be the agent of *nemesis* in this context.

Equally, however, a Platonic text cannot be thought without reading, that is, it is only through giving the text its due *as text* that the thought there at play can be disclosed. It is the determinacies of text that must be given their due *as determinacies of text*. Arguments—texts, *logoi*—have a momentum, a potential, of their own, and they await a torchbearer, a vehicle for their self-propulsion. In the story of Themistocles and the Seraphian (329e–330a), we see that Athens has a momentum of its own but that it needs an appropriate respondent to deliver its identity. Plato is like Athens. Plato is a textuality with a momentum of its own, but it needs an appropriate reader to deliver its message.[8] In our readings of Plato, we must be the agents of *nemesis*, working to deliver the text of its meaning by receiving as a question what initially appears closed. The just reading receives the text—the tradition—as a question. It is the reading that, as *nemesis*, provides the place—the receptacle—within which the text can judge itself and can pay for its injustices, according to necessity. The text must be given a chance to—and made to—answer for itself.

It is this question of what it is to read the Platonic text and of what else is written within the manifest discourse of the dialogues that is, in general and in specific, the question that guides the essays collected in this volume. The four essays in part 1, Plato's Other Writing, focus especially on the character of Platonic textuality and on the relation between this and the way writing is characterized within the dialogues.

How does this injunction to just reading that I have read in the *Republic* reflect on the manifest discourse of the characters in this dialogue? In the course of the discussion narrated in the *Republic*, writing—a certain poetic writing in particular—is accused of political wrongdoing, of a certain corrupting of the young, and its expulsion from the city is proposed. In chapter 1, "Another Apology," Claudia Baracchi finds inscribed in Socrates' discourse in Book 10 of the *Republic* an apology for the injustice done poetry within the *Republic* and, indeed, by philosophy itself. Baracchi reads in the Platonic text an invocation of an ultimately unpresentable source of all presentation, a mythic background to the entire realm of logical determination. The challenge to philosophy is to acknowledge justly this ground of indeterminacy that rationality and argumentation—*logos*—always necessarily cover over by resolving tensions into clear determinations and subordinating conflict and difference to the rule, that is, to the originariness, of a pure intelligibility untouched by dependence, by imitation, by repetition, by *mimesis*.

Taking as a clue the opposed portrayals of the problem of *mimesis* in Book 3 and Book 10—*mimesis* suffering from too much immediacy in Book 3 and from too much mediation in Book 10—Baracchi traces out the "logic," so to speak, of *mimesis* as it is portrayed by Socrates. In fact, *mimesis* is not discardable, but is the inevitable and necessary characteristic of any discourse that aims at the *eidetic*, at the intelligible. In other words, *mimesis* is not the characteristic of a certain class of discourses, but is the core of all discourse, all texts. Furthermore, justice itself—the *eidos* sought in the *Republic*—must itself have the character of a text, must itself be *mimetic* in its very heart. In sum, Baracchi reads in this Platonic text a vision of the creative power of *mimesis,* a creativity the very form of which is to create itself as a *re-creating,* a creating that creates itself as image, an image that retroactively enacts an original of which it is the imitation. Socrates' *mimesis,* then, is itself originary: Its own act of unveiling is itself formative of the form it unveils. This rereading of the nature of *mimesis*— of textuality—points to a reevaluation of the Platonic interpretation of the world of becoming, of time, of human affairs: It is this latter realm that in its play, in its re-creation, is the place of origination of intelligibility, of meaning. The "apology" of Book 10, then, is philosophy's admission of its betrayal of its own nurse, its own most intimate source, in its attempt to banish myth.

This essential role of the mythical is the subject of chapter 2, "The Discourses of the *Phaedrus,*" by Graeme Nicholson. The *Phaedrus* identifies three modes of discourse: myth, rhetoric, and dialectic. Nicholson first specifies the characteristics of each mode of discourse: *Myths* are a prolongation of a cultural discourse that springs from the very nature of the soul and provides the ground of rational discourse; *rhetoric* is a discourse of personal power that endorses a clear-cut ontology of clear-cut entities and is fully lodged in the present; *dialectic* is that mode of discourse, distinctive of Socrates, geared to clarification and self-understanding. Plato's philosophical discourse, however, cannot be characterized as any one of these, but is a synthesis of all three. Nicholson finds in the discourses of the *Phaedrus* Plato's most profound statement of the nature of the human soul as a complex, nonunified, not-fully-rational being; such a soul will never be capable of a discourse of pure reason, but will always be entangled with the myriad modes of discourse, especially those mythical modes that do not invoke a self-contained author.

Through further study of the *Phaedrus,* Walter Brogan, in chapter 3, "Socrates' Tragic Speech: Divine Madness and the Place of Rhetoric in Philosophy," carries forward this emphasis on the problematization of authorship and textuality in the Platonic texts. Just as the *Republic* enjoins us, as it were, to redistribute it, Brogan, describing the *Phaedrus,* notes the following:

> [T]here is an internal interpretive aspect already interwoven into Platonic writings, despite the notable absence of authorial privilege in Plato's texts. This is especially true of the *Phaedrus,* whose speeches are reinscriptions of one another. In other words, it may be fair to say that there is no original

text of the *Phaedrus*. That is, the *Phaedrus* and other similarly complex dialogues are themselves the enactment of a rewriting of a text.

This conception of the text leads to a particular conception of philosophy.

Brogan finds in the *Phaedrus* yet another reenactment of Socrates' trial, but this time it is Plato's own philosophy of writing that is forced to defend itself. Specifically, what Brogan finds in the *Phaedrus* is a notion of writing as that which disrupts the apparent self-containment of the soul and throws it beyond itself. It is specifically its metaphoric capacity that allows writing to be this chariot of the soul, and this characteristic of writing means that a rejection of the notion of the self-containment of the author and its replacement by the notions of *enthusiasm,* of having the god in one, or of *ecstasy,* of being outside oneself, is implicit in writing, by its very nature. Indeed, the failure to acknowledge this is the real failing of Lysias's speech in the *Phaedrus,* for Lysias's speech enacts the illusion of direct communication, where direct communication is what is forever made impossible by the emergence of writing. The philosophic voice, then, is never a voice of direct communication: It is a voice of madness, of myth, of the uncanny; it is "the philosophical equivalent of taking the hemlock."

If these readings are just, they seem to point to a non-Socratic vision of the philosopher: They point not to a philosopher of direct discourse in the *agora,* but to an alien philosopher of writing. Who is this philosopher? This philosopher, according to Abraham Schoener's "Not the Sophist," chapter 4, is inscribed by negation in the text of the *Sophist,* woven into the dialogue as textuality itself. Platonic philosophy is the philosophy that has shown textuality itself to be the self-concealing and de-centering ground of politics and of Socratic conversation. The philosophy of writing undermines both the presence of direct conversation and the self-presence of the author. Indeed, the philosophy of writing, with its attendant epistemology of *phantasia,* brings with it a metaphysics of the undermining of presence as such; that is, it brings with it the metaphysics of non-being hinted at in the *Sophist,* the metaphysics of *to heteron.* What is this other metaphysics, this metaphysics that is other to the study of the present determinations of an already resolved being, the metaphysics of "other" invoked by the almost inhuman surface, the very texture (*sumploke*) of Platonic textuality?[9] What is this other metaphysics, and, in its turn away from the immediacy of direct engagement between individual souls, what does it leave of Socratic practice? This is the torch passed on from part 1, the questions for which the essays in part 2, "Plato's Other Metaphysics," and part 3, "Plato's Other Socrates," try to read answers.

In part 2, "Plato's Other Metaphysics," the metaphysics of form and imitation traditionally attributed to Plato is subjected to a rereading. In chapter 5, "Traces of the *Chōra*," John Sallis considers the complex relations between the elements and the receptacle in Timaeus's second speech from the *Timaeus*. In particular, the very difficulty in identifying which element is which points us backward, behind the familiar Socratic opposition of image and original, to the *chōra*, a necessary third metaphysical player, the very nature of which is to be incapable of becoming present as a theme—a posited object—of reflection and analysis, but which shows itself backwardly in the indeterminacy that haunts the heart of the determinate identities it nurtures. Like that ineluctability discerned by Baracchi that can only be read in the very backward-referring mimetic character of all determinacy, the *chōra* functions as a sort of ground for the very determinacy that points back to it, but "it" is not "itself" one of the beings it grounds, not some other thing lying underneath, not a *hupokeimenon;* this "ground," rather, is, as the Germans say, *Abgrund,* (an) abyss, (a) non-being that, in its falling away from being, makes being possible; indeed, it is the very possibility of being. In this speech by Timaeus, the realm of intelligibility, of image and original, is itself cast into a relation of tension and struggle with this third that is both nurse to and the permanent threat of the dissolution of this intelligibility. How, then, are we to understand determinacy—presence—in the context of this ineluctable non-presence, this abyss that manifests itself in errancy, that only exists as a backward reference from that of which it is the background?

In "We Sense That They Strive: How to Read (the Theory of the Forms)," chapter 6, John Russon addresses the theme of determinacy using the claim in the *Phaedo* that learning is recollection. Russon follows out Socrates' remarks to argue that the very form taken by our immediate experience is recognition of the determinacy that embeds itself in tension-filled relations with others, all in the context of a mutual striving and measurement that inescapably invokes a context of goodness, beauty, and truth. In other words, we already sense things *as* participating in a Platonic universe. The central structure of this universe is the phenomenon of *being-with*, the *duas* of the *Phaedo*. This "with" has the form of a harmony—the "backward turning" *palintropos harmoniē* of Heraclitus—itself the necessary form of *nous*, "mind," which has not the bloodless character of abstract logic, but is more like the bacchic revelry in which Socrates says all philosophers participate. The Platonic *nous* is not a flight to another world, but is the very self-organizing and self-dismantling dynamism of this very world of embodiment, speech, strife, and *mimesis*.

If the other metaphysics of the *chōra* does indeed invoke a conception of *nous* as the contested space of reciprocal striving for the good, how are we led to read the Platonic metaphysics of "the Good"? In chapter 7, "The Idea and Mixture of the Good," Günter Figal argues that the Platonic idea of the good is inseparable from a metaphysics of human freedom. Specifically, the good is the objective by striving toward which we are able to introduce *distance* into our lives—a distance between our being as striving and the being that is our immediate determinateness. This distancing, perhaps the space of *phantasia* identified by Schoener in chapter 4, is the very space of self-questioning, of philosophy; it is the very space that resists the ultimacy of an Aristotelian opposition of practical and intellectual wisdom and allows our practice, the *vita activa,* to open onto the space of self-interpretation and clarification, the *vita contemplativa.* This metaphysics of the good, and the light it shines on human practice, thus raises again the question of the virtue of the Socratic life.

To the Stoics and most other Hellenistic philosophers, Socrates was ascetic, logical, and otherworldly. To many recent interpreters of Plato, Socrates is simply a mouthpiece for a series of doctrines, and the dramatic details of the dialogues are largely irrelevant decorations. Are either of these the Socrates written in the Platonic texts? If the Platonic dialogues invoke an "other" metaphysics of writing that leaves us always beyond the city walls before we have even begun, what is left of the Socrates who converses in the *agora*? In part 3, "Plato's Other Socrates," the character of Socrates as he is depicted in the dialogues is studied.

The image of Socrates is the central focus of chapter 8, "Retracing Homer and Aristophanes in the Platonic Text," by Bernard Freydberg. Like Baracchi in chapter 1, Freydberg begins with a reconsideration of the treatment in the *Republic* of the ancient quarrel between philosophy and poetry. Freydberg argues first that poetry and philosophy are shown by Plato to have a kinship and an opposition: a *kinship* in that they are both routes of distancing oneself from the city, and an *opposition* in that they perform this distancing in fundamentally different ways. Hinting of Figal's association of freedom and distance in chapter 7, Freydberg marks this distancing as the essence of the liberation of the soul, and poetry and philosophy both incite one to this liberation and can speak to the soul thus liberated. It is only a "city-based literalness" that is unable to take inspiration from each mode of discourse according to the specific liberatory riches it offers.

This pairing of philosophy and poetry is shown in relation to epic and tragic poetry through their operation within a variety of dialogues, but this pairing in relation to comedy is marked by Freydberg as especially revelatory of the natures of philosophy and of poetry and is to be found on display primarily in the *Apology*. Freydberg shows that Socrates' contest in the *Apology* with the "old charges" is not the contest between the real Socrates and an (Aristophanic) image of Socrates, but is rather the contest between two images of Socrates: the serious and the comic. Freydberg argues that it is the demands of a certain political situation that require the writing of such an extreme opposition of the serious, righteous, and angry Socrates of the *Apology* with the playful, mischievous, and frivolous Socrates of the *Clouds,* an opposition of images that is mediated by the less one-sided images of Socrates in the other dialogues. Freydberg shows, in sum, that the Socrates we are concerned with is an assemblage of images, but, as the political events of 399 B.C. show, these images are very much the stuff of reality.

This theme of the image of Socrates is carried forward by Francisco J. Gonzalez in chapter 9, "Giving Thought to the Good Together: Virtue in Plato's *Protagoras*." Gonzalez contrasts the characters of the *Protagoras,* Socrates and Protagoras, in their roles as images of human conduct. Through careful attention to the dramatic detail of the dialogue, Gonzalez shows Socrates to be the champion of *sunousia,* the "with" studied by Russon in chapter 6. This *sunousia,* or "being together," is understood by Socrates as dialogue (*dialegesthai*), as the shared commitment to the pursuit of the good through expression and understanding (*dia-logos*). Gonzalez shows that, rather than setting forth doctrine, all Socrates' utterances—including his violent misinterpretation of Simonides' poem—are to be understood as attempts to talk with Protagoras, that is, as utterances the meaning of which cannot be ascertained outside of their dialogic context. In particular, Socrates' question of the unity of the virtues is the key to understanding the teaching of the text, for it is the asking of this question that simultaneously discloses the duplicity of Protagoras's position and invites us to recognize the primacy of *sunousia.*

It is as such a philosopher of dialogue that James Crooks also reads the character of Socrates in chapter 10, "Writing Conversion: Notes on the Structure of the *Phaedo.*" Crooks emphasizes the theme of conversion: the turning of the soul described in *Republic* Book 7, in which the earlier identity and significance of one's whole situation is redefined. As with the traditional inheritance to which we must do justice by being appropriately active in our reception, so do our own earlier selves and personal histories set upon us demands for their responsible appropriation, and it is such a reappropriation of our own past that is that conversion of the soul that is education and philosophy. Drawing especially upon the dialogue's use of Theseus as an image of Socrates (or Socrates as an image of

Theseus), Crooks reads such a turning back upon itself as the very structure of the writing of the *Phaedo*. Indeed, the Socratic practice of midwifery and dialectic seems the practical counterpart of what Schoener identifies as the Platonic metaphysics of writing and *to heteron*, for each is the demand actively to remember—to heed the agreement we made yesterday, according to the *Sophist*, or to recollect the route that led us to our particular place in the argumentative labyrinth, according to Crooks's reading of the *Phaedo*—but to remember in a way that risks patricide, that risks a fundamental transformation of the substance of our own past. Conversion is rereading of our own selves, a self-translation that must be both faithful to determinacy and also forward-looking in its hindsight: It must be a translation that is faithful, but faithful to the living possibilities awaiting liberation, of the not-yets implicit in or on the horizon of the determinacy, and not just a dead repetition of positivities, of already closed-off meanings.

Crooks's reading of the *Phaedo*, then, and indeed all the essays in this volume, would seem to point to the art of translation as the ultimate art. In the end, the torch these essays pass on is the task of how to read Plato, of how to translate Platonic writing into education. It is this issue with which we complete (so far as we are able) our retracing of the Platonic text, with the essay that serves as the volume's conclusion, "On Translating Plato," by Eva T. H. Brann, in which that specific mode of translation that is rendering Plato into English serves as a *paradeigma*, a paradigm, for the translating—the reading (*nemein*)—of a Platonic text.[10]

It is the forward-looking character of Platonic writing and its translation that is specially addressed in "On Translating Plato." This textual prescience is the educational character of writing: It is always about to let the reader know something; it is always saying something that cannot be finished, cannot be said, without the reading partner. Brann's essay builds its interpretation of Platonic writing primarily from a project of translating the *Sophist*, the very dialogue that, as Schoener indicated, develops a metaphysics of non-being, a metaphysics that can accommodate not-yets, futures, possibilities. It seems a translator must learn this rejection of positivism, must adopt this other metaphysics, for it is this tradition of forward-looking that the translator is responsible for carrying on; and, like the Eleatic Stranger, the translator should seek partners in discourse and should not fear to offend his or her father in this project of advancing a tradition, the real significance of which is beyond his or her own ken.

This ability to transport the translator and the reader beyond themselves is the character Brann calls the "pedagogic generosity" of the Platonic writings, and it is the central feature on which all the essays in this volume draw: The Platonic writings are ready to teach the reader who is ready to learn. The contributors to this volume have many differences in their interpretations of Plato, but they share a commitment to the readability of the Platonic texts: They are commited to the possibility and the necessity of attending to the rigorous demands of accurately measuring the determinacies and of being swayed by the errancies of the text,[11] that is, of attending to the rigorous demands of reading. The writers in this volume also share a commitment to the value of the last two hundred years of European philosophy for an education into how to read in general and how to read Plato in particular. These essays are informed by an understanding of the philosophical insights of such figures as Hegel, Heidegger, Derrida, Strauss, Gadamer, and Baudrillard. It is in part through the study of these figures that the contributors to this volume have learned how to let an author like Plato teach us. In this volume, we have tried to carry the torch of Platonic philosophy by means of our appreciation of European philosophy and to pass this torch on, in the hope that a stronger English-language tradition of such a study of Plato might develop.

Notes

1. For *nemein* as reading, see Jesper Svenbro, *Phrasikleia*, trans. Janet Lloyd (Ithaca: Cornell University Press, 1993), chapter 6.

2. For a good introduction to these themes, see Gregory Nagy, "Poetry and the Ideology of the Polis: The Symbolism of Apportioning Meat," in *Greek Mythology and Poetics* (Ithaca: Cornell University Press, 1990), chapter 11; and the essays collected in Marcel Detienne and Jean-Pierre Vernant, eds., *The Cuisine of Sacrifice among the Greeks*, trans. Paula Wissing (Chicago: University of Chicago Press, 1989).

3. Fragment 1 (Diels-Kranz numbering).

4. Socrates invokes *adrasteia*, the synonym of *nemesis*, at the beginning of Book 5 of the *Republic:*

> To speak knowing the truth, among prudent and dear men, about what is greatest and dear, is a thing that is safe and encouraging. But to present arguments at a time when one is in doubt and seeking—which is just what I am doing—is a thing both frightening and slippery. It's not because I'm afraid of being laughed at—that's childish—but because I'm afraid that in slipping from the truth where one least ought to slip, I'll not only fall myself but also drag my friends down with me. I prostrate myself before Adrasteia, Glaucon, for what I'm going to say. I expect that it's a lesser fault to prove to be an unwilling murderer of someone than a deceiver about fine, good, and just things in laws. It's better to run that risk with enemies than friends. (450d–451b)

Socrates here alludes to the story of Adrastos (Herodotus 1.34–45). See also *Laws* 717d.

5. See Diskin Clay, "Reading the *Republic,*" in *Platonic Writings, Platonic Readings,* ed. Charles L. Griswold, Jr. (New York: Routledge, 1988), 19–33.

6. See lines 357a–b; Socrates denies that the argument was incomplete at 368a–b; in any case, this text shows that the issue can still be raised as a question and, for those who haven't been persuaded, it must be (see 337c).

7. This injunction to read by rewriting could also be read in the *Parmenides,* in the Platonic rewriting of the Eleatic philosophy, in the *Phaedrus,* in the repeated rewritings of the speech of Lysias (on which see Walter Brogan's discussion of the *Phaedrus* in chapter 3), in the *Menexenus,* in the rewriting of Pericles' (Thucydides') funeral oration, and so on. Compare Proclus, *Commentary on Plato's Parmenides,* trans. Glenn R. Morrow and John M. Dillon (Princeton: Princeton University Press, 1987), 29–30.

8. Compare the logic of the midwife, *Theaetetus* 149a–151d.

9. On the metaphor of weaving, see John Scheid and Jesper Svenbro, *The Craft of Zeus,* trans. Carol Volk (Cambridge, MA: Harvard University Press, 1996), passim.

10. See *Sophist* 218c–d.

11. See *Republic* 394d; *Sophist* 236d.

PART   I

PLATO'S OTHER WRITING

1

Another Apology

Claudia Baracchi

> [C]e qui serait vraiment surprenant, c'est que le son *ne pût pas* suggérer la couleur, que les couleurs *ne pussent pas* donner l'idée d'une mélodie, et que le son et la couleur fussent impropres à traduire des idées.
>
> —*Charles Baudelaire*
>
> . . . forêts de symboles . . . synergies . . .

This essay is oriented by the question of apology. The apology here at stake is not the self-defense one delivers in the courtroom, for instance, in order to preserve oneself from (or to confront?) slanderous accusations and the blind rage of public opinion. Rather, the apology here considered has to do with the acknowledgment, in speech (*logos*), of an injustice inhering in the order of speech itself.

This other apology takes place in Plato's *Republic* and has to do with a certain injustice committed against poetry. For such an injustice is, indeed, committed in the course of this discussion, whose crucial task is addressing the question of justice. (There is an injustice inhering in the pursuit of justice as purely eidetic.)

In Book 10 of the *Republic*, following the argument on imitation and before the narration of the story of Er with which the dialogue concludes, Socrates is compelled to recognize the necessity of an apology and to respond accordingly. "Well," he says,

> since we brought up the subject of poetry again [*anamnēstheisi peri poiēseōs*], let it be our apology that it was then fitting for us to send it away from the city on account of its character. The argument [*logos*] determined us. Let us further say to it, lest it convict us for a certain

3

harshness and rusticity, that there is an old quarrel between philosophy and poetry [*palaia men tis diaphora philosophiai te kai poiētikei*]. For [sayings such as] "that yelping bitch shrieking at her master," and "great in the empty eloquence of fools," "the mob of overwise men holding sway," and "the refined thinkers who are really poor" and countless others are signs of this old opposition [*palaias enantiōseōs*].(607b–c)

In this context, Socrates' apology is an inconspicuous one—self-effacing and uttered in passing. In fact, however, it constitutes a crucial punctuation in the development of the conversation.

In this essay, I will try to demonstrate the twofold and dynamic character of this other apology. Such apology, in its movement of recognition and acknowledgment of an injustice, moves beyond itself, redoubles itself, as it were—or else it displays a transformative power.

First of all, the *almost invisible* apologetic gesture takes place in *logos.* In *logos,* Socrates articulates, perhaps elusively, but unmistakably, the admission of an injustice committed against poetry. But then, second, such apology presents rather noteworthy consequences. It transfigures discourse. It makes possible a discourse in which the apology is not simply uttered, not simply pronounced or delivered. It makes possible a discourse other than the one from which the apology would simply be expelled—other than the *logos* which would relegate the apology to the exteriority of the signified and, through this simultaneously objectifying and discharging strategy, remain unaffected.[1] It opens the way to a discourse that is changed, in its structures, mode, and mood, by its *content.* It calls for a discourse that, in its unfolding, allows its own limits and injustice (the limits and injustice of discourse) to shine through, to show themselves—as such.

I should like to indicate the *muthos* of Er as such a doubling of this other apology, as that *logos* transfigured in and by the movement of the apology, as discourse (*logos, muthos*) presenting itself *as* apology.

Considering the movement of this apology will involve showing the dialogue on the *politeia* in its being at odds with itself, in its not quite matching or being adequate to its own expectations, in its failing to accomplish the task it had assigned to itself beforehand. It will involve showing how this discourse must finally (late at night) apologize for the brutality marking certain moments of its unfolding and yield (open up) to that which cannot simply be expelled, repressed, or mastered.

And yet, it is as if, in this apologetic exposure and acknowledgment of limits, discourse would open itself up and give itself according to its most proper possibility. It is as if the *apologia* of *logos* would be of *logos* in an essential way, as if it would stem from (*apo,* indeed) *logos* and interpret (that is, reveal) *logos* in one of its most essential modes. Through this movement of *apologia, logos* lights up, without, however, taking fire, but, in fact, taking place before the funeral pyre and indeterminately deferring its all-consuming ceremony.

So, I will have discussed another apology after all. And yet, before doing so, because of the nature of this other apology, I will have to discuss the *vexata quaestio* of *mimesis.* For it is because of its mimetic character that poetry is attacked, to begin with.

Thus, in order to gain an insight into the essence of the apology taking place in the *Republic,* it is necessary to turn, yet another time, to this classical philosophical *topos.* Perhaps we are still in need of a reassessment and reformulation of this issue. Perhaps the Platonic text in which the question of *mimesis* is paradigmatically discussed may give us further indications concerning this problem—it may even, perhaps, surprise us.

Mimesis

To the question of *mimesis,* then. As we all know, the problem of *mimesis,* paradigmatically in Plato's discussion, has to do with distance. The imitator's work is compromised by an excessive distance from the truth of what is. Suppose, however, that *mimesis* were a matter not so much, or not simply, of that remoteness from the source which blurs and distorts the presentation of being. Suppose, rather, that *mimesis* were a matter of a distance, broadly speaking, *inappropriate* to the bringing forth and to what is to be brought forth—a matter of being either too far from or too close to the source, a matter of missing that degree of proximity *and* of detachment which, alone, would allow for the correct contemplation (apprehension) and presentation of what is.

Suppose, then, that *mimesis* were a problem because of the inability it designates—an inability properly to negotiate between exceeding intimacy and detachment. Suppose, in other words, that *mimesis* were a matter of loss of boundaries, on the one hand, and of myopia, on the other, that is to say, of con-fusion and dimly lit outlines fading into the distance—a matter, in both cases, of a certain blindness. What would it mean, then, to speak or otherwise bring forth in a way that is free from this flaw? Can bringing forth (creating, re-creating, and procreating) ever occur without, in its very operation, disseminating deformity? If not, can speaking, *legein,* sever itself from *poiein* and, therefore, determine itself as pure gathering, as purely autonomous (because correctly distanced) presenting of what is, unaffected by the dangers of *mimesis* (*poiēsis*)? And *how* would such *logos* operate otherwise than mimetically? Perhaps, one will say, such *logos* would have to be understood as that speaking which knowingly keeps at the right distance, neither too close nor too far—as that speaking appropriately positioned with respect to being(s) and, hence, entitled to let being come forth and come through, without deformations and lies—maybe, even, as object.

Logos would, in this way, demand to be understood as that correct distancing and positioning which would resolve into pure transparency and thereby allow being to shine forth in the splendor of its truth, without any further residue.

But let us proceed in an orderly fashion. To begin with, let us briefly recall that moment, late in the *Republic*, at which Socrates develops a discussion of *mimesis* in terms of excessive distance from the origin(al). This elaboration has rather consistently been the point of reference for generations of scholars seeking Plato's conclusive and most comprehensive treatment of the issue.

Here, after having illustrated the making of the *phutourgos* (the nature-begetter), of the *dēmiourgos* (the craftsman; literally, the begetter of the or a people), and of the *zōgraphos* (the painter, a "quite wonderful sophist" [596d] and *mimētēs*), Socrates points out that the imitator, whether a painter, a "maker of tragedy," or any other such thaumaturge, is "at the third generation from nature." Indeed, "he is naturally third from a king and the truth" (597e). The imitator displays a certain mastery, a certain ability to evoke images, even in speech, as if they were alive, as if they were at all. But his mastery does not stem from his frequentation of the truth. Rather, it has the character of sorcery. It is because of an obscure (in fact, occult) power that the imitator can so effectively deceive, telling lies that sound as if they were the truth. His skill (in speaking, singing, or otherwise creating images) is joined with the danger and the power of seduction, with his ability to cast spells. Socrates claims, however, that it is possible—if one can discern—to defend oneself against this dark and darkening power. His art resting on illusion and not on the right reception of the truth, the imitator is a wizard—in no way a king. One can and must, Socrates insists, preserve (make?) this distinction.

Parenthetically, one can see here very clearly that Socrates is not concerned with "aesthetics" or with "art" in any specialistic or specialized sense, let alone with "art" or "literary criticism." What is at stake, rather, is the possibility of discerning the king from the impostor, the one whose authority rests on his being-in-truth from the one who merely seems to have some kind of commerce with truth, but in fact only exploits and perverts it, covers it over and makes it inaccessible. The problem, of course, arises because the imitator-magician is an actual challenge. Thanks to his charms, he does, indeed, have authority. His work does, indeed, have a shaping and directing power. In virtue of his cunning, he may appear as if he would preside over (*epistamai*, 597b) the truth, whereas only the king does—or should.[2]

The pronouncement against imitation is further deepened. Imitation is not even of what others created or produced, but, more precisely, it is of the way these creatures and works look. It is of their surfaces and shrouds. The mimetic procedure, we are told, does not aim at grasping the truth animating and sustaining beings, but remains essentially involved in "the phenomenon as it appears [*to phainomenon, hōs phainetai*]." *Mimesis* is not "of truth [*alētheias*]," but of phenomenality, "of the phantasm [*phantasmatos*]" (598b).

There is, thus, a blindness characterizing the imitative procedure. Such a procedure does not allow (the) truth (of being), being itself, to manifest itself in its brilliance. So remote from truth and from a genuine concern with the truth is the imitator, so absorbed is he in the play of phantasms, that his operation only allows for the faintest (most superficial) presentation of being. In the imitative work, what remains of truth is a spectral outline, a dimly lit fleeting appearance. *Mimesis* is an exceedingly distancing, hence obscuring operation. It brings forth the shadow(s) of the light.

It is worth noticing, in passing, that all making, all *poiēsis*, whether poetic or not, shares this same problem, to a degree. The craftsman, too, operates at a certain remove from the truth of being and his work, consequently, falls somewhat away from it. To a rather hesitant Glaucon, Socrates has just said that even the work of any manual artisan (*kheirotekhnēs*) "turns out to be a dim [*amudron*] thing compared to the truth" (597a). An adumbration of the truth, the work of craftsmanship, too, retains in itself a moment of obscurity, a spacing, a shadow veiling the glow of being. But the maker of images or of poems, this masterful wizard, exacerbates the problem of the darkness harbored within what is brought forth.

Socrates, thus, concludes:

> imitation is surely far [(too far) *porrō*] from the truth; and, as it seems, it is due to this that it produces everything—because it lays hold of a certain small part of each thing, and that part is itself only a phantom [*eidōlon*]. For example, the painter, we say, will paint for us a shoemaker, a carpenter, and the other craftsmen, although he doesn't understand the arts of any of them. But, nevertheless, if he is a good painter, by painting a carpenter and displaying him from far off [*porrōthen*], he would deceive children

and foolish human beings [*paidas te kai aphronas anthrōpous*] into thinking
that it is truly a carpenter. (598b–c)

Further removed from the truth (the source) of the living and even from
the degree of vision accorded to the artisan, blind to the being which
sustains all that appears and to the laws guiding the craftsman's work, the
imitator brings forth a crowd of lifeless ghosts—visions for the visionary.
The *eidōlon* is what remains of the *eidos,* after even the integrity of the
phainomenon has been lost.

This fruit of distance, however, possesses a strange power. It may
appear to be true, to be alive, to be guided by understanding and vision.
This is the case when such fruit of distance is, in turn, perceived from a
distance, by the many foolish (myopic, mind-less) human beings, or, say,
by children, whose souls, in their receptiveness, are especially defenseless
(and who so unabashedly delight in the plays of phantasmagoria). Here
lies the sinister threat of the imitative work. Itself the result of a heedless
drifting away from being, it induces further departures in those it charms.
Like the sirens' singing, it can seduce those exposed to it and bring about
hallucination, aimless wandering, errancy. Even shipwreck.

We all know this very well. We've heard them say it innumerable
times. But where does the maker of *logoi* stand in this connection, he
whose project was (and is), in and through *logos,* to bring the just city
into being? Again, can *logos,* under any circumstance and in any of its
modes, give itself in a simply and purely nonimitative fashion? Even if it
brings forth cities? Even if the enterprise of bringing forth cities takes
place within the city, in a place where the city as such is already somewhat
in view? In brief, what do Socrates' reflections on the problem of distance
in imitation reveal concerning Socrates' own *logos* as it unfolds in the
Republic? A brief detour is necessary, at this point, in order to address
these questions.

The task undertaken in the *Republic* is to gain an insight into the
essence of justice. What does this have to do with the making (building)
of the city? Is such making accessory or necessary?

The founding of the just city is undertaken only for the sake of
the investigation of justice. At the end of the founding effort, in Book
4, Socrates will notice that, precisely because articulated by reference
to the extrinsic dynamics of the city, the determination of justice thus
achieved (justice as attending to one's own) is merely "a kind of phantom
[*eidōlon*] . . . that is also why it is helpful" (443c). The procedure of the
political founding is, then, on Socrates' own terms, mimetic. It is a *mimesis*
of the being (*idea*) of justice. The just city is a ghost of justice.

At that stage of the dialogue, after having attained a first provisional
determination of justice, Socrates readily dismisses that in virtue of which

such insight was gained. He does so by minimizing and dissimulating the importance of the path, the *hodos*, which led to such realization. He reminds his interlocutors that the just city founded in speech is, after all, but an image, a figure, a ghost of justice—an imitation. As such, it is but a stage in the ascent to the contemplation of justice, that is, to the determination of the essence of justice in *logos*. This will be the philosopher's reminder, at the end of the founding exercise—as if the founding moment could and should be left behind, as if, in fact, it should be forgotten, shown as inessential and, consequently, dispensable. As if, again, *logos* could be purified from its imitative-poietic diversions, and be brought simply to say (to present) the truth of justice.

And yet, at the beginning of the enterprise, the founding of the city appears to be not so much a helpful stratagem as the *conditio sine qua non* for something like an investigation of the essence of justice to take place at all. Indeed, according to Socrates' own words, the city (phantastic and phantasmatic as it may be) comes *first* in the order of vision (of the vision of justice), and it grounds that order as such in its manifoldness. The truth of justice is harbored within the city brought forth in *logos* and can be glimpsed at only through the figure of the city. Far from being the derivative (merely helpful) semblance of justice, then, the spectral city appears to be indispensable for the contemplation of justice. Even more precisely, it appears to be that through which justice originally gives itself to contemplation and becomes at all visible (imaginable). This is the truth of the ghost town.

Would it be the case, then, that the making of the just city in *logos*, rather than representing (imitating) justice, would bring justice forth— as such? Not quite, not simply. The disconcerting complexity of the issue at stake demands utter caution in proceeding.

The just city is brought forth as a figure of justice. For it is only through the envisioning of such a figure that justice can be *found* and *captured*. Indeed, as Socrates points out at the outset, the investigation concerning justice "is no ordinary thing, but one for a man who sees sharply." He adds, however, "since we are not clever [*deinoi*]" and don't see sharply enough to "read little letters from afar," it will be necessary to consider "the same letters . . . but bigger and in a bigger place . . . if, of course, they do happen to be the same" (368c–d).

The turn to the founding of the just city is precisely that through which justice can be brought closer, as it were, and made visible. There is no other way of reducing the interval separating one from justice, of positioning oneself closer to justice itself. The making of the just city is the unavoidable detour which those must take who, like Socrates and his interlocutors, are not *deinoi* enough to discern justice itself. Because of their structural myopia, the construction of the city becomes that which, *alone,* can provide them with an access into the exceedingly removed, unreadable essence of justice. This is why, after surmising that there is "justice of one man" and, surely, "of a whole city too," Socrates concludes:

> So then, perhaps there would be more justice in the bigger and it would be easier to observe closely. If you want, first we'll investigate what justice is like in the cities.(368e)[3]

It is secondary, after all, whether the question of justice be observed in the human being (in the order of the *psychē*) or in the organism of the *polis*—whether, that is, this question be approached through a psychological or a political synecdoche. What is crucial is that the question of justice cannot be answered with a direct, unmediated turn to justice. *Justice itself eludes the gaze,* and insight into it can be gained only in terms of something other than justice in which justice belongs, only by turning to that which justice informs, that whose order justice is—namely, the *eidōlon* of the *eidos.* But then, is the *eidōlon* still to be understood as a fallen image?

It should also be emphasized that a continuity is clearly implied between the order of the essence of justice and its *eidōlon,* the *polis.* No separation or essential distinction is posited between them—no contrast between the invisible region of the objects of noetic contemplation and the diaphanous (yet brightly imaginal) domain of becoming in which the city belongs.[4] The riddle of justice itself is simply written in letters too small and too far to be read. The nearsighted, looking out into the distance, can discern only confused, shimmering shadows—hence the necessity of observing the text of justice there where it is presented in a magnified version, as if through a converging lens. The elaboration of the just city is such a tele-scopy. No bridge between radically discontinuous orders is involved, not even a transliteration: The letters of justice are simply brought closer and to a "bigger place." Imitation, then, far from merely representing (and in a distorting way) the bare remnants of truth, emerges as *that thanks to which the truth of justice, justice in its being, can be at all divined.*

But, in this way, *finding* the essence of justice appears to be intimately intertwined with the *founding,* with the making of the city-*eidōlon.* The determination of justice would be crucially involved in (indeed, indistinguishable from) the emergence and construction of the city. Even more precisely, the *destiny (history)* of the eidetic (the eidetic, then, has a destiny) would depend on the becoming of the city that is being produced. And finding, dis-covering, contemplating would no longer be clearly distinct from founding and in general from the deep involvement in becoming which characterizes all making.[5]

But what has *mimesis,* in this way, come to designate? In order to read (find, determine) justice, the just city (at once magnifying device and magnified image) must be built. But such a building would have to presuppose what it must make readable. That is to say, it would have to presuppose justice itself as a model of the city, if the city has to be just and prepare (foreshadow) the apprehension, the coming forth of justice. It would have to assume what it cannot read, in order to make it readable. Or perhaps such a making would proceed in the dark, without a model or guidance. But then, how would a making, a production proceeding in this way be that through which the letters of justice are brought closer, as it were, and read?

One begins to wonder whether mimetic production, *mimesis tout court,* is at all a matter of the idea (the truth of being) guiding the more or less adequate making (re-presentation) of the *eidōlon,* or whether the building may perhaps take place in the dark, blind, without directives, only retrospectively allowing for the emergence of the idea (abstracted from the creation). And one wonders, too, whether the alleged inadequacy of *mimesis,* its obscuring operation and failure to see well may in fact be recast in terms of originary lack, of a radical withdrawal of eidetic directives—directives which *mimesis* would paradoxically be called to re-present but, properly speaking, would invent (re-present *and* present). Otherwise, one wonders how, if not as a purely and discernibly eidetic directive, the idea of justice would *inform* the building of the just city. Indeed, what is it that would guide a making even in the dark, where and when vision fails and guidance is not in view—since proceeding in the dark might still not amount to pure errancy, to a random development? Perhaps, the knowledge of the user, rooted in the practice and experience of the user, would provide (be) such guidance? (But what or who would be the users of justice? How to speak of the use and user of justice, how to bring together the thought of the user and the question of justice, without remaining caught in the embarrassment of this semantic awkwardness?) A final difficulty: What would that idea be like, which would be originally—written? Is justice always already a text, a script, a scripture, an inscription—written letter(s)?

We must leave these questions open, for now. Here we should limit ourselves to emphasizing the inevitability of *mimesis* at the heart of that discourse whose aim is to find an access to the eidetic, to (the) truth (of being). It turns out that Socrates, too, who makes the just city in *logos,* is a *mimētēs,* a *mimētēs* who, thanks to the making of the political *eidōlon,* achieves a certain determination of the *eidos*—if not its production. His determination elucidates, and in this sense un-veils, justice—but does so *originally,* in a somewhat originary fashion. And this occurs despite

Socrates' own dictum according to which "none of the craftsmen [let alone the imitators] fabricates [*dēmiourgei*] the idea itself [*idean autēn*]" (596b).

Unless, of course, Socrates' "logical" founding (founding in *logos*), in its power literally to found the eidetic, is to be considered as divine making (begetting). For, in fact, the *theos-phutourgos* of the *Republic* is the author of nature—and not of nature as the shadow of being, as is the case with the celestial *dēmiourgos* of the *Timaeus,* but of nature as that which is (being is, therefore, created).[6] He is the maker of *phusis* as being, of the eidetic as such (597d). In fact, he *desires* (*boulomai*) to be such *poiētēs* (597c–d). Socrates' making, however, is the making (invention) of the eidetic thanks to the necessary detour through the *eidōlon*—in *logos.* Hardly a divine deed, or perhaps, indeed, one so divine that it would demand a radical rethinking of the *theos,* of *logos,* and of making (even divine), in the light of a certain necessity encompassing and presiding over them. It would demand a rethinking of making as a creating which is, to *begin with,* re-creating. And this not in the sense of re-presenting, but rather in the sense of making *again,* never out of nothing.

Between divinity and sorcery, between creation, thaumaturgy, and visionary evocation, Socrates hovers, bringing together modes of making which are inextricably intertwined and may in fact be virtually indiscernible—if certainly not the same. And certainly not brought out of nothing.

For isn't the city already there, with its order and disorder, as the vision of the just city is brought forth in *logos*? Does the dialogue not take place within the embrace of the living city? What if it were *this* city, *this* life which envelops and sustains (grounds) all dialogue, all gathering, and consequently all making (of being and of its alleged images)? What if being (the *eidē*), and not simply its phantoms (*eidōla*), would come to manifest itself in and through the palpitating and becoming of the city in deed? How to understand this other kind of priority, this other origin whose ineffability would be other than that of the transcelestial realm?

As Socrates also asks,

> Do you suppose that if a man were able to make both [*amphotera dunaito poiein*], the thing to be imitated and the phantom [*eidōlon*], he would permit himself to be serious about the crafting of the phantoms and set this at the head of his own life as the best thing he has?

Certainly not, we are asked to reply. Rather, Socrates adds,

> if he were in truth a knower [*epistēmōn*] of these things that he also imitates, he would be far more serious about the deeds [*en tois ergois*] than

the imitations and would try to leave many fair deeds behind as memorials of himself and would be more eager to be the one who is lauded than the one who lauds.(599a–b)

Can these words of Socrates, he who divines *and* invents being through its *eidōlon* (justice through the just city), be heard as an acknowledgment of the priority of deeds (becoming)? Of this realm which, in the light of a certain intertwinement (if not con-fusion or collapse) of the mimetic and divine comportment, turns out to be more *and* less, other than the middle in a tripartite hierarchy? Such an acknowledgment might be the gesturing toward the unsayable priority of that which hosts the dialogue—the priority of that locus (a *shared* place) always already in sight whenever a dialogue (*dia-logos*) takes place: the priority of the dwelling where the gathering occurs, of the city above and its movements, of the agitation down at the port—and of all-embracing night, brightened by the flickering lights of the torch race for the goddess. Of everything which is, in deed; which is and works; which lives.

However we are to understand and resolve the riddles posed by *mimesis,* the pervasiveness of its operation is now evident. But this, to tell the truth, was already intimated in Book 3. This early discussion of *mimesis* presents quite unique features, irreducible to and even in tension with the later thematization. Here we will not be able to do justice to the argument, but will briefly recall it in order to problematize the notion of *mimesis* even further.

In Book 3, it is a certain immediacy that Socrates names *mimesis.* Imitation would have to do with a lack of distance, with an excessive, compromising intimacy with truth—with too direct, hence blinding, an exposure to truth. The imitative logic of con-fusion, in Socrates' view, essentially informs the speaking of poetry—dramatic as well as epic. The problem of *mimesis* is illustrated by reference to the Homeric *epos.* A distinction is drawn between the opening lines of the *Iliad,* in which "the poet himself speaks," and what follows this inception, in which the poet speaks "as though someone other than he were speaking" (393a).[7] It is this coinciding of the poet and the character, this speaking in one voice, that Socrates proceeds to call mimetic. For "isn't likening himself [*homoioun heauton*] to someone else, either in voice or in looks [*skhēma*], the same as imitating [*mimeisthai*] the man he likens himself to?" It seems, then, that "he [Homer] and the other poets make the narrative through imitation [*dia mimēseōs tēn diēgēsin poiountai*]" (393c).

On the one hand, through this erasure of distance, the voices and deeds evoked emerge in their brilliance and directness. The self-subtraction of the poet, then, is for the sake of a more vivid bringing forth. As the poet recedes and disappears toward the background, those he sings of acquire their own voice, as it were, and seem in fact to sing themselves, of their own accord.

On the other hand, though, the dazzling clarity of this way of poetic elocution involves a delusion, an occultation which, in Socrates' account, *seems* to be deliberate and unnecessary. Indeed, Socrates observes that "[i]f the poet nowhere hid [*apokruptoito* (*apokruptō*)] himself, his poetic work and narrative as a whole would have taken place without imitation" (393c–d). Perhaps, then, this cryptic operation would be—dispensable?

What Socrates seems to be pointing to, as he discusses *mimesis* in terms of direct speech, is a certain indifferent, indiscriminate readiness to (re)produce everything and anything—to consider "nothing unworthy of oneself," and hence to undertake "seriously to imitate in the presence of many everything we were just mentioning—thunder, the noises of winds, hailstorms, axles and pulleys, the voices of trumpets, flutes, and all the instruments, and even the sound of dogs, sheep, and birds" (396e–397b). Just so do children act in their plays (plays which, parenthetically, disclose the world to them and, through mimicry and repetition, open them up to learning the ways and correspondences of the world). And yet, time and again the impossibility imposes itself of simply excluding imitation and its danger. Time and again we are reminded by Socrates that even the diction of the one who is "beautiful and good" may have to be imitative to some degree or other. Such a diction "will participate in both imitation and the other kind of narrative, but there'll be a little bit of imitation in a great deal of speech [*en polloi logoi*]" (396e).

As the shadow of a cryptic receding from pure and full manifestation, the ghost of imitation would, thus, haunt even these discourses. Even Socrates' own. After all, let this be said in passing, the dialogue on the *politeia* is narrated by Socrates. And it is preeminently by resorting to direct speech, to the mimetic evocation of other voices, that Socrates recalls the conversation which, we are told, took place the day before. And what to say about that other narrator behind Socrates, that other one who makes Socrates remember and narrate, even write? What to say of this one, who writes dialogues but himself never speaks, who never says anything in his own voice, and rather speaks "as though he had become" someone else, indeed, many others? If the dialogues of this narrator behind Socrates are, in general, the locus of the hiding of their maker, this dialogue (on the *politeia*) unfolds thanks to a double gesture of self-dissimulation—that of Socrates, through whose voice the interlocutors are enacted, and that of Plato, as always completely disappearing behind the scene.

But then, if the mimetic element (however one is to understand *mimesis,* at this point) cannot simply be expunged from discourse; if, that is to say, (logos) never seems simply to position itself at the appropriate distance, neither too close to nor too far from the truth—then the whole question should be recast in terms of *comportment toward the ineluctable*. In this case, however, the charge of mimetic obscurity brought against poetry appears to be impertinent, merely contentious, even irrelevant. For in no way does the contamination of *mimesis* concern poetry alone. The preoccupation surrounding poetic power is now revealed as exquisitely ethical. The problem is that of the comportment, the *ēthos*, toward the irrepressible and unassimilable remainder of darkness harbored within saying, any saying, and constantly threatening to resurface with its unrest and disquiet. Yet, in Book 3 and Book 10 as well, it is the thematization of *mimesis* which dominates the argumentation-accusation concerning poetry.

That is perhaps why, albeit so inconspicuously, in the end (to be sure, very late in the dialogue), Socrates clearly intimates the necessity of an *apologia*. In the end, as a transition from the last remarks on imitation and poetry to the presentation of the *apologos* of Er. It has become evident that, in condemning poetry on the ground of its mimetic character, Socrates has let himself be carried away and determined by those concerns which now appear to have been merely strategic. Hence the necessity of his apology. Let us again recall its inception:

> Since we brought up the subject of poetry again, let it be our apology
> that it was then fitting for us to send it away from the city on account of
> its character. The argument determined us. Let us further say to it, lest it
> convict us for a certain harshness and rusticity, that there is an old quarrel
> between philosophy and poetry. (607b)

Socrates allows his own argument against essentially imitative poetry to appear in its one-sidedness and vulgarity—to appear in its error and purely contentious character, that is, in its injustice.

Apologia

Thus, in Book 10, after it has become clear that the "greatest accusation against imitation" concerns, in fact, the dangers of the use and misuse of this uncanny (uncontrollable) power, Socrates apologizes for having been carried away by *logos* in his determination to expel or control poetry.[8] The argument, as he now recognizes, determined his line of inquiry in advance. The ancient quarrel between poetry and philosophy, the question concerning how to distinguish the king from the magician (impostor), the preoccupation with the invocation of the poets' authority in order to authorize (hence crystallize) existing practices and *nomoi*[9]— all these concerns have determined the unfolding of the dialogue and the per-verse assertions against poetry. The accusation, the *katēgoria* must therefore be withdrawn or, at least, qualified. Emended by an *apologia*— an *apologia* put forth not as the self-defense of the accused but as a realization of the accuser.

What the accuser now realizes is, most importantly, his own inability simply to determine the essence of justice—to secure the thinking of justice to a purely eidetic order and to say (to present) the truth of justice. Only thanks to such determination and such securing would it be possible to subtract the exercise of justice, once and for all, from dangerous impostors and charlatans.

This other apology, then, articulates the acknowledgment that the *logos* is indebted, and indebted in such a way as not to be able appropriately to give back what it owes. It promised, in advance, to give something that it cannot give. What surfaces is the inadequacy of the *logos* to give back "in full" the essential determination of justice owed to the just ones.[10] If *mimesis* (its darkness and blindness) has obscurely, if variously, accompanied the unfolding of the dialogue, the dialogue could not possibly accomplish that which it set out to, namely, the determination of justice in its essence.

Hence, this other apology is necessary not simply in order to emend the attack against poetry, but because of a structural inadequacy of the account (*logos*) itself. This is not, therefore, the apology of the discourse retaining a certain sovereignty, a certain mastery over itself (as if the apology were either a formality leaving the *logos* unaffected or a game of auto-affection). Through this apology, the *logos* comes to show itself beyond its self-possession and self-legitimation. *Logos* comes forth in the admission of its own limits, of limits it does not even properly own and therefore cannot appropriately account for.

The lie of *mimesis* (if it is a lie) is not simply controlled, like a necessary but dangerous *pharmakon* safely in the hands of a doctor (389b).

And the apology takes the form of a letting be, letting poetry be— of a becoming-poetry, even, there where *logos* ceases, remains mute. Socrates' other apology, then, will have been less a defense than an exposure, a self-exposure, and a defenseless one at that. An openness. A letting poetry (*muthos*) shine forth—and not in order surreptitiously to achieve, by all means necessary, the much pursued far-reaching vision and closure, truth lighting up in its fullness. Letting poetry be—even in its own shadow, darkness, blindness. For this is what the *muthos* of Er (this myth of *lēthē*) intimates: *muthos* as *logos* lighting up, but not as full illumination, unable simply to burn and do away with what resists, challenges, obscures. Such is the story Er is said to have told—a story in the midst of which a moment of irreducible blindness (*lēthē*) operates and surfaces *as such*—immeasurably punctuating the movement of birth, the coming into the light.

It is in this way, among other things, that the systematic, often violent repression of poetry, on which so much of the project of the dialogue rested, is interrupted. It is interrupted even in its transposition as purely logical *agōn*, as conflict in speech. It is interrupted even as the sublimation of *agōn*. What remains (or, perhaps, thereby begins) is a wandering discourse, illegitimate in many ways. It is a discourse exposing (enacting) the quarrel (*diaphora*), the *diapherein* (an ancient one, of philosophy and poetry) as such, a discourse agitated by an irresistible movement of divergence, an irreducible antagonism, giving itself, *also*, as a secret intimacy.

Notes

1. This is the dream of the transparency, disappearance, and, hence, of the formality of *logos*.

2. *Epistamai* is revealed as a matter of nearness, of proximity. Hence, knowing becomes manifest as a matter of ruling (presiding over) from a position of intimacy.

3. Notice, here, the theme of the foreignness of that which is near, the invisibility of it. Indeed, the distance here at stake should not be thought (measured) as if it were a merely spatial problem.

4. With respect to this point, see contrasting passages such as *Phaedo* 79a.

5. We must read *inventio*, in its twofold sense.

6. Accordingly, the task would be to think being as *ergon*.

7. It is worth noticing that at this juncture Socrates neglects the invocation opening the Homeric poem whereby the Muse is called to sing through the poet. In this light, the speaking of "the poet himself" should be understood in terms of divine inspiration, indeed, possession, that is, in terms of the self-dispossession characterizing the experience of *enthousiasmos*. Socrates later on mentions dithyrambs as exemplary of the nonimitative mode of speaking that proceeds "by the poet's own report," unlike tragedy and comedy, which proceed in a thoroughly mimetic fashion (394c). This very remarkable moment in the dialogue cannot here be given the attention it deserves. In this context, suffice it to present a couple of observations in outline. In the first place, according to Socrates' remarks, one would most properly be oneself and speak in one's own voice precisely when *undergoing* the experience of the Muse speaking through one, that is, when *becoming* the place of the resonance and momentary dwelling

of the divine. Second, by introducing a distinction *within* poetry, a contrast between imitative and nonimitative poetic modes, Socrates is complicating the issue, making it impossible merely to attribute the mimetic function to poetry in general and to reduce the contrast of imitative and nonimitative discourses to the contrast of poetry and philosophy.

8. In Book 3, at the beginning of the discussion leading to the expulsion of poetry from the just city, Socrates had observed, "You see, I myself really don't know, yet, but wherever the argument, like a wind, tends, thither must we go" (394d).

9. See, for example, Book 1.

10. Socrates introduces the *muthos-apologos* of Er concluding the dialogue as an attempt at gesturing toward "the prizes, wages, and gifts" awaiting the just ones after death. "And these things," he says, "should be heard so that, in hearing, each of these human beings will have gotten back the full measure of what the argument owed [*ta hupo tou logou opheilomena*]" (614a).

2

The Discourses of the *Phaedrus*

Graeme Nicholson

n considering discourses here, I have in mind two different things. First
of all, following the most natural sense of the word, I mean the three
main speeches of the *Phaedrus:* the speech attributed to Lysias in which
a man not in love praises nonlovers over lovers; then the first speech of
Socrates that continues to diminish lovers; and finally Socrates' second
speech that restores lovers to a place of honor. Socrates and Phaedrus
themselves discuss the three speeches in the later pages of the dialogue,
and in this way I'm just continuing the discussion that they began.

Second, I have in mind a contemporary philosophical sense of the
word *discourse* to signify a certain *kind* of speech or a certain *way* of using
language, and I mean to bring into the foreground three different kinds
of speaking that occur in the *Phaedrus,* three modes of discourse that
Plato himself calls myth, rhetoric, and dialectic. There will be a fair
amount of coincidence between my two senses of the word *discourse,*
because the three modes of speech can be treated in connection with the
three speeches. I'll be considering rhetoric mainly in connection with
the speech of Lysias; dialectic mainly in connection with the first speech
of Socrates; and myth in connection with Socrates' second speech.

In dialogues such as the *Euthyphro,* the *Ion,* and the *Gorgias,* I
understand the figure of Socrates to represent philosophy itself, and in
his encounters with the advocates of religion, epic poetry, and rhetoric,
we see a line of demarcation that Plato is drawing between philosophy and
other forms of learning and culture. In fact, Plato's works have remained

influential in establishing for succeeding centuries the distinct profile of philosophy—lines of demarcation between philosophy and poetry, philosophy and religion, philosophy and rhetoric. But my thesis is that the *Phaedrus,* probably belonging to Plato's middle or late period, is no longer engaged in drawing lines of demarcation. Socrates is still very much the philosopher here, and he continues to practice his accustomed art of questioning, the art of dialectic, but he is able to mix the voice of myth and the voice of rhetoric with the voice of dialectic.

First of all, Plato has put him into a scene of great natural beauty along the river Ilissos, and, inspired by the beauty and divinity of this scene, Socrates is led into discussions about mythology. In his own great speech, he will launch into a vast mythological discourse about the soul. He is bringing his dialectic into the closest connection with myths. Moreover, the dialogue shows Socrates ready to enter into a rhetorical competition with a famous orator, Lysias, and the subsequent discussion will show a Socrates who is not nearly as hostile to rhetoric as he had been in earlier works such as the *Gorgias.* Indeed, his own speech is a highly polished work of rhetoric and is so described and so praised in later pages of this dialogue.

The *Phaedrus* is a dialogue in which Plato, confident of the integrity of philosophy, confident of the strength of his dialectic, does not need to resist other forms of culture, but is ready to accommodate them and assimilate them. A philosophy that turned its back on poetry, myth, rhetoric, and religion would never come fully into its own, for the very highest topics are not open to treatment by a merely analytical philosophy or a merely dialectical one. In the *Phaedrus,* it is the polyphony of myth, rhetoric, and dialectic that is able to reveal the true nature of Love.

Early in the dialogue, the two speakers, Socrates and Phaedrus, have an exchange about mythology: Phaedrus asks Socrates about the story of the capture of Oreithuia by the god of the north wind, Boreas, and then he asks him directly if he thinks this bit of mythology is true. If this myth should not be true, it's not because of details peculiar to it, but rather because of something about the whole class of myths. Phaedrus's question has inaugurated a philosophical discussion, and he is speaking for his generation. Socrates' reply makes it clear enough that Phaedrus's question was a commonplace of the intellectual life of the time. A whole *kind* of speech, it seemed, mythology, might not be true. In Plato's text, myths were a prolongation into the current time, the time in which the dialogues were set, of a discourse stemming from an earlier time. Whereas Socrates in the *Euthyphro* and the *Republic* was pictured as being fully on the side of the contemporary Enlightenment, in its suppression of myth, the *Phaedrus* depicts him instead as unwilling to follow in this direction anymore. He is happy to preserve mythic discourse. Socrates' reply to Phaedrus's question regarding Boreas (229c6) is deeply wrapped in irony. He lends no support to what Phaedrus has just suggested, that stories such as this aren't true. Rather, he says with some scorn, disbelieving the story is exactly what smart people, cultivated people, the *sophoi*, tend to do these days. Socrates won't identify with those scholars who try to explain away the centaur—he feels more at home identifying with the centaur. He wants to follow the Delphic oracle and look into himself to see if in his own soul he's really more like one of these monsters, such as the Typhon. Or maybe, after all, his soul is really a very gentle animal. The Typhon reference shows Socrates making use of an item of mythology in his inner self-searching. Though he is employing a myth, it is in the course of a study that he has defined for himself, a self-scrutiny, and this is an intelligent and literary use of an item of myth—converting it into an image or a metaphor.

Rhetoric

The rhetoric of Lysias is an utterly different mode of discourse, and I would like to highlight its very opposition to myth. At the beginning, Phaedrus reads to Socrates a speech supposedly written by Lysias that is the *ne plus ultra* of contemporary oratory. His rhetoric is sharp, bare, and analytical; it is, in other words, intellectual. There are no figures of speech in this address, and if there is rhythm, it is very close to what we hear when people are doing business. Nothing is vague. This rhetoric has excluded everything that might be uncertain or cloudy. This is the mode of discourse that has shut out mythology from the start. While mythology persevered into lyric and drama, there can be no trace of it in Lysian rhetoric. All of its vaguer entities, the Wind-god, the Maiden-princess, are long since gone from the mind of Lysias. No gods are present. Nothing is left that remains uncertain as to date or place. In mythic discourse, some say Oreithuia was carried off from the Ilissos by Boreas; others say it happened at the Areopagus. Not so in the discourse of Lysias. Rhetoric is a form of discourse that is quite clear on what entities it can recognize, including abstractions such as *advantage,* and what entities it excludes, gorgons and centaurs, for sure. It is a successor-discourse, consciously displacing the preceding form of discourse and culture.

Lysian rhetoric excludes the cloudy mythology, with its familiar emotions and its colorful figures, partly because of how it is created. The myth has no text, and it has no author, but rhetoric is the work of a definite orator and has a fixed text, the material biblion or scroll that Phaedrus can carry away. The author who gave it its form is very much present to us in the rhetorical mode of address. It is not that "Some say she was carried off." Now it is "Lysias says . . ." Rhetoric is not only the assertion of some thesis or other; it is even more the instrument of the speaker's self-assertion. Rhetorical persuasion is, in practice, a form of personal power; it is ultimately a political category. As the vehicle for a self-assertion, a rhetorical address has as its key word *I*. When the issue at hand is that of persuasion, the question, "Of what have they been persuaded?" is not as important as the question "Who did the persuading?" The concept of *advantage, sumpherein,* the central concept of Lysias's speech, is central to rhetorical culture. Where I persuade you of what is to your advantage, I am also advancing my own advantage as a leader.

In ascribing the present view of love and lovers to Lysias, then, Plato makes it clear that such would be the profile of love to a forensic and rhetorical culture. Thus we are able to see that the rhetoric of Lysias not only excludes the discourse of myth, but that in so doing it shows its own narrowness from a human point of view. Lysias's speaker is seeking a *victory* in the oratory of love, trying to win over a boy by the force of a series of legal-style *arguments*. Plato's intention in this respect is quite plain: to expose the blind spots that inhabit the rhetorical discourse and culture by exposing how it would treat the matter of love. As soon as Lysias's address is over, and Phaedrus asks him about it, Socrates' first reaction (235c) is to think of two lyric poets, Sappho and Anacreon, who had much more adequate things to say about love.

Socrates, speaking as a philosopher, certainly expresses criticisms of rhetoric immediately after the reading and later in the dialogue. On the other hand, the *Phaedrus* shows us that Plato is by no means determined to squash or exclude every form of rhetoric. He does not deny that there are assemblies and law courts that require some form of rhetorical address, and this must point us to the figure of Isocrates, who looms large in the concluding pages of the *Phaedrus*. Isocrates was of Plato's own generation, and in founding a school of his own in Athens, he, too, made the claim of imparting "philosophy." In the written orations that he circulated, he never ceased to polemicize against Plato and the Academy, with the argument that the Platonic education, requiring detailed study of geometry and astronomy, logic and metaphysics, was illiberal and esoteric.[1] It was rhetorical *philosophia* that would shape leaders and rulers, and Isocrates was especially interested in forming a pan-Hellenic ruling class. We can hear these sentiments expressed by Callicles, the third main interlocutor in the *Gorgias,* beginning at 484c. And what Isocrates (and Callicles) said is surely true, at least in part. It is certainly true that the persuasion exercised in political rhetoric or forensic rhetoric cannot be reduced to the conviction accomplished through formally valid logical argument.

At the time he wrote the *Gorgias,* Plato was not prepared to cede one inch of ground to those, such as Isocrates, who advocated education in rhetoric. His posture was one of total combat, and the reason is surely that he saw his kind of philosophy in an embattled position, his teacher condemned to death, the partisans of rhetoric claiming to represent culture as such, the whole of *paideia* comprehended under rhetoric— precisely the claim of Gorgias and his followers in that dialogue. The rhetoricians, as we said above, excluded myth rigorously from their discourse. Unfortunately, they did not grant the validity of philosophy, either—philosophy, that is, as Plato understood it, stemming not only from Socrates, but also from Parmenides, the Pythagoreans, the students of nature. In return, therefore, arguing on behalf of philosophy, Plato wanted to defeat rhetoric completely.

But with the *Gorgias* behind him, and after he had founded his school devoted to rigorous philosophy and science, he still had to confront the world of public affairs: law courts, assemblies, and the arts of government. His first hypothesis, it seems, was that public affairs might be run best, after all, by those who had received precisely his kind of rigorous education in mathematics, science, and philosophy: This was the hypothesis of the *Republic,* which he had had to abandon by the time he wrote the *Phaedrus.*

The *Phaedrus* recognizes that rhetoric is the instrument of law and government, and more clearly so in a democracy than in any other regime. The subtle task Plato has taken on, then, is to rebuke rhetoricians, such as Isocrates, who aim to undermine rigorous philosophy and science by puffing up their own art, while at the same time recognizing that there is a legal, political territory in which rhetorical art is necessary. But even as Plato continues his critique of the pretension of rhetoric to stand free of philosophy, he abandons his own high-handed way with rhetoric, and we see that rhetoric must be admitted a still further vocation, a role to play even outside politics, even in pure philosophy. The philosopher cannot abandon the will to communicate. Thus philosophy must now admit rhetoric into itself, it must accept a pluralism in its own constitution in place of its earlier search for discursive purity. And this is one of Plato's greatest moments. It has permitted him to offer the content of his philosophy to a whole world of readers and listeners who would never dream of listening in to purely dialectical discussions, as Socrates conducted them or as they were conducted within the walls of the Academy. It is the rhetorical address in the middle of the *Phaedrus* that has won Plato his readers—indeed, Plato's concessions to rhetoric in the present dialogue are only the recognition of what he had done in practice already, for instance, in the great speeches of Aristophanes, Socrates, and Alcibiades in the *Symposium.* The *Apology of Socrates,* for that matter, standing at the head of Plato's corpus, was already a work of rhetoric, with only a few dialectical passages entered as interruptions. The philosophy that has recognized its own rhetorical voice will now be the effective corrective to the historical rhetoric that was the enemy of philosophy.

Dialectic

Let me attempt to show that rhetoric preserves a positive vocation even in the treatment of love, where rhetoric must be fused with dialectic. In the course of his critical treatment of rhetoric, Socrates makes repeated reference to the alternative that he calls dialectic (269b, 276c; see 278d, 279a). Dialectic is evidently what is *distinctive* of Socrates, what marks his thinking off from that of Phaedrus and Lysias and differentiates him as well from those who continue to circulate the old myths. It is the instrument peculiar to philosophy. But does that mean that where dialectic is pursued there can be no myth or rhetoric? To this the answer is no. We can show that elements of myth and rhetoric can be integrated into it to constitute the full chorus of philosophy.

Socrates proposes (269a–272b) to rebuild rhetoric on the foundation of dialectic, but we must see the double character of dialectic. It is not only a certain technical operation; it has a moral and personal meaning, an existential meaning, for Plato. Dialectic is introduced here as the corrective to the practice of politics and law that was driven by the rhetorical ideals of glory and influence. Rhetoric itself was not a mere technique of speech but a culture of its own, and when Plato wants to reconstitute rhetoric by way of dialectic, he is seeking to instill virtues such as truthfulness and honest inquiry, which are not merely habits of speaking, but virtues of the soul. They inform the character that Socrates exhibited in his encounters with Callicles and Thrasymachus. Dialectic, in this text, then, has inherited all the aura that Plato generally accords to philosophy itself. Dialectic is the form of discourse used by philosophy alone. Yet there is a fusion of rhetoric and dialectic that I shall illustrate this way.

In our first reading of the *Phaedrus,* we come upon the first speech of Socrates as a companion piece to Lysias's speech, contrasted with it in point of form but not content, since Socrates was to make the same points, but make them better. The first reading takes it all rhetorically. As we read on, however, and proceed into the retrospective analysis of the speeches at 265–266, we are invited to compare this speech with the palinode that followed and therefore to read it dialectically. In the first, rhetorical reading, there was no hint that the *erōs* under discussion might not be the whole of *erōs*, but precisely this is the point made at 265 and in the discourse following: The Lysian speech and Socrates' first speech had dealt only with one half of love, the bad half, leaving the other, good half to be treated in the palinode. Dialectic has taken us to a sovereign, elevated standpoint where, looking downward, we comprehended the generic unity of things that seemed otherwise to be in contention: love in both its heavenly and earthly forms. When we read the palinode in a first reading, we took it rhetorically, as well; that is, we took it as an outright attack on the two speeches that had insulted *erōs*—it was the vindication of *erōs*. Socrates did not state at that point that there was a bad kind of love which Lysias and he had been right to attack. The rhetorical effect of the palinode was that it was treating *erōs* as such, *erōs* as a whole. Thus the atmosphere was one of contending with the earlier speeches. This rhetorical effect cannot be removed by the subsequent dialectical reading, for we do not forget that Socrates had to do penance for his blasphemy of Eros. And in the impact of the dialogue as a whole, this rhetorical point remains important. It would be a misunderstanding to suppose that the good kind of love and the bad kind were two neutral species or divisions of love, indifferent to one another. The truth is that the bad kind of love is a corruption of the good kind, a disorder of love. A dialectical discussion of the two kinds of love that did not see that point would be a faulty dialectic indeed. Therefore, the rhetorical force of the palinode remains. Though there may be a bad kind of lover, there is something even worse, namely a false rhetorician who condemns love as a whole by failing to see that the bad kind is a corruption of the good kind. Lustful and selfish love is bad, but even worse is the blasphemy that attacks love itself and rules out the spiritually creative love as well as the possibility that a human being could be led on to the good love even after beginning with the bad.

Mythology

In a discussion of this mode of discourse, I'll focus on the extended passages of mythology that we can attribute to Plato himself—and the

Great Speech of the *Phaedrus* is the climactic member of that group. This is a dialogue that celebrates Eros as a god, not a mere demon or spirit intermediary between gods and mortals as in Diotima's speech in the *Symposium*. That is the cumulative point of the three speeches in the *Phaedrus*. The first two constitute an abuse of the god and create a need thereby for Socrates to make the third speech in vindication of the god. The vindication of Eros undertaken by Socrates is a speech that is a dialectical triumph as well as a rhetorical one. The speech itself is a work of love, inspired by the god Eros (243d3–4), offered to him at the end in a prayer (257a–b), and throughout spoken as if to a young man in a kind of love speech (243e4–8). Love's divinity is a theme for philosophy once it is no longer wedded to the purity of an abstract dialectic and can recognize its own kinship with myth and rhetoric. When Socrates is compelled to break off his anti-erotic discourse, he will be reminded of ancient truth in the ancient myths and will introduce Phaedrus to the place of Eros among the whole panoply of gods. And pondering the gods leads Socrates into new and unaccustomed depths in the study of the human soul. Before Socrates can give his definitive reply to Lysias, he must chart the eternal homeland of the soul, its own kinship with truth and true being. Then he will be able to offer the true and adequate account of love and beauty.

In discussing the mythic discourse of the great speech, I'd like to take a cue from a remark of Socrates at 246c–d that seems to offer a guideline for the use of our imagination. Socrates says we often imagine a god in the form of a mortal creature, as having both a soul and a body: absurd, of course, and springing from ignorance, from our not having ever seen a god or given adequate thought to the gods. We treat the immortal being not as purely immaterial and spiritual but as a combination of soul with a body that would last forever—absurd! According to Socrates, our present condition, our human condition as living creatures, *zōa*, is the result of a fall from heaven and our acquisition of an earthly body. This fall has resulted in a fallen form of imagination and thought, as well. When we suppose that the gods are like us, just bigger and more beautiful, we exhibit a fallen form of thinking, specifically the fallacy of attributing bodies to the gods, but equally the mistake of attributing bodies to the mortal souls in advance of their fall and incarnation. Socrates is calling on Phaedrus (and the reader) to make use of the horse-and-charioteer imagery in another way altogether—to dematerialize the images when we hear them and especially the image of the wings.

And I think that this remark has a still broader application, not only to the soul-imagery of horse and chariot, but also to the heavens and the earth, the outer rim of the heavens, and to the space and time that are assumed in the mythic narration. I shall argue that the import of

Socrates' remark is that we would be wrong to make any *cosmological* use of the myth: Its meaning, I shall argue, is restricted to the circumstances of the *life of the soul.* This narrative that even opens up a place *above* the heavens cannot be interpreted in cosmological terms. The meaning of this image will become apparent only if we dematerialize it in accordance with Socrates' warning.

In the *Phaedo* (107c and following), Socrates speaks of the souls going down into the underworld. At the end of the *Republic* (614c–d), the souls of the dead are shown proceeding either into the earth or up into the heavens after they have received judgment. In the *Phaedrus,* the soul is likened to a charioteer and horses soaring through heaven and even (if they are divine) gazing out beyond it. These texts all separate the soul from the body rigorously—they relate encounters undergone by the disincarnate soul. So we can't visualize this "underworld" and this "heaven" in physical or cosmological terms. This heaven and this underworld constitute an environment for a purely immaterial soul: They are an *imagined* heaven and an *imagined* underworld and an *imagined* earth that constitute a sort of location for an *imagined* soul. We are imagining the heavens that we traversed before we became incarnate. These heavens, and the things that lie beyond the heavens or outside the heavens, are to furnish a background for the explanation of the human experiences of love and knowledge toward which Socrates is making his way in the narrative, experiences that befall the human beings in their location here on earth. It is noteworthy that much of the recitation of the myth takes place in the present tense (for example, 246c–249b). But at 249b–250d, where attention has turned to the experiences human beings have during their lifetime here on earth, the mythical material is presented in a retrospective style, by way of the philosopher's recollection of those supernal scenes, and those scenes are narrated in the past tense, the aorist.

The flight of the souls takes place in an imagined space. Where Plato treats the creation of the world in the *Timaeus,* he conceives an earthly space or a material space, a Receptacle (*hupodochē*) and a Space (*chōra*)—see *Timaeus* 49a–52b—where bodies can be extended and which is governed by the main polarity of heaven and earth. But in the *Phaedrus* the imagined space has now been expanded into a place *beyond* the heavens.

And this story runs on through an imagined time. It was untold aeons ago that our souls were soaring on high in that happy company. Then chaos and confusion arose among the mortal chariots. Then the decree of destiny was uttered. The imagined space and time are the dimensions for the adventures of *the imagined soul.*

How do we read such a discourse?

The nineteenth-century philosophers explored mythology in a way that entered deeply into the Greek myths in particular, the place they take in Plato's work, and the problem of Plato's own mythical compositions. Hegel attempted, in his *Philosophy of Religion,*[2] to interpret ancient Greek religion largely through the records of the Greeks' mythology, a program of interpretation that was grounded in his own philosophy of spirit. What the spirit or mind first grasped by way of pictures and mythical stories— that is, *Vorstellungen,* representations, such as Zeus—was the very truth about the spirit itself and its world, but it was not expressed in the final and adequate *form.* That was to be accomplished by concepts formulated through rational thinking.

Hegel's rival F. W. J. Schelling went a very different route. In his later years, Schelling delivered several courses of lectures on the philosophy of mythology.[3] He did not regard myths as fictions or inventions. They are not produced by any consciousness, neither individual nor collective; they should not be treated as *Vorstellungen,* tales or pictures, and even less are they available for translation or transposition into some other discourse, supposedly superior, such as a philosophy that operates with concepts and ideas. Schelling's central thrust against rationalizing in-terpretations is that mythical discourse originates in a preconscious and nonrational "potency" of the soul.[4] Although scientific and philosophical discourse spring from the same soul, they express another and different "potency" of it.

And everyone's soul has these same "potencies." Therefore, every-one has the capacity to respond to the myths just as the ancients did. Thus, for Schelling, philosophy and science do not appropriate the myths, but stand beside them. The myth is in this way parallel to the work of art. Schelling argues at the end of his 1800 *System of Transcendental Idealism* that there is more in the art work than was placed there by the conscious intention of the artist; the work is only in part a product of consciousness, and, where there is genius, an unconscious "poetry" has been at work. This "potency" operates in advance of consciousness and its controls, and the work of art, like the myth, is created through the cooperation of the conscious and the preconscious potencies. Schelling's doctrine of the interaction of the conscious and unconscious potencies accords with many phenomena of mythology, in that it does not promote hasty interpretations and translations. It lets the myths be; the notion of a separate potency in the soul for myth recognizes that there really was a need for mythical expression as such. Schelling's view is particularly appropriate for grasping the place of myth in Plato's philosophical texts. Plato found that a myth could be the best way of saying something that he wished to say. Why then should we interpret the myth?

We never find a myth pure and simple in any text of Plato; it is always joined to a passage of nonmythical reasoning, whether dialectical or rhetorical. A number of key words, especially *soul* and *god,* move easily among these kinds of discourse. The fact that the myths are already set within a dialectical framework inhibits readers from adding new allegorical interpretations of their own to the myths, and, indeed, it inhibits myth interpretation altogether. The myth that accompanies a passage of dialectic addresses us in a different way; or, rather, it addresses some other part of ourselves, adding to the instruction of dialectic the delight of narrative, and the narrative is itself instructive in a different way.

We need to be aware precisely of the harmonies of these voices in the text of Plato and to understand why he wrote that way. Can we give the reason for it? As we apply the thought of Schelling to that of Plato, we are drawn above all to the manifold constitution of the *soul.* What Schelling spoke of as different potencies have already appeared in Plato, especially in the *Republic* and the *Phaedrus* as the three parts of the soul. Our question about the status of myth in relation to reason is initially a question about two forms of discourse, two possibilities of language, but upon closer scrutiny it turns into a question about the composition of the soul or the mind. Plato's tripartite soul offers the grounding for a doctrine of different modes of discourse, each an expression of the soul but not reducible to one part and one mode, in the ways usually sought by philosophers of pure reason. Phaedrus and Euheremus wished to substitute something different for myths that are not rational. Hegel will elevate pictures into concepts and ideas. But Schelling is closer to the Socrates of the *Phaedrus* by hearing the discourse in its own terms and *expanding* philosophical reason to accommodate it, including the myth within the philosophy.

The Unity of the *Phaedrus*

I believe that this offers a clue to the question of the unity of the *Phaedrus,* a question that is so important for the relation of Plato's early work to his late work. The account offered in the Great Speech of our supernal vision is not contradicted at any point in the later pages on rhetoric and dialectic. Indeed, the dialectician's study of the soul (270b–272b) actually invoked the psychology of the Great Speech. The main passages of the *Phaedrus* that treat dialectic (265a–266c, 269b–272b, 276e–277c) would be descriptions of the philosopher's daily encounter with various interlocutors and various themes and situations. But the secret, hidden, and higher condition for this practice of dialectic would be the soul's primordial vision. One consequence of this reading of the *Phaedrus* is that the account of the primordial vision would not lend itself to dialectical treatment, since it is exploring the very ground of the possibility of dialectic. It would be appropriately treated, instead, by myth and rhetoric. We undertake dialectic under the normal conditions of everyday life—it is one form of discourse, as is rhetoric, one way in which we encounter one another through speech—but the condition for our attaining truth through dialectic lies in our having been exposed to the ideas in advance of all experience and all dialectic. Could there be a dialectical treatment of the preconditions for dialectic, then, or was it inherently necessary for Socrates' account of the soul to be mythical? The answer to this question, I think, is twofold. It seems that Plato himself never attempted a nonmythical, dialectical treatment of the pre-empirical formation of the soul. On the other hand, if we look to later centuries of philosophy, we find different routes taken to validate a Platonic doctrine by dialectical means. There is the neo-Platonic doctrine of the procession of the soul from *nous,* the Leibnizian preformation of the monad, the Kantian *a priori,* the doctrine of the Absolute in Schelling and Hegel, and Heidegger's "pre-ontological understanding of being." But these later variants should not be brought into an exposition of the *Phaedrus.* They are a part of its *Wirkungsgeschichte,* that is, they illustrate the depth of its influence in Western thought, and they counteract any tendency in the reader to dismiss the mythical account as a mere fairy tale, uninteresting to philosophers. But to apply these doctrines retroactively to the text would disturb the balance Plato struck in his writing between myth and dialectic.

So is it necessary to distinguish the imagined soul of the mythical narration from the actual and true soul, the topic of philosophy? I wish to answer no. Philosophy is the inquiry into truth that is able to employ and interweave different discursive modes, the mythical, the rhetorical, and the dialectical, taking each of them to be one style or mode for the disclosure of what is. A philosopher of pure reason (Hegel, perhaps) might wish to demonstrate the integrity of the imagined, mythical soul and of the real soul, the object of philosophy, by reducing the former to the latter, that is, to interpret the myth by restating its point nonmythically. But another route, closer to Plato's, would, I believe, work the other way around: It would not reduce the mythical imagery to something else, but, rather, would show that there is a *reason* for our use of mythical discourse, a reason rooted in the nature of the soul. The myth of the soul in the *Phaedrus* shows us a soul whose rational part is in struggle with the other parts symbolized by the horses, and it shows the limits of vision achieved by this charioteer. The human soul, then, is such that it will never be capable of a discourse of pure reason. There is a reason, rooted in our nature, why philosophy must express itself at points in myth. It would be altogether too literal, of course, to trace the mythical voice back to the black horse or the rhetorical voice to the white horse, but we can grant, more generally, that the finite and divided soul is what gives grounding for philosophy's need to employ more than one voice.

Notes

1. Already in his *Against the Sophists,* dated around 390 B.C., Isocrates diminished the ideal of pure research in favor of a humane education focused on the art of forceful speech; see chapters 16 through 18. This is also the burden of his later *Antidosis,* chapters 80 through 84 and 258 through 275, that explicitly attacks Plato's program of theoretical study and dialectic.

2. G. W. F. Hegel, *Lectures on the Philosophy of Religion,* one-vol. ed., *The Lectures of 1827,* ed. Peter C. Hodgson (Berkeley: University of California Press, 1988).

3. See F. W. J. von Schelling, *Philosophie der Mythologie,* vols. XI and XII in *Saemmtliche Werke* (Augsburg: Cotta, 1856 and 1857; reprint, Darmstadt: Wissenschaftliche Buchgesellschaft, 1966). I am indebted in this exposition to the excellent study by Edward A. Beach, *The Potencies of God(s): Schelling's Philosophy of Mythology* (Albany: SUNY Press, 1994).

4. See F. W. J. von Schelling, Sixth Lecture, *Philosophie der Mythologie,* vol. XII in *Saemmtliche Werke* (Augsburg: Cotta, 1857; reprint, Darmstadt: Wissenschaftliche Buchgesellschaft, 1966), 108–31. See also Beach, *The Potencies of God(s): Schelling's Philosophy of Mythology* (Albany: SUNY Press, 1994), 184 and following.

3

Socrates' Tragic Speech: Divine Madness and the Place of Rhetoric in Philosophy

Walter Brogan

> If any person comes to the gates of poetry without the madness
> of the Muses, persuaded that *techne* alone will make him a
> good poet, then shall he and his works of sanity [*sophrosune*] be
> brought to nought by the poetry of madness.
>
> —*Phaedrus*

In the *Phaedrus* dialogue, we witness Plato's magnificent ability to interweave form and content. Eva Brann refers to Diogenes Laertius and other ancient sources to verify that Plato "combed and curled" his dialogues with utmost care. One story had it that at his deathbed were discovered several rewritings of the beginning of the *Republic* that Plato had been working on. In the *Phaedrus,* as in many other dialogues, there is an interdependence of structure and interpretation, such that an interpretation of any section of the dialogue requires that we look backward and forward in order to understand it. Furthermore, there is an internal interpretive aspect already interwoven into Platonic writing, despite the notable absence of authorial privilege in Plato's texts. This is especially true of the *Phaedrus,* whose speeches are all reinscriptions of each other. In other words, it may be fair to say that there is no original text of the *Phaedrus.* That is, the *Phaedrus* and other similarly complex dialogues are themselves the enactment of a rewriting of a text. The content of the dialogue, the issue of rhetoric and *logos,* is about the form of the dialogue, and the form of the dialogue demonstrates the content. This backtracking onto itself, this reflection on its own progress as a way of writing, is the method of Platonic philosophy. It is a method particularly suitable for one who would want to destabilize the tendency of philosophy to solidify its findings into sophistic doctrines.

The *Phaedrus* is perhaps the most self-effacing and at the same time the most self-conscious of Plato's writings. If the *Apology* thematizes the trial of Socratic philosophy, the *Phaedrus* is the trial of Platonic philosophy and of the relationship between Plato and Socrates, between writing and speaking.

It is commonplace to distinguish Socrates from Plato on the score that Socrates did not write. Only in the *Phaedo*—within the horizon of the death of Socrates and thus at the advent of Plato's need to reincorporate and reinscribe the Socratic gesture that began philosophy—is there any indication that Socrates ever wrote anything (60D: Evenus wants to know what induced Socrates to write lyrics now, when he had never done it before). This connection of the *Phaedrus* with the *Phaedo* becomes more pronounced if we keep in mind that both the *Phaedo* and the *Phaedrus* thematize the immortality of the soul and that, before delivering his second speech on *erōs,* Socrates specifically mentions Simmias, one of the characters from the *Phaedo.* What is the connection between the death of Socrates and the need to write? And how is the *erōs* of or for philosophy related to this theme? Socrates understands philosophy as a preparation for death. He says in the *Phaedo* that, "true philosophers make death their profession" (67e). Philosophy is being ready to die. Socratic philosophy, therefore, requires the awareness of radical separation, of otherness, of death. We might recall in this regard the image of making a good crossing of the river (the river Styx) that Socrates suggests in the interlude between his two speeches on love in the *Phaedrus.* What then is the interconnection between *logos* (especially in its repeated and inscribed form), *thanatos* (death), and *erōs?*

Perhaps, then, the art of writing is our way of carrying on philosophy after the death of Socrates—in the face of the mortality and finitude of the human condition, in acknowledgment of the loss of the father. Toward the end of the *Phaedrus,* at 275d, writing is considered dangerous because it can disown the author and go off on its own. It is no longer accountable for itself. The offspring becomes unfaithful. This wandering away from the homeland is symptomatic of the illegitimate birthright of writing. If Socrates disowns his voice by insistently attributing what he says to the *daimōn* and claiming not to know enough to speak on his own, then Plato, in turn, finds himself disowning his writing as the source of truth. In the *Theaetetus,* Socratic midwifery is premised on his incapacity to give birth to ideas of his own. Similarly, in the *Phaedrus,* writing is said to be dead discourse. It cannot produce children of its own. Writing "pretends to contain important truth and permanence" (277a) but is not able to achieve immortality because it sows its seed on the surface.

One possible reason for the sterility of writing is that writing has an ambiguous relationship to the human soul, which alone can gain passage to the divine banquet that is the true homeland for human beings. The *Phaedrus,* in Socrates' second speech, reenacts this procession of the soul to the divine banquet. But even here it is a question of a reenactment. The human condition is one of separation, of needing to recover what one has forgotten and lost. There is no original, immediate access to truth and being—this is reserved for the divine condition. Not even the philosopher can lay claim to this. The fatherland, the plain of truth and being, the proper soil and food of human *logos,* lies beyond the activity of *logos* itself.

To demonstrate this, we can recall the character of Socrates' *daimōn,* his inner voice. Socratic discourse is a response to the command of this voice. But the voice needs to be interpreted; it never directly commands. It provokes. It is the command to practice philosophy, but it does not say what philosophy is. Socratic philosophizing is without guarantees.

The second speech is motivated by this inner voice. The voice prohibits direct passage at noonday to the other side of the river. The voice only weighs what is not true—in this case, his first speech about love. So, all Socratic philosophy begins with awareness of the *not.* This awareness holds open the relationship between being and non-being, between appearance and reality, between image and original. These relationships are, in fact, the central themes of the second speech. The second speech is offered as an atonement for the deception and falsity of the first, but the need to deliver the second speech is tied to the need for recovery. All philosophical speech is recovery and recollection.

Can writing, despite its evident threat to Socratic philosophy, be said to be such a genuine way of philosophizing? In the *Phaedrus,* we find that there is a kind of writing that helps us to recover from the condition of forgetfulness. Remember that the second speech is said to be the speech of Stesichorus, thus a repeated speech, and that the central part of the speech is offered through the metaphor of the charioteer and the divine procession. Good writing acknowledges its task as a recovery of what has been closed off. It does not close off and then try to control our relationship to truth, but rather precisely disrupts the apparent self-containment of the human soul and conveys us beyond itself. Good writing is the chariot that transports the soul. Its power to transfer us is metaphorical.

In speaking of tragedy in his *Poetics,* Aristotle argues that tragic poetry is especially akin to metaphor. It is through metaphor that what appears at first to be ordinary can reveal its strangeness. To be capable of such metaphoric transference is, Aristotle says, the gift of genius that belongs to the poet. This gift, according to Aristotle, is akin to madness (*manikos*) and requires that the poet be *ekstatikos,* ecstatic, outside of himself or herself (1455a30). Socrates, of course, gives his speeches under the spell of the cicadas in a state of dithyrambic frenzy. He attributes his second speech, for example, not to himself but as having been evoked by the muselike power of the tragic poet Stesichorus, who sang in order to atone for his loss of sight and his desecration of beauty and love. So metaphor, such as the metaphor of the chariot, is the kind of *logos* that frees *logos* from the ordinary grip of rhetoric and allows it to express what is uncanny. And the Socratic speaker and poet, similarly, is the one who is mad enough to be physiologically inspired, to be ecstatically affected and thereby drawn outside of himself or herself. The philosophical voice of such a speaker is never one that could be characterized in terms of immediate and pure presence. It is always a voice that is written over and a voice of repetition. Such metaphorical speaking/writing requires madness and a kind of physiological and psychical ecstasy such as that which was inspired in Socrates by the presence of Phaedrus.

I want to suggest that Socrates' second speech is especially metaphorical in this sense; that is, it embodies a poetic madness that in Dionysian fashion unravels the multiple threads of the apparently well-constructed verses of the previous speech and provokes an ecstatic transference of genuine erotic openness to what is beyond and other than itself. In other words, it is a kind of *logos* that does not lay claim to the truth it reveals. In this sense of metaphor, Plato's physiological condition has a direct bearing on the style of writing. Metaphorical, philosophical writing is embodied, besouled writing. It gives expression to the physically painful embrace of death and life on which Socrates meditates in the *Phaedo.* In acknowledging the place of the blind Stesichorus in the second speech, Socrates indicates that his ode to beauty may help to recover sight but will not shield him from the scarring and blinding that occurs when staring with tragic vision at the divine spectacle of life. Socrates' Dionysian turn toward madness in this speech is not just childlike play, dancing, and mirth; it is the philosophical equivalent of taking the hemlock. One becomes dismembered, torn apart, and disfigured. It is a writing that is violent, painful, frenzied, and erotic.

The danger of writing alluded to at the end of the dialogue is twofold. It is the danger of rhetorical and nonphilosophical writing; it is the danger of sophistry, of a rhetoric that is false and deceptive, that is, one that is disembodied, non-ecstatic and already dead. But it is also the danger of a philosophical kind of writing that will inscribe itself into the body, that will be traced on the soul of the interlocutor.

The first kind of dangerous writing is exhibited in the speech of Lysias, conveyed by Phaedrus. In the relationship between Phaedrus and Lysias, Phaedrus is the one who reflects beauty but has not himself grown wings. He is the passive follower, without inwardness, with no distance from the self that *erōs* opens up. Phaedrus is the beloved rather than the lover. But the nonreciprocity in his relationship with the *logos* of Lysias, the lack of any transfer, makes him truly the counterimage of the nonlover rather than the lover. Phaedrus is the perfect receptacle. He memorizes and recites and becomes a mirror image of the other. Phaedrus is the embodied presence of the beautiful form that shines through him; he is the receptacle, the *sōma* of the form, the surface upon which beauty can write. In contrast, with the philosophical *logos* of Socrates, Phaedrus is drawn out of himself. Their relationship becomes one in which the stream of beauty flows between them, a relationship of lover and beloved.

Diogenes Laertius reports that Lysias wrote a speech for Socrates to deliver after his condemnation and that Socrates refused to do so on philosophical grounds (DL 2.40–41). Lysias was, in fact, a ghostwriter for the Athenian courts. He was the son of Cephalus (who also argues for the primacy of the non-erotic). The power of Lysias's writing was that it could appear to be direct discourse when spoken by another. It offered the illusion of communication without any relationship between the composer and the listener. This detachment is the essential power of rhetoric. It assumes the stance of universality and gives the advantage to the nonlover who is impartial and out of touch with who and what is under discussion. Lysias says his speech is to be preferred for this reason.

In his renunciation of the speech of Lysias, Socrates lays out three criticisms: First, the order is random and the speech is repetitive; second, there is no central definition of love; and third, everything is at the same level. The irony of these accusations is that the speech condemns *erōs* as an obstacle to objectivity and artful control. Thus it is ironic that Lysias is accused of having no control over his discourse. There is a contradiction between form and content. Elsewhere, Socrates argues that the eristic success of the sophist relies on this disorder and confusion, that he requires it in order to ply his trade. In contrast, dialectic tries to sort out the confusion through its method of proper collection and division.

The model of love in Lysias's speech is *epithumia*, physical, appetitive desire or lust. In contrast, the model of the nonlover is an economic model. The underlying assumption of Lysias's speech is that the only human motivation to relate to others is selfish desire. In this context, one can get ahead better with a nonlover than a lover because there is at least a level playing field, whereas the lover needs to have the beloved inferior to himself and is jealous, exclusive, petty, and destructive of the possessions and wealth of the beloved. Both love and nonlove are selfish desires. But with the lover, the hope for recompense is destroyed by the lack of control of the lover, who is not a free agent. The lover has poor judgment, since he cannot transcend the immediacy of his situation or control his conduct. He is sickly, since he neglects his affairs and discourages the beloved from associating with others, which would be to his advantage in the long run. He engages in false flattery and is motivated by fear and frenzy about the relationship. Furthermore, the lover has no stability of character, and the relationship is, therefore, inevitably transient, leaving the beloved who sacrifices everything with the short end of the deal. Afterward, he feels only remorse for his ignoble condition and for his self-forgetfulness due to passion, and he flees without paying his debts.

The nonlover's stance is one of indifference. Yet he has desire. The difference between the desire of the lover and that of the nonlover is that the nonlover replaces private *erōs* with a kind of public, impartial, and indiscriminate desire whose approach depends on persuasion and opinion, *doxa*. The public written word used in oratory is now crucial to successful pursuit. There is a complicity between written rhetoric and non-erotic relationships. The only two alternatives in the speech are desire and opinion, whereby desire is tethered to a kind of *logos*, the *logos* of persuasive opinion.

In the third speech, love is also a kind a madness, but not the indiscriminate, wanton madness ascribed to *hubris* and lust. For love is also a god. Thus, madness has something to do with divinity. In the Diotima speech in the *Symposium*, *erōs* is said to be half mortal and half immortal, born of *penia* and *poros*, lack and excess. *Erōs* is said to be halfway between knowledge and ignorance. *Erōs* has to do with the movement of the soul and with the *between*. Thus, whether erotic madness is good or bad depends on the nature of the soul. So Socrates proceeds to prove the immortality of the soul, proving that the movement of the soul is ungenerated and does not go outside of itself. Yet, according to myth, *erōs* and *psychē* are lovers, and the madness of their love is a kind of movement *beyond* itself. How then can the soul be defined as a principle of self-movement that is so self-contained that it would seem impossible for anything to be written on it?

The soul is understood as movement. But it is a specific sense of movement. It is not the movement from place to place or from cause to effect. It is movement as such; the being of movement: perhaps *physis* or *genesis*, rather than *kinēsis* (245d).

Remember that in Socrates' first speech the soul was said to be guided by two leading but antagonistic principles or *archai: doxa* (*epithumia* with *logos*) and *hubris* (*epithumia* without *logos*). Love was said to be this wanton desire that has no *logos* and therefore no self-control. But this second speech raises again the question of the *archē* of the soul. Is madness really divorced from *logos*, as was assumed in Lysias's speech and again in Socrates' first speech? Can the movement of the soul that bears fruit, that is responsible for *genesis,* for coming into being, for the making manifest of something new, be without the excess that goes beyond the mere comic mastery of oneself that Lysias promised and promoted? On the other hand, is erotic madness reducible to the excess of tragic *hubris* that weakens and dissipates the soul without allowing it to reach beyond itself? Or is *erōs* neither doxic nor hubristic?

This third position is hinted at already in the beginning of the dialogue when Socrates repeats the myth of Boreas. In the myth, Pharmacy is playing with Oreithyia when Boreas sweeps Oreithyia to her seduction and death. The sophists and scientists interpret the myth of Boreas as a story about death rather than a mythical story about being swept away by love. In contrast, Socrates' position is ambivalent with regard to the choice, the either-or, that is presented between *erōs* and *thanatos*. He says that his concern for self-knowledge precludes choosing between the sophistic and mythological accounts. So for Socrates, the central issue with regard to *erōs* and *thanatos* is the issue of self-presence, or, in other terms, the self-movement and immortality of the soul. The human condition lives under the threat of losing itself, of being utterly overwhelmed by what is beyond itself, and yet lives, too, under the possibility of participating in the full and self-contained presence of being. Might it be the case that the question is not either-or—*either* overwhelming mythical forces *or* the closure of the self-contained competence of human *logos?* Might human *logos* also contain a spark of the divine vision that allows it to play between these two alternatives?

To open up an understanding of this third possibility, Socrates' second speech tells the story of the fall of the soul and its loss of wings: the story, that is, of the soul's embodiment. In this story, the divine procession to the vision of truth and being is accomplished without struggle or competition. There are only good, obedient horses. But there is no *erōs*. In humans, the unruly horses cause confusion and blindness. The journey is thwarted. The souls fall to earth. Like the divine, it is the soul's knowledge of the truth that constitutes its humanness, as opposed to the souls of beasts. On the other hand, it is the soul's forgetfulness of truth that distinguishes the human soul from the divine soul. The extent to which, before the fall, the soul participated in the vision of truth determines the destiny of its human life. The speech goes on to tell the story of the soul's return to the divine banquet. The philosopher is the only soul whose way of life shortens its bondage to cyclical development on the way to a return to the divine procession. The philosopher, as the standard of excellence, is not just the highest human soul-type, but is radically disassociated from the natural condition of the others. The soul of the philosopher is not defined in terms of just another specialization bound to its inner dynamics. The soul of the philosopher transcends the natural condition of embodiment and its cyclical destiny. For this reason, the philosopher is out of touch with the goods and services of the ordinary human soul. He or she is a wanderer who is disenfranchised from the human community. On the other hand, it is this soul that is most human because it is most capable of remembering the realm to which all human souls belong. The philosopher can stand above his or her human condition and therefore sees the true place of all souls—their harmony and belongedness to a whole. Plato says:

> For only the soul that has beheld truth may enter into this our human form—seeing that the human being must needs understand the language [*legomenon*] of forms [*eidos*], passing from a plurality of perceptions [*aisthēsis*] to a unity gathered together by reasoning [*logismos*]—and such understanding is a recollection [*anamnēsis*] of those things which our souls beheld aforetime as they journeyed with their god, looking down upon things which we now suppose to be, and gazing up to what truly is [*to ontōs on*].

Is this Plato's theory of forms? What does it mean that Plato here in this passage substitutes *eidos* for the beingness of being (*to ontōs on*)? Plato defines *eidos* as the seeing that comes before and gathers the many. But here we see that this oneness of being is forgotten by the human *logos* but recollected by the philosopher who is attuned to the divine while looking both upward and downward, from the plurality of *aisthēsis* to the oneness of *nous*. A proper human banquet must recollect; it must recover the oneness, the beingness which allows beings to be known as they are in themselves.

The essential question here is whether this double vision of the philosopher is a vision hostile to the sensible realm. For sure, mere reliance on sensuous visibility seems inadequate for the philosophical soul. Plato tells us in the passage with which we began that only if the artist can somehow achieve a relation to *physis*—to what arises and comes forth of itself (here *eidos* and *physis* are the same)—can he or she be a great artist. Mere *technē*, as evidenced in sophistry—the skill at making things appear to be without any attunement to their being—leads to a false illusion. Its power to deceive comes from the ambiguity of the human condition because we *are* the beings who are forgetful of being.

Art, henceforth, must see its end in the philosophical vision of the truth. But only if the poet is seized by divine mania will she or he be a good poet. So, if art is to be subservient to truth, this cannot mean that art is to become conceptual or even a mental image. The philosopher is rather depicted in the *Phaedrus* as the truly sensuous person who is inspired by divine madness. The artistic vision of the beautiful does not come entirely from ourselves but from beyond, overwhelming the person and threatening to tear one apart. But it lures and captivates one and leads one to reach beyond and toward that which provokes this passion in her or him. It draws one to see the source of one's enraptured state. It shakes one out of one's comfortable and familiar relationship to beings and provokes one to ask what it is one sees there. The philosopher's relation to being and truth, his or her vision of the *eidos,* is a far cry from the serene contemplation of the forms. The philosopher's vision awakens *erōs,* the desire to see what we had taken for granted and therefore had not seen before.

Erōs and beauty are required for this turning of the soul to the revealing of beings in their true being. Thus, in conclusion, we will turn briefly to a description of the kind of *erōs* which allows beauty to shine forth in the midst of beings.

In a significant way, the *Phaedrus* can be considered a dialogue on remembrance. It is a dialogue about our awareness that we have a need, suffer a loss; it is the recognition that something is not there. Such an awareness is provoked by *erōs.* For human beings, it is the sensuous that first provokes our openness to being, that recollects for us the divine feast in which even as mortals we are able to participate. *Erōs* is the desire to know the being as itself, that is, in its being, rather than as semblance, as what it is not. The desire is said to be divine, yet it is not painless. The erotic physical struggle to see the other as itself is a beautiful story in the *Phaedrus.*

It may be important to note that this delirium of vision which lets the other be itself is provoked by the absence of the beloved, when the beloved is held in memory and the outlets begin to close up. The ecstasy and anguish that this play of presence and absence provokes, this being held apart, allows the lover and beloved to achieve a unity that preserves their identity. Truth, as the unconcealment and unveiling of being, and the human being whose essence is the view upon being, are opened up in beauty. But the site of beauty is the *mē on,* the sensuous, the place where non-being occurs.

4

Not the Sophist

Abraham Schoener

A t the center of the dialogue, the *Sophist,* somebody is responsible for a death. The person responsible is not the Sophist.

Beginning

It is hard to know where to begin reading these dialogues. The beginning itself so often insists on placing us somewhere else, at least in some particular context, that is outside the present dialogue. The *Sophist,* like the *Republic,* and then the *Timaeus,* begins by reminding us of yesterday's conversation. I do not know just what to make of this, but it is surely a device related to the written character of the dialogues. It is so different from the way that Xenophon often begins his Socratic writings: for example, "At one time, [Socrates] said this."[1] The Platonic beginning, with the reference to yesterday, makes clear that what we are about to read is not the mere record of a conversation that we will somehow rehearse or review. "We said this yesterday" is such a self-conscious way to speak and oddly against the apparently living character of the dialogues. If the essence of the dialogues is in the dialectical motion and not in the doctrines (god forbid) therein expressed, then what difference what we said yesterday—what agreement we reached? This seems especially so when what we said yesterday is not merely recollected as a starting point for a new discussion, but is preserved and manifested in a written document—a "dialogue"—which we have just read or must now read in order to grasp the self-proclaimed context for the present "discussion." This is not what we expect. The sun is new each day in the land of Socratic inquiry; yesterday's conversation ought to be the way that corpses are for Heraclitus: more fit to be thrown out than dung. There is a sign within the words of such dialogues as these that their permanent written character was always primary, that the dialogic form, and its exaltation of living and ephemeral speech, is misleading—or partial, at best. Lurking strangely behind this realization is the rebirth of the possibility that the dialogues do embody doctrines like any other philosophic text, that they are hardly unique in their form or function—that the dialogue really might as well be a "Platonic letter."

This is an awful beginning. It falsifies my deepest and oldest experience of the dialogues and undercuts what I suppose brought most of us to Plato: the sense that these dialogues are the preeminent philosophical *texts*, that is, that they are *the* ones that most call the *textuality* of all and any philosophy into question. So let me not begin by dismissing this sense.

The *Sophist* suggests another beginning, not in the yesterday of dead discourse, but in the still-living roots of all Greek speaking: in Homer.

Penelope

Theodorus begins the conversation innocently enough, reminding us of yesterday's agreement to meet again today and introducing a "sort of stranger" from Elea—whom Theodorus calls "a very philosophical man." Theodorus, as always, is plain in his speech, but Socrates responds more than playfully and insists, rather demonically we might say, that the guest is a god—and he gives a text for this insistence. It is Homer, whom Socrates cites by name and alludes to at least twice in the following exchange. He weaves two passages from the *Odyssey* into his remarks, suggesting that the guest is a god come down to observe the deeds of mortals, with an interest in their dialectical, not civil, virtue. Theodorus straightfacedly denies that the guest is a god, but allows that, because the guest philosophizes, Theodorus does indeed consider him to be "divine."

Socrates congratulates him for this (one can sense that they are already mocking each other, but it is not clear why they should be) and continues his conceit with enthusiasm. He now compares all such philosophical men to the previous gods and claims that these men are no easier to recognize than gods are. This is a curious claim,[2] and suggests a suspicion on Socrates' part whether the stranger really is philosophical. Now Socrates also insists that these men, like the gods before, will be inspecting the lives of their fellow humans—in fact, "looking down" upon them, an expression he adds to Homer's account. This is all very odd, and very much worth sorting out.

Let me begin by citing a full translation of the beginning of the dialogue.

> **THEODORUS:** According to our yesterday's agreement, Socrates, here we are (quite properly, too), and we are also bringing this sort of stranger. His kind is from Elea, and he is a companion of those who follow Parmenides and Zeno, and is very philosophical.
>
> **SOCRATES:** Has it really escaped you that you are bringing not a stranger, but a kind of god—as Homer's saying goes? He says that not only do different gods accompany those men who have a share in just shame, but that also, in fact, the god of strangers most accompanies them, and that they gaze down upon the acts of violence and lawfulness of men. So perhaps whoever this is who accompanies you is one of the higher powers, come to observe us, poor as we are in speeches, also to refute us—being a kind of Refuting God.
>
> **THEODORUS:** No, this is not the stranger's way, Socrates; rather, he is more measured than those who are eager for contention. And though, in my opinion, the man is not a god at all, he is nonetheless *divine*—for I address all philosophical men in this way.
>
> **SOCRATES:** Yes, that is fine, my friend. However, this kind is probably not much easier, as they say, to discern than that of a god. For certainly these men appear in all sorts of guises—through the ignorance of others—and roam the cities. I mean those who are philosophical not through contrivance, but in their being: They look down, from above, on the life of those down below, and they seem to some to merit nothing, and to others to be worthy of everything. And at some times they appear in the guise of statesmen, and at others sophists—and then again there are some to whom they might furnish the opinion that they are completely crazy.

At the beginning of his response to Theodorus, Socrates uses a phrase from the *Odyssey* and cites Homer by name. The first passage that Socrates cites is in the scene with the Cyclops Polyphemos. Polyphemos is already a kind of namesake for Odysseus. Odysseus is called *PolyTropos* in the first line of the poem: the man of many turns. *Polyphemos* means the man of much fame or who talks a lot—both of which are preeminently true of Odysseus in this story. Now this reflection of names does not end here. The episode culminates with Odysseus's famous grammatical trick, in which he tells the Cyclops that his name is "Nobody," foreseeing, I suppose, that the Cyclops will not be able to make a use/mention distinction later when Odysseus attacks him (9.360 and following). I should note that Homer's word play involves at least a double pun: in certain grammatical constructions, the Greek word for "nobody" (*mē tis*) is nearly homonymous with the word for "craft" or "guile" (*mētis*), and when Polyphemos's companions ask him about how it can be that "nobody is killing him," what they say in Greek is no less than "Aha! Craft is killing you!" This is right, of course; they say the truth without knowing it. But most deeply, what this pun, contrived by Homer, points to is not just that Odysseus is Craft embodied (this is obvious), but that Odysseus's craft, at its craftiest, resides in his understanding of the textuality of language. His trick depends on the possibility of citation and on the recognition that quotation marks—or whatever in a language would signify citation—do not appear in speech. One might then add that his craft depends on his understanding not just the textuality of language, but the crucial role the distinction between spoken and written utterance plays in that textuality. His *mētis,* craft, is not knowing how to trick brutes but knowing how to work words.

Now this first allusion points to a story in which a man is recognized precisely for what he is; the Cyclops makes no mistakes about Odysseus's divinity or humanity. For this reason, it is not clearly apposite to Socrates' question about Theodorus's guest. Yet there is some kind of mistaken identity in this story: Polyphemos does not recognize Odysseus as Odysseus, but is deceived into thinking that Odysseus is Nobody. This suggests that Socrates' real concern here is not whether we mistake a god for a man, but whether we recognize a man for who he is. This is precisely the way that Theodorus takes Socrates' prodding (Theodorus might be staid and rather prosaic, but he is not altogether dumb): He responds by claiming that he recognizes the stranger for what he is—that is, as very philosophical.

We should note that in responding in this way, Theodorus politely accedes to the rather monstrous terms of Socrates' comparison. In the *Odyssey* episode, the person whose *recognizing* is at stake is the brutal Cyclops; the person whose *recognition* is at stake is, of course, Odysseus. Theodorus's response thus casts himself as the Cyclops and his guest as Odysseus. But the comparison cannot end here: In the first allusion, Socrates makes *himself* the speaker of Odysseus's words that suggest to the Cyclops that he ought to honor his guest for who he is. This is clearly Socrates' own role in the present conversation, and so he obscures from the beginning the difference between himself and the stranger. This is not surprising. But when Socrates casts himself in this scene as Odysseus, the admonitory speaker, he accords himself a particular aspect of Odysseus's character. Odysseus knows *who he is* here—he *is* Craft, and so will crush the brutish Cyclops. When Socrates casts himself as Odysseus, he gives himself the excellent resource of knowing who he is himself. His allusion thus suggests that he knows just what kind of man the stranger is and just who he is himself. This is not shocking, but it emphasizes from the beginning that the Socratic "Know Thyself" has already been decided.

The allusion to the *Odyssey* clearly suggests that we take Odysseus as the model for the hard-to-find philosopher. It also seems to suggest that Socrates is making some kind of pathetic allusion to his own case: We cannot forget that Socrates had to bring the previous day's conversation to a close in order to address Meletus's suit. The brutish Cyclopes around him do not recognize him for what he is, but mis-take him for a mere nobody. This could be the last suggestion of this allusion. But—on the slightest reflection—this misrecognition is not pathetic: If the allusion is truly apposite, their mistake is due to his knowing guile. He is only "Nobody" because *he* says he is. If the Cyclopes of Athens misunderstand him, that is his work—his *easy* work.

But this is only the beginning of the allusions that Socrates insists on. He twice refers to a passage much later in the *Odyssey*, paraphrasing it two different ways and changing it substantially and emphatically, but in the same way, each time. After Odysseus returns home, he disguises himself as a beggar and insinuates himself among the suitors besieging his home. The worst among them is named Antinoos (as if eager new students at the Academy were naming the characters); Antinoos hurls a stool at the disguised Odysseus and threatens his life. When he does so, some of the more moderate, or less daring, among his companions upbraid him. One, nameless, says:

> Death to you if he turns out be some kind of god, down from heaven.
> You know the gods appear as all kinds of strangers, and wander the cities,
> beholding both the violence and lawfulness of men. (17.484–487)

This too seems to be not quite apposite. Socrates might be reminding Theodorus that the stranger could be a god, checking on them, just as the nameless suitor was reminding Antinoos. But the beggar in the reference turns out not to be a god, but a mortal. On the other hand, he *does* turn out to be other than he seemed. The reference thus becomes much more fitting once Theodorus claims that his guest is no god, but a very philosophical man. Socrates could then be suggesting that philosophers are not recognized by their insolent inferiors, just as

Odysseus was not, and that they eventually turn out other than they seem. But this does not pay enough attention to the story.

In each reference, Socrates seems to put Odysseus forward as some kind of model for the hard-to-recognize philosopher. In both cases, Odysseus disguises himself or withholds his identity. When, in this second case, he is not recognized for who he is, the cause for this, once again, is his own self-disguise. One may blame the suitors for their insolence, but not for their failure to recognize their philosopher-king come home from the wars. This emphasizes that the undetected existences of the philosophers are due to their own work—indeed, Socrates uses the strange verb *phantazontai* to express the way that philosophers appear to *us*; it means something like "appear disguised, fashion themselves in the images of." But the thrust of this second allusion goes further still, beyond even this rather surprising language.

Three things are worth noting about the way that the story of Odysseus unfolds after this passage. First, two people *do* recognize him, despite his disguise and deceits. Second, after he reveals himself, he purges his home of the suitors and their followers and does so in a merciless bloodbath. Third, even after the house is purged and Odysseus reinstated, Odysseus, upon seeing his old father, lies to him and disguises who he is.

This is a crucial point: Otherwise, we might think that the philosopher only disguises himself because he must, to protect himself against the violent threats in his own house. We would be left with the already familiar image of the philosopher disguising himself against the stupid and inimical forces in his own city. The allusion to the *Odyssey* pushes us beyond this.

Two people recognize Odysseus: his wife, Penelope, and his aged nurse, Eurykleia. Eurykleia simply sees a distinguishing scar on Odysseus's ankle. This suggests that the true philosopher can be recognized by physical marks, external appearances, his cheap and tattered cloak, perhaps, or his use of sandals in winter. This suggestion cannot be wholly sarcastic. Penelope does not so much recognize Odysseus as force him to prove who he is. She does so by tricking him, by referring to his bed in a way that suggests that someone had ruined it. She is indirect. Her suggestion causes him to betray himself by leading him to say something that no one but he could have known. She tempts him, by appealing to his sentimentality and his vanity. The appeal works, Odysseus reveals himself utterly; they kiss, in a chilling but touching moment.

Penelope is Odysseus's perfect match. We may confirm this by stepping outside of this episode and asking simply: For what is Penelope most famous? The inevitable answer: She is the weaver.[3] Odysseus and Penelope are king and queen of their own textualities.

The repeated and insistent allusion to the hiding and discovery of the identity of Odysseus sets an odd but still clear context for the *Sophist* and its search: The philosopher is a weaver of words, capable of hiding within the tissues of his own fabrication; the person best able to make him disclose himself is the other weaver, the weaver of images. Lastly, these wandering philosopher-gods bear clear physical signs of their identity— you only need to know the signs. On the whole, the allusion suggests that, if you are not vicious or brutish, it is not hard to recognize the philosopher. This context does not make Socrates' eventual question— that is, "Are sophist, statesman, philosopher, one, two, or three?"—less interesting or serious, but it does make it easier in a certain way. This beginning assures us that there is a definite answer to the question. (We can answer the question, "Is that a beggar or is it Odysseus?") It assures us that the philosopher can be counted on to give himself up, that his disguise depends on his craft with words, but that a certain counter-craftiness with words will flush him. We will see that the philosopher is our Odysseus; Plato is his Penelope.

This is just a beginning, a mere preliminary result that demands rigorous testing. Let me just give one sign that this is right. I think that no matter how difficult the question of "What is the Philosopher?" becomes in the course of dialogues such as the *Sophist*, we never have any doubt about *who* is a philosopher. We never have any doubt that Socrates is; part of the reason for this certainty are the mere physical marks that we immediately recognize with some sentimental satisfaction.

The Patricide

Let me say right away what these preliminary results portend for the reading of the rest of the *Sophist*. They allow us to escape being mesmerized by the search for the philosopher and prepare us to accept without utter shock the apparent trapping of the Socratic philosopher in the nets woven to catch the Sophist. I am thinking here of the increasing resemblance between the successive appearances of the Sophist and the figure of the Socratic philosopher. The resemblance begins superficially and would result in identification, we suppose, only at the hands of Socrates' more shallow enemies; but when the hunt finally characterizes the Sophist as a purifier who educates through the refutation of vain opinion-wisdom, we can hardly keep from seeing Socrates caught in the nets set for the Sophist. Just in case we do not notice this catching—or do not take it seriously—Plato has the Stranger and Theaetetus reiterate their divisions. In the reiteration, Theaetetus confuses the fourth division, and the Stranger multiplies the confusion, for some reason, by calling the original fourth division "the fifth." He then calls the last one, which they had originally called the "fifth"—that is, the purifying educator— the "sixth" appearance of the Sophist. One never knows what to make of numerology in the dialogues, but this much is for sure: If someone counts something that we can count, too, and gets the number wrong, we must attend not only to the miscounting but to the number specified. Six is the first perfect number, and so not a bad one to sew on the back of Socrates' jersey.

Theaetetus and the Stranger then begin their final assault on the Sophist—as an image maker. This is the one that enmeshes them in the questions of being and non-being. It is only at the end of the dialogue, af- ter their great incursion into non-being, that they distinguish the Sophist as an image maker who dissembles his lack of knowledge. Until that point, they are engaged in a discussion of the foundations—the possibility—for an image-making that may or may not depend on knowledge. Until we introduce the traditional distinction in terms of knowledge, the genuine philosopher, caught in the fifth net, remains entangled in the shroud of likeness, apparition, and non-being that the Sophist throws out. The early figure of the Odyssean philosopher is helpful here: Through his allusions at the beginning of the dialogue, Socrates has prepared us for the thought that the tribe of genuine philosophers, too, is not inexperienced in disguise and dissimulation.

Now, though we are prepared to see the philosopher enmeshed— enshrouded—in a web of appearance and mere likeness, this gets us no closer to understanding the *meaning* of this web. We are still left with the shocking and serious problem of *why* the philosopher should enmesh himself in phantasms. I will but broach this question in the remaining part of this essay. The path to the answer is through the remarkable image of the Stranger's patricide.

At the center of the dialogue, the Stranger begs Theaetetus not to take him as a sort of patricide. He does this because he foresees clearly having to deny—having to violate utterly—his father Parmenides' teachings on being and non-being. He must do this in order to catch the Sophist in his lair of likeness. This is the central image of the dialogue: If Penelope were weaving the dialogue's representation, the image of the Stranger's patricide is what would seize and hold our vision.

I will suggest several wide implications of this central image. They are grounded, vaguely and imprecisely, in my overall sense of what Theaetetus and the Stranger engage in and accomplish in the rest of their discussion. Let me summarize it this way: They agree in what way "what is not" may be said to be; it is "other." They say further that this understanding does not depend on language, but, rather, that this state *is* the necessary ground for language itself. Lastly, they prove on this basis that there are such beings as false speech and false opinion—and since these things exist, they feel confident pursuing the Sophist into their territory. I must say how shocking I have always felt these results. No matter how closely we pursue the dialogue's subtle distinctions, these metaphysical moves remain startling: How far we have come from the discussion of the previous day, in which we could not tolerate the threat that change in nature posed to knowing. Now we take as a foundation a children's prayer that "all things be unmoved and moved at once" and proceed from there to consider the inseparability of being, same and other, rest and motion. This willingness marks a triple patricide.

First, it overthrows the teaching of Parmenides. Being no longer stands alone, august and holy (compare 249a). It is now mixed—corrupt. In the aftermath of this fundamental mixing, nothing can remain pure and absolute. This seems to destroy Parmenides' thinking at its foundations: No thinking is possible once we take this path. We should note that Parmenides' teaching was apparently not dialogic at all, but resided in written verses. It is these verses, and not any spoken, unversified, sayings, that the Stranger cites in the dialogue. In the dialogue, Parmenides is represented entirely by his written text. He is killed through a contradiction of his text.

Second, the progress toward otherness abandons and tramples the teaching of Socrates himself. Perhaps I should have said "of a certain Socrates"—I mean by this the Socrates of dialogues like the *Republic,* the *Symposium,* the *Phaedrus,* even. This Socrates teaches a metaphysics and epistemology based on unchanging forms, pure and powerful. I do not mean to claim that this teaching was ever simple or unambiguous—that it was ever intended as doctrine—but it did mark a certain path. Even the *Theaetetus* seems to follow this path. But this move not only deviates from that path but renounces and destroys it. The fundamental inseparability of *same* and *other* means that there are no transcendental originals, no pure beings—just mixed beings, with no clear ontological differentiation between originals and images. Toward the end of the discussion, Socrates rather blandly proposes that the "attempt to separate everything from everything is not only in bad taste, but belongs only to a man who is completely uncultivated and unphilosophical." This is because such a separation would lead to "the complete obliteration of all discourse"

(259d9–259e5). Theaetetus finds this claim to be "true." Such a move would be not only, say, questionable in the context of the central books of the *Republic*, but would be unimaginable. The analysis of non-being that follows the renunciation of Parmenides' doctrine thus destroys a certain Socratic teaching as well.

The third patricide is the most serious, the most instructive, and the only one tied ineluctably to the textuality of this and every other dialogue.

The inquiry of the dialogue abandons the political early. Once it broaches the question of likenesses, it moves into and easily and energetically inhabits the realm of the "pre-Socratic" philosophers, and exceeds even their wildest speculations. At its center, it focuses on the most abstruse and abstract questions and ignores both the soul and the city. In the end, the dialogue rejects the "Socratic turn" and inaugurates instead a fundamental inquiry into what is being, alone, without even the pre-Socratic grounding in nature.

The dialogue thus marks the murder of an older Socrates. This murder can be a *patricide* in only one way: Plato must be the perpetrator. The Stranger's patricidal rejection of his father is thus mirrored by Plato's rejection of the "political" Socrates. This rejection takes two interrelated forms: First, Plato rejects the Socratic turn to the city, away from metaphysics; and second, Plato rejects the Socratic mode of teaching through speech.

The first rejection is nearly obvious; I do not mean to say that it is complete or permanent, but any indulgence in pure metaphysics of the sort exemplified in the *Sophist* after the patricide would be a serious rejection of the "Socratic turn," no less serious than the stranger's rejection of Parmenides' injunctions. But this is not the most interesting form of the rejection.

I might be wrong in imagining for myself a purely "political Socrates" whom Plato rejects and leaves behind, but I am not wrong about the way that Socrates (whether he is involved in metaphysics or not) teaches. We do not pay enough attention to this one remarkable tension in the dialogues: They present the deeply personal, spontaneous interaction of idiosyncratic human beings as the paradigm of human teaching and learning, but do so in written treatises. We are familiar, whether we are troubled or not, with the way that the *Phaedrus* raises this question—but I think that even this does not go far enough. The dialogues are not merely written; they are written as artfully as possible—and in a way so deep, intricate, and seductive, that we cannot resist reading them. But I do mean *reading* them. They are written in such a way that the text never disappears; in fact, in my experience, at any moment that I simply become involved in reading and thinking, the text calls me back and reminds me that it is referring to itself, or to Homer, or that somebody has miscounted something—and that I need to *re*read—as if reading were never enough. The text is thus like a jealous and insatiable lover: No attention is enough, it always calls out for more.

In this way the text becomes central, primary, and is never merely some kind of vehicle for preserving, or conveying, or perhaps simulating Socrates' teaching. Socrates' teaching takes as its form "We are engaged in this inquiry together." Plato's teaching, on the other hand, takes this form: "You are reading me now, and you had better pay attention." Everything seems to me to turn on this: Once the dialogues become written *in this way,* Socratic learning and teaching becomes impossible. We cannot concentrate on our souls, on the city before us, on our shared conversation. Our concern becomes, instead, the text and its challenges.

Let me give you one sign that the writing of the dialogues *alone* is intimately tied to the loss of their political character. The dialogue on writing, the *Phaedrus,* takes place outside the city walls. It can do so precisely because it is based on a written text that can be carried around. Once a dialogue is embodied in a written text, it can be removed from the agora and addressed and engaged in private. It will engender reading and reflection—two activities that depend on and are perfected by *solitude.* The *Phaedrus* thus makes explicit the nature of all of the Platonic dialogues: They are indifferent to the city.

The first ramification of the turn from conversation to text is that the students of Plato (and, consequently, of Socrates) focus on images rather than originals. It is no accident—nor a mere stroke of artistry—that the dialogues are full of images. The dialogue itself is an image—and I do not mean of a conversation. That is treating them too simply, credulously. We know that in almost no case do they mimic a possible discussion—they almost always present themselves as something perfectly choreographed and composed—no "realistic" image of any human conversation. I do not think that they represent "ideal" discussions, either—they are not like great statues, inaccurate representations altered from the originals so that they seem beautiful to us (236). No, they are not *representations* of anything. They are teaching tools, or manifestos, or poetry—but not images *of* anything. Yet images they are—surely. They cannot be originals by the ontologies of the *Republic* or the *Phaedrus.* They are squarely in the Sophist's realm of not-being. So the first crucial ramification of Plato's turn to writing is the focus of philosophy on images.

Let me mention one way in which this is obviously true. As students of Plato, the frequent focus of our attention is the figure of Socrates. We ceased asking long ago about the degree to which this figure corresponds to the historical or actual Socrates. We are content to examine him as a factitious—fabulous—image. The very Socrates that we love and follow as some kind of beacon of true philosophy is an image—a character. I am not cretinously suggesting that we do not recognize this—just the opposite. We know it full well. I suspect only that we often draw no conclusions from this.

Now a second ramification follows inevitably from the first. Once philosophy takes up residence in the realm of images, it has, as it were, two choices: to investigate everything else but its own domain, or to subject its own domain to inquiry. Just as every patricide aims at securing some patrimony, Plato claims this prize from his father's house: Philosophy must inquire into its own realm or fail to know itself. Thus, as soon as Plato turns to writing, the investigation of seeming, the encounter with non-being, the ontology of *same* and *other* is inevitable. The dizzying metaphysics of the *Sophist* is decided in advance by the written form—the textuality—of the very first dialogue.

I want to state three corollaries to this. First, the written text says "something is not here, something is absent." It always presents itself as incomplete and other—even if we cannot say clearly what would complete it or what it is other than. Thus we always ask: What does this passage mean? It is never complete. For this reason, Plato's metaphysics must take seriously not just seeming, but non-being.

Second, Plato's text is *pure* image, or, perhaps, *phantasia*. It has no transcendental original. The metaphysics of this dialogue allow for no such originals for any being. We must seriously question whether the soul, for instance, is not equally an image with the same ontological status as the text. It would be a kind of pure production. The soul—and, perhaps, the *eidē*—would be images no less than the city or the cave is in the *Republic*. A small sign that this is true is that by the end of the dialogue the Stranger (openly) uses *eidos* (and not *eidōlon*) for that which appears in the reflections of bright surfaces (266c).

Third, philosophical practice cannot focus on the recovery of or return to originals.

What work then is left for the philosopher? The end of the dialogue provides the obvious answer, in the obvious way. On their way to closing in on the last appearance of the Sophist, the one Theaetetus calls "the completely beingly sophist," the Stranger makes the following suggestion:

> Let us assign [the art that employs one's own voice or body as an
> instrument for making *phantasiai*] to the class of the "mimetic," but as for
> [the class that produces *phantasiai* by other instruments], let's be soft and
> let it go, and leave it for someone else to unify it and give it a fitting name.

This omission is a flag; we cannot avoid asking what that fitting name would be and who would apply it. To note the omission and attempt the supplement is to know the answer: The name is "philosophy," and Plato applies it precisely by not writing the expected dialogue entitled "The Philosopher." The omission of this name, and elision of the whole dialogue, constitute and demonstrate the textuality of the dialogue, of the question, and of the practice of philosophy itself. It is precisely in moments like this, reflecting the beginning of the dialogue, that Plato shows what he understands philosophy to be. He does so by fashioning images—but not mere representations. The images show the place of philosophy in the netherworld *of* images; they show philosophy's roots in the creation of texts. In this way we see that despite Socrates' suggestion of the philosopher's many resemblances to Odysseus, Plato is the reflection of *Penelope*—the master weaver.

We must pause for a moment to recall just what Penelope is weaving. It is a burial shroud for Laertes, the father of Odysseus—the father of the image of the philosopher—who is not yet dead. This is a sign that, for Plato, the writing of the dialogues is not a supplement or marker for the dead, defunct Philosopher, but that the writing precedes and even announces his death. Plato's Socratic dialogues are Socrates' Penelopean burial shroud, tolling the death of conversational, "living," philosophy.

This brings us to our last question. This is a very vexed one and seems to be addressed with the greatest seriousness in all of the literature on the *Sophist*. The question is: Who is the (real) Philosopher?

Our answer must now be "Nobody in particular." Stop worrying about the question. It is a question left over from the pretextual era of philosophy. Once philosophy becomes and recognizes itself to be textual, the question for now and all time is: What is being? This displacement is the deepest form of the patricide of Socrates by Plato.

Notes

1. Compare *Oeconomicus* 1.1; *Memorabilia* 2.1.1, 2.3.1; and so on.
2. We might suppose that gods are relatively easy to distinguish and concede from the beginning that philosophers are not. This calls Theodorus's judgment into question from the very beginning. On the other hand, we ought to keep in mind the remarkable story told by Herodotus of Athena's visit to Athens (1.60). An aspiring demagogue, only a few generations before the time of this dialogue, wanted to impress the Athenians with the divine support for his rule and so dressed a tall and striking country girl as Athena and had her wheeled into Athens

on a fancied-up oxcart. Her name, according to Herodotus, was Phue, but she convinced the city she was Athena. Even close to Socrates' own time, it seems, his fellow citizens could not distinguish a god from a mortal. Now, Socrates' response to Theodorus cuts two ways; the first is insulting to him. It calls into doubt not whether we should miss a god among us, but whether we, like the mass of Athenians, should mistake another mortal for a god—or another sophist for a philosopher.

   3. Compare 2.85 and following. Penelope is weaving a burial shroud for Odysseus's father, Laertes, who is not yet dead. We will return to this point. We should note that a burial shroud would have been a tapestry not only of threads but of visual images.

PART II

PLATO'S OTHER METAPHYSICS

5

Traces of the *Chōra*

John Sallis

he *Timaeus* abounds with indications concerning the character, structure, and direction of its various discourses. Among the many passages where the dialogue thus turns upon itself, there is one that pertains in particular to the question of beginning. The passage occurs near—though not precisely at—the beginning of that part of the dialogue in which Timaeus presents his long monologue, or rather, his three long monologues, which constitute the greater part, though by no means all, of the *Timaeus*. The passage immediately precedes and is linked to a much longer one in which Timaeus insists on the kinship that makes discourse like its object, that makes discourse on likenesses—discourses such as those Timaeus is about to present—likely discourse (*eikōs logos*). But the particular, immediately preceding passage on which, here at the beginning, I want to focus is a passage about beginning, an injunction declaring how one ought to begin. Timaeus says: "With regard to everything it is most important to begin at the natural beginning" (29b).

Let me follow this injunction forthrightly, assuming—in order not to defer beginning—that the natural beginning of the dialogue *Timaeus* is to be found in its opening words and its opening scene.

The opening words are spoken by Socrates: three words, the words *one, two, three*. So, then, a counting, here at the beginning, a counting to three. In the same way, at the center of the dialogue, Timaeus counts to three, counts the three kinds, calling them, among many names: one, selfsame being; two, that which is generated; and, three, the (receptacle) of all generation. What is decisive at that point and hence for the entire dialogue is precisely that the counting must proceed to *three,* that to the twofold of paradigm and image there must be added a third kind, which is called by various names, among them *that which receives,* or simply *the receptacle.*

The opening scene and deed of the *Timaeus* prefigure this third kind. The scene is one of reception, of Socrates' being hospitably received by those three hosts whom, at the outset, he counts off: Timaeus, Critias, and Hermocrates. Having himself entertained them on the previous day, Socrates comes now as their guest, eager to receive the feast of discourse he has been promised. Therefore, the scene of the dialogue and what is enacted in deed from the beginning correspond quite precisely to what comes to be said at the center of the dialogue. In all these dimensions, it is a matter of reception, of receptacle. Or, as it is finally called in the brief discourse around which one can gather the entire dialogue, the *chōra.*

Despite the injunction Timaeus issues, it turns out that in the first of his three discourses he does not begin at the beginning. Rather, his discourse gets ahead of itself; or, more precisely, the discourse is ahead of itself from the beginning, since it fails to tell of a certain beginning that precedes the production about which it does tell, the production by which the *dēmiourgos,* the artisan god, came to make the heavens, the cosmos. Thus, Timaeus is compelled to break off his first discourse and to make a new beginning, to launch a second discourse that would turn back to the beginning with which the first discourse failed to begin. It is in this second discourse, indeed at the point where he has just come as close as he ever will to saying the beginning, that he uses the word *ichnos,* which I translate as *trace* (53b). This is the sole occurrence of this word in the *Timaeus.*

The context is one in which Timaeus is speaking of fire, air, water, and earth. These are precisely the primary bodies that were taken for granted in the first discourse, assumed to be simply there to be used by the artisan god in his fabrication of the cosmos. Thus it was that, when Timaeus broke off the discourse so as to make a new beginning, he specified that it was imperative to consider the nature (*phusis*) of fire, air, water, and earth as they were before the generation of the heavens. But the context in which they are called traces pertains to a time that precedes not only the productive deeds of the god but even his very arrival. Timaeus says that in the absence of the god these four (fire, water, earth) were not yet even themselves; or, more precisely, he says that they had only some traces (*ichnē*) of themselves. In the absence of the god, fire, air, water, and earth were not yet themselves but only traces of themselves. Only when the god arrives on the scene and informs them with the shapes of the regular solids do they become fire air, water, and earth as such.

For Timaeus's second discourse and indeed for the dialogue as a whole, nothing is more decisive than the strange involvement that these (traces) prove to have with the *chōra*. When, breaking off his first discourse, Timaeus turns to consider fire, air, water, and earth as they were before the generation of the heavens, it is precisely this strange involvement that leads him on to a consideration of the *chōra*, turning the discourse into a chorology. And this strange involvement is what in a certain way even enables this discourse, makes chorology possible. It is precisely this involvement that would be said in the phrase "traces of the *chōra*"—a phrase that one does not find as such in the dialogue but that allows one (as I shall undertake to show) to gather up with appropriate coherence and articulation certain of the most decisive segments of Timaeus's discourse.

Three segments, in particular, will require attention. In the first segment fire, air, water, and earth come to be apprehended as traces of the *chōra* in such a way that Timaeus's discourse, having turned to these traces, is compelled also to address the *chōra*, to become chorology. The second segment is divided from itself, occurring in part before and in part after the chorology proper. Here too fire, air, water, and earth are addressed as traces of the *chōra*, but now in the sense of its appearance, indeed appearance in a sense best expressed perhaps by a word that recurs often in the *Timaeus*, the word *chalepon*, that is, "difficult," "troublesome," even "dangerous." The third segment is the entire remainder of the dialogue beyond the point at which the god returns and forms the traces into primary bodies. Here, the question becomes one of replacement: once fire, air, water, and earth are no longer traces, then what traces of the *chōra* remain, even in an extended sense of trace? Where can the effectiveness of the *chōra* be traced in the cosmos, once the god has bestowed measure and intelligence (*nous*) upon it?

The first segment of discourse on the traces of the *chōra* occurs shortly after Timaeus has broken off his account of the production of the cosmos and made the new beginning that would turn back to the beginning passed over previously. Timaeus has declared that to the twofold of paradigm and image a third kind must now be added; or rather, more precisely, he has said that the *logos* seems to necessitate attempting to reveal such a kind. Also, he has characterized this third kind as the receptacle of all generation. Only then—and, indeed, not before uttering again the word *chalepon*—does Timaeus turn to the fire, air, water, and earth for the sake of which the second discourse has ostensibly been undertaken. The difficulty is not long showing itself. The difficulty lies in saying which of these is to be called, for instance, water rather than fire. The difficulty lies in saying which is to be called which and in doing so in a saying that is trustworthy and stable. Timaeus explains the difficulty by referring to sight and to a kind of circle that can be observed in what one sees of fire, air, water, and earth. One sees what is called water becoming, by condensation, stones and earth. One sees it also dissolving into breath and air and these, in turn, through combustion, becoming fire. One can follow the circle in the other direction, seeing fire become air, air condensing into cloud and mist and then water, and then again water becoming stones and earth. Timaeus says, "Thus, in a circle they give generation to one another, as becomes manifest [*hōs phainetai*]." He poses the question, "Thus, since no one of these ever makes its appearance as the same, which of them can one affirm to be this, whatever it is, and not something else without incurring ridicule?" He answers: "There is none" (49c–d). And he prescribes the way in which one could, then, most safely speak of them. Whatever one sees constantly becoming other, one should call not *this* (*touto*) but *suchlike* (*toiouton*). Nor should one speak of any one of them as though it possessed stability. For they *flee* from all names that would mark them as stable. And whereas they can only be called *suchlike*, that in which, being generated, they appear and from which, in turn, they perish can appropriately be called *this* and *that* (*touto kai tode*).

The passage I have just outlined is one the specific sense of which has been vigorously disputed. In its most recent form, the dispute goes back to Cherniss's 1954 paper "A Much Misread Passage of the *Timaeus*."[1] The main point in the dispute concerns *what* exactly cannot, according to Timaeus, be said, for instance, of fire, what word cannot be applied to it. Specifically, the question is whether it is the word *this* that cannot be applied to it (as the traditional interpretation and Cherniss's critics would have it) or whether it is the word *fire* (as Cherniss argues). Fortunately, it is not necessary in the present context to enter this dispute or to make a choice between the two interpretations. For, regardless of which reading one assumes, the main point remains the same: fire, air, water, and earth flee from *logos*, are fugitives from *logos;* that is, they lack sufficient stability or selfsameness to be called *this* or *that* (or *fire* or *water* and so on). Because they are always becoming something else, they can only be named by a name that simultaneously releases them from naming, a name such as *suchlike*.

One begins to realize that Timaeus was not speaking loosely when he declared that the *logos* seems to necessitate attempting to reveal a third kind. One could even say that, for the move from the twofold to a third kind, *logos* is the touchstone. When it touches or attempts to touch fire and the others, they take flight in a manner that is incomparable to anything that occurs within the compass of the twofold. However imperfect a couch may be in comparison to its paradigm, it can be called *couch* without proving already to have been becoming something else. Not only the paradigm but also the product made in its image is sufficiently selfsame and determinate that they can to a degree sustain the name; later Timaeus will say explicitly that the image shares both the name and the look of the paradigm (see 52a). Only fire, air, water, and earth are fugitives from *logos,* indeed in such a way that their very flight points to a third kind that would harbor them outside the twofold. One could say that the flight of such self-extinguishing indices as fire traces a way beyond the twofold of paradigm and image. Their flight traces a passage, a way out to the receptacle in which they would be received and held. It is thus that they are traces of the *chōra,* namely, as traces indicating the way to the *chōra.*

It is by taking up this way, by following these traces, that Timaeus comes to speak of the *chōra.* His initial strategy is to present a series of images of it (nurse, mother, gold, and so on), thus to address it in a likely discourse (*eikōs logos*) improper to it. As he proceeds it becomes increasingly evident that what he says of it has the effect of putting in question the very possibility of saying anything binding about it. Though, unlike its traces, it can be called *this* and *that,* it turns out that discourse on the *chōra* is no less problematic than that on its traces. When finally Timaeus ventures the discourse in which it comes to be called by its proper name, this chorology proper, turning upon itself so as to indicate its own character, declares itself to be a sort of bastard reckoning (see 52b). In Athenian usage a bastard (*nothos*) was the child of a citizen father and an alien mother. As here, where the bastard discourse is fathered by Timaeus and is to be borne by the maternal *chōra* in all its alien elusiveness, its alterity, its strangeness.

Stopping short of that discourse, holding back from the chorology, from which it would be most difficult for us to find an exit leading back to the traces that are our concern, let it suffice to mention only three things that Timaeus says about the *chōra* as his discourse moves toward the chorology.

First of all, Timaeus says that it is all-receiving, yet itself formless (*pandeches, amorphon*). He says this against the background of several images that he has just offered: the gold that can be molded into all sorts of shapes, but is not itself any one of these shapes; the matrix (*ekmageion*) on which, as on wax, all sorts of figures can be stamped without its being any one of these figures; the base for a fragrant ointment, which must itself be entirely without fragrance. So must it be with the third kind, the receptacle, that which will eventually be called the *chōra*. It has itself none of those forms, shapes, or determinations that can be stamped on it or received by it. Since it is all-receiving, this is tantamount to saying that it itself has no form, no determinations whatsoever. It can receive all the forms represented by the paradigms or intelligible *eidē*, but it is not *itself* determined by any of them; it cannot itself have any of these determinations, cannot have them *as determinations of itself*. The ramifications of this nondetermination are profound, not to say abysmal: If the *chōra* has no determinations whatsoever, then how can anything be said of it? For, presumably, to say something of it would be to ascribe to it some specific determination. Little wonder that the discourse will eventually designate itself as a bastard sort of reckoning.

Second, Timaeus calls the third kind *invisible,* or, more precisely, he says that if we call it invisible (as well as formless and all-receiving) "we will not be speaking falsely" (51a–b). Its invisibility can be regarded as linked to its formlessness: Since it is not determined by any intelligible *eidos,* it has no look by which to present itself to one's vision. Yet its invisibility is different from that of the intelligible *eidē.* It is not an invisibility that, as with the intelligible *eidē,* is just the other side of another, higher visibility; rather, the invisibility of the third kind is a more insistent invisibility. Not transparency and excess of light, but utter darkness.

Little wonder, then, that Timaeus says, third, that this invisible, formless, all-receiving third kind is "most difficult to catch." Or rather, if we say that it is most difficult to catch, "we will not be speaking falsely" (51a–b).

It is to this difficulty that the second of the three segments of discourse on the traces of the *chōra* is addressed. For if it were simply and unqualifiedly invisible, if it offered nothing to vision, the discourse on the *chōra* would be utterly blind, would be a discourse completely unbound by anything beyond itself, a discourse that could not but fall back into itself. This is why it is of utmost consequence that the third kind somehow *appear,* show itself, become manifest. It is precisely such appearing that is announced in the second segment on the traces of the *chōra.*

This segment of the discourse is itself segmented into three passages. The first occurs in conjunction with the image of the third kind as a matrix that can receive all things. Timaeus says, "Being moved and shaped by those things that enter it, through them it appears [*phainetai*] different at different times" (50c). Even if different at different times, even if never as the same, nonetheless it *appears.*

The second passage occurs a bit further on, just after Timaeus has called the third kind invisible, formless, and all-receiving, just before the chorology proper. At this point in the text, it is as if the significance of the appearing were underlined by the way its declaration is framed between two textual indicators. The first announces the intention of speaking, as Timaeus says, "most correctly." The second indicator announces the intention of presenting the discourse on these matters that most thoroughly distinguishes what is to be distinguished among them. Between these two indicators stands Timaeus's declaration regarding the appearing of the third kind: "That part of it that is made fiery appears [*phainesthai*] as fire" and likewise for the other three (51b). The third kind, which is about to be called *chōra, appears as fiery*, that is, it appears as and by way of the fire that is only a trace. The *chōra* appears, shows itself, becomes manifest, but never *as itself*, never without holding itself as such—if it has an itself as such—in concealment.

The third passage comes almost immediately after the chorology proper. Reverting to the image of the *chōra* as the nurse of generation and referring again to the traces of fire, air, water, and earth held in it, Timaeus says that it "appears [*phainesthai*] manifoldly to sight" (52d–e). This reaffirmation of the appearing of the *chōra* then launches Timaeus's account of how the *chōra*, filled with the traces (as they are now called), sways unevenly, shaking and itself being shaken by the traces, beginning to sort them out, as in winnowing. The scene is thus prepared for the arrival of the god and for the resumption of his productive deeds.

In a sense Timaeus's discourse has now caught up with itself, though one would hardly expect it merely to revert to the mode and structures that were operative before it broke off and opened the abyss toward which it was drawn by the traces of the *chōra*. What, then, about the segment of discourse that ensues once the god has formed the traces into the primary bodies used by the god in fabricating the cosmos? Once the traces have thus been assimilated, once they are no longer traces, do there remain any traces of the *chōra*? Is the *chōra* in any way traced in this third segment of discourse, running from the account of the primary bodies to the little comedy with which the dialogue concludes?

It is an old complaint, a complaint made by one of the earliest readers of the *Timaeus*, the complaint that having introduced the *chōra* Plato then makes no use of it in the remainder of the dialogue. It is Aristotle's complaint, for instance, in the passage in *On Generation and Corruption* where he says:

And what is written in the *Timaeus* does not distinguish sufficiently. For it is not clearly said whether the all-receiving [*to pandeches*] is separate

> from the elements. Nor does he make any use of it, after saying that it is a
> substratum [*hupokeimenon*] prior to the so-called elements, just as gold is
> the substratum of works made of gold. (329a)

Whatever reservations one might voice about the appropriateness of such
words as *hupokeimenon,* the complaint is clear and has continued to be put
forth even by some recent commentators on the *Timaeus.*[2]

But what about the complaint? Is it sustained when one turns to the
dialogue itself and reads with care and discernment?

In fact, there are several places in the *Timaeus* where statements of
intent or reflections on the account under way would seem to indicate
quite the contrary of what Aristotle says. For instance, at the beginning
of Timaeus's second discourse, where he has just broken off and made a
new beginning, he declares that the generation of the cosmos came about
as a mixture, from the combination of intelligence (*nous*) and necessity
(*anagkē*). The discourse that follows makes it manifest that *anagkē* is a
name for what comes to be called, finally, *chōra*. And, more carefully and
discerningly translated, the passage speaks, not just of combination (as
if *nous* and *anagkē* were simply united), but rather of a standing-together
in which there can also be hostility, conflict, as with two soldiers in close
combat. Thus, the specific sense of the passage is such as to suggest that
the necessary or choric moment will not be simply assimilated once the
god returns, that this moment is not to disappear from the dialogue from
that point on. Another instance is found just after the account of how the
god assigned the figures of the regular solids to the traces. Reflecting on
the account, noting that it is a likely discourse, Timaeus observes that
indeed the god shaped the primary bodies in just the way described,
at least—and this is the decisive indication—to the extent that *anagkē*
permitted (56c). There are other, fairly direct references to the *chōra* in
the epichorological discourse, as when, for instance, Timaeus says that
the motion of the receptacle serves to keep the primary bodies apart in
their respective regions (57c). And that is to say nothing of the fact that
even in Timaeus's third discourse various names for the *chōra* and the
name *chōra* itself are sounded.

There can be no question, then, but that the *chōra* will remain to
some extent in force after the god's return. At the very least it will limit
what the artisan god can achieve in his cosmic fabrication; it will limit the
productive operation of divine or noetic causes. And yet, unlike what is
produced, unlike even production itself, the *chōra* cannot become a *theme
to be presented,* something to be presented, say, along with the operation of
nous. Why not? Precisely because the *chōra cannot be presented*. It does not
itself become present, but only appears as something else, not as itself. It

cannot be presented even in the sense of being the theme of a discourse that would determine it, for it withdraws from all determination and allows only a bastard discourse. The consequence is that the chorology *cannot be integrated* into the likely discourse that resumes following it and that continues to the end of the dialogue.

In a sense, then, Plato could not have made use of the *chōra* in the rest of the dialogue. Yet this does not mean that the *chōra* is not in force beneath the production of the various things the god will fabricate, but only that it is not in force as something present that could be represented, that is, imaged in a likeness in a likely discourse. How, then, is the *chōra* in force? And how is it said in—or, in a sense, along with—the likely discourse that runs on to the end of the dialogue?

The word that names its way of being in force is introduced at the very beginning of the second discourse when Timaeus describes the kind of cause that at that point has to be brought into consideration, not having been considered in the previous discourse. He calls it an *errant* kind of cause, errant (translating *planōmenon*) in the double sense of wandering and erring. How, then, is the *chōra* in force? It is in force as errancy: as hindering, diverting, leading astray the work of *nous,* as installing indeterminacy into what *nous* would otherwise render determinate. And the *chōra* is said in the epichorological discourse of the *Timaeus* by the way in which this discourse traces the errancy, that is, marks the traces of its operation in the very midst of the god's productions. The discourse marks the traces of the *chōra* by marking the traces of its errant, indetermining operation.

In the epichorological portion of Timaeus's second discourse, there are several such traces marked. Let me mention three.

The first occurs near the end of Timaeus's account of how the primary bodies are produced by the assignment of the figures of the regular solids to the traces of fire, air, water, and earth. In the course of that account, Timaeus explains also exactly how these figures are themselves constructed from two kinds of triangles, right isosceles triangles and triangles each of which consists of half an equilateral triangle. What is unusual in the account—and what marks the operation of errancy—is that, just at the point where it would seem that complete order had been constituted, Timaeus suddenly mentions that these two kinds of triangles occur in all different sizes (57d). Thus there proves to be an unlimited, indeterminately great variety of combinations.

The second such trace occurs at the point where, as Timaeus is discussing the four kinds of primary bodies, there suddenly appears a kind of gap in the discourse, an indeterminacy, a certain silence within it. In speaking of air, he notes that there are different kinds of air, since

JOHN SALLIS

the triangles that compose it can be different sizes. So, there is ether and mist and, he says, "other *eidē* [of air] without a name, produced because of the inequality of the triangles" (58d). But since, as he just mentioned, there are indefinitely many different sizes of triangles, he has now in effect introduced into the very eidetics of air an indeterminate proliferation. Proceeding to discuss water, he mentions the names of several kinds, but then says regarding the various mixtures of various kinds of water, "Most of the kinds thus generated are without names" (60a). The structure of the text is here most remarkable. Right between a passage in which he gives the names of some kinds of water and the passage in which he admits that many others have no names, Timaeus abruptly turns the discourse upon itself, calling it, not an *eikōs logos,* but an *eikōs muthos* and characterizing such storytelling as a pleasant, measured, and mindful play (*paidia*). Presumably the discourse here becomes, if it has not, indeed, already become, a matter of play, of playful stories, because of the indeterminacy, instability, wandering, and vacillation that belongs to things of the kind he is describing. He says even: Let us give free rein to this play, and go on with such stories. The question is, how far does this self-determination of the discourse as playful story extend? Does it extend only to the end of the discussion of the primary bodies? Or, perhaps, to the end of the second discourse? Or even to the end of the dialogue?

The third trace is marked in Timaeus's discussion of sensible affections. For in the course of this discussion, some things turn up that not only have no names but have no *eidē,* thus sensible things of a sort that are not even images of the intelligible. Timaeus mentions especially odors and declares that they "do not allow *eidē*" (66d). He calls them "halfkinds" (*hēmigenes*). Since they have no *eidē* they cannot but lack names even more insistently than in the cases discussed earlier.

In Timaeus's third discourse, also, such traces of the *chōra* are marked, this wandering, errant indetermination that haunts the works of the god and, perhaps even more, the works of the engendered gods to whom he delegates the task of making the other living beings, except for their immortal part. Nowhere is such a trace more unmistakably marked than in Timaeus's description of the making of the mortal part of the human soul. He says that the mortal soul has within it passions that are both fearful (*deinos*) and necessary (*anagkaia*). Then he tells how the mortal soul came about: "And blending these with undiscursive sensation and with all-endeavoring *erōs,* they compounded, in the manner of necessity, the mortal kind of soul" (69d). Thus are *anagkē* and its errancy (errancy itself) operative within the human soul from the very formation of its mortal part.

In Timaeus's discourse on the human body, there are numerous indications as to how the *chōra* is duplicated within the body itself and, through its double, put in play there. Such duplication is unmistakably indicated in the case of the liver: It is made dense and smooth and bright and sweet, yet containing bitterness; and so, as Timaeus says, "the power of thoughts that proceed from *nous* move in the liver as in a mirror that receives impressions and provides visible images" (71b). Also, the lower belly, the abdomen, is explicitly called a receptacle (*hupodochē*) for food and drink; its purpose is to prevent them from passing through too quickly, that is, to secure them in their flux. Timaeus observes that, without this receptacle, we would be plagued by insatiable appetite; and then, because of our gluttony, we would be rendered devoid of philosophy. So, then, Timaeus supplies a playful story about how the belly—a double of the *chōra*—makes philosophy possible. One could add perhaps another kind of story, about how philosophy requires images, which the *chōra* makes possible. But that would be another story!

Even the word *chōra* is found in Timaeus's discussion of the origin of disease—appropriately so, since the description pictures disease as like a reversion to that state of imbalance and shaking that was said to prevail when, before the arrival of the god, the *chōra* was filled with the traces of fire, air, water, and earth. Referring to these four, but now as the primary bodies from which the human body is composed, Timaeus says: "When, contrary to nature, there occurs an excess or deficiency of these or a change in the *chōra* from the proper to an other, then the body loses its selfsameness and there results disease [*nosos*] and unlimitedness [*apeiron*]" (82a). When Timaeus goes on to speak of the treatment of disease, specifically of the restoration of symmetry between soul and body, he declares that this involves imitating "the nurse of the universe" (88d); that is, recalling the earlier role of the image of the nurse, it involves imitating the *chōra*. This is to be accomplished by never allowing the body to be at rest, by continually producing internal vibrations keeping it in movement, thus duplicating the state of the *chōra* filled with traces being winnowed out.

Timaeus's third discourse contains numerous touches of comedy. One example lies in the picture of someone making himself like the *chōra* and its traces in order to treat his illness, especially in the case of a man, considering the maternal nature of the *chōra*. Several of the comic touches have, indeed, to do with sex, with the difference and relation between the sexes.

But let me touch only on the remarkable way in which the third discourse, and hence the *Timaeus* as a whole, draws to an end. Just short of the end, the discourse appears to reach a kind of climax, to culminate in an ascent. Timaeus comes to speak only of the divine part of the soul (housed in the head) and of our looking to the harmonies and revolutions of the cosmos in order to make the revolutions in our head, disturbed by and at birth, like those of the cosmos. The ascent is nothing short of a reversion to the sphere of Timaeus's first discourse; both in tone and in content, it sounds very much like the injunction issued at the end of the first discourse, just before that discourse was interrupted for the sake of the turn back toward the *chōra*. In this ascent, as previously, it is a matter of mimesis and of the structures within which mimesis operates; it is a matter of an imitation that looks to a paradigm in order to make something (now one's divine part) like the paradigm. Most remarkably, it is at precisely this point that a kind of comedy breaks out, a kind of sex comedy, which comes thus to interrupt the ascent. Timaeus, of course, is speaking:

> And the marrow that we call seed, inasmuch as it is animate and has been granted an outlet, has endowed the part where its outlet lies with a love for generating by implanting therein a lively desire for emission. Wherefore in men, the nature of the genital organs is disobedient and self-willed, like a creature that is deaf to *logos*, and it attempts to dominate all because of its frenzied desires. And in women again, owing to the same causes, whenever the womb or uterus, as it is called—which is an indwelling creature, desirous of child-bearing—remains without fruit long beyond the due season, it is vexed and becomes errant; and by straying all ways through the body and blocking up the passages of the breath and preventing respiration, it casts the body into the utmost distress and causes, moreover, all kinds of maladies; until the desire and love [*hē epithumia kai ho erōs*] of the two sexes unite them. (91b–c)

Thus, at the very moment of ascent—or in the moment of its interruption—there comes a comic transition from male to female, to the prospective mother, whose womb can become errant, wandering (*planōmenon*). And then, there comes also a comic transformation of the way up, the ascent, the flight. For, as soon as the woman has given birth, Timaeus continues, "Now, as for the race of birds, they are derived by transformation, growing feathers in place of hair, from men [males: *anēr*] who are harmless but light-minded" (91d).

So then, Timaeus provides not only playful stories, but comic ones, comedies that interrupt the high-minded ascent of those who would fix their gaze upward or suspend themselves in the clouds. These comedies release the play of *erōs* and draw us back toward the abyss. It is with such comedy that the *Timaeus,* this most abysmal of dialogues, comes fittingly to an end.

Notes

1. Harold Cherniss, "A Much Misread Passage of the *Timaeus* (*Timaeus* 49c7–50b5)," *American Journal of Philology* 75 (1954): 113–30, especially 118–19; reprinted in Harold Cherniss, *Selected Papers,* ed. Leonardo Tarán (Leiden: E. J. Brill, 1977). An extensive discussion of this debate is provided in John Sallis, *Chorology: On Beginning in Plato's "Timaeus"* (Bloomington: Indiana University Press, 1999), chapter 3. Several other discussions in this essay are developed more extensively or within a more elaborated context in *Chorology.*

2. See, for example, Edward N. Lee, "On the Metaphysics of the Image in Plato's *Timaeus,*" *Monist* 50 (1966): 349.

6

We Sense That They Strive: How to Read (the Theory of the Forms)

John Russon

The *Phaedo* seems to equate Socrates and Theseus. Reading the dialogue well would require careful attention to how these two biographies are made to harmonize, but that is too big a task for this essay. I will, in fact, pay relatively little attention to the drama or the mythology of the dialogue except to follow out one thread: the question of the minotaur. If the *Phaedo* shows Theseus in the labyrinth, what is the monster that he must slay and from whose lair he must make an escape? Along with James Crooks, I believe the minotaur to be misology, the fear of argumentation, so I will follow Socrates' advice and use thinking to find a way out of the labyrinthine arguments of this most puzzling dialogue.[1]

Indeed, one reason why reading Plato seems different from reading most other dramatic texts is that the drama of the Platonic dialogues is largely conceptual. Whatever else is involved, rigorous conceptual thinking remains one of the main abilities required to read Plato. Plato is to be *studied,* to be read over and over, and it is only after many and careful readings that the texts are sufficiently contacted, that we are "with it" enough, so as to let their treasures—their meanings—show themselves. Reading Plato requires work. It requires active hunting. And one of the major dimensions of this work is thinking through the explicit arguments made by the various characters.[2] Ultimately, this essay will address only a few lines of the *Phaedo,* that is, 74d9–75b2, but to begin to do this—and this essay will only get to this beginning—requires thinking through some arguments. These arguments are presented in three of the key speeches of the dialogue; they are the argument that knowledge is recollection, the argument that the soul cannot be a harmony, and the discussion of mind as cause. It is what we will learn from a philosophical study of these themes that will allow us to return to a few lines from the discussion about recollection and to open up a road to reading them powerfully and in a way that has a chance of making us turn to thinking yet again. I will begin by recalling (of course) the argument about recollection, and I will end by recalling what *aisthesis* is like, and, particularly, what it is like to read a text—say, a text of Plato's.

Recollection and Equality

We all recognize various situations of equality.[3] This stick, we say, is equal (in length) to that stick; this shoe is equal (in size) to that shoe; this woman is the equal (in strength of body or strength of mind) to that man.[4] How do we know what equality—not just some equals, but equality itself—is? We might first think that we develop this knowledge by moving (perhaps by abstraction) from these various equalities, as evidence, to achieving a knowledge of equality itself, as a conclusion. But this cannot be, for it is only by virtue of already knowing what it is to be equal that we have the ability to recognize the various equalities *as equalities* in the first place. Consequently, an ability to recognize equality as equality must be possessed in advance, and any discovery of equals or of equality itself can only be a recollecting of this that we already know: Only one who already knew what equality was would be capable of recognizing equals. Rather than pursue the further details of this argument from *Phaedo* 72e–77a or the consequences that Socrates and his partners derive from this, I want to linger a moment over this notion of equality. The point of this argument about equality and recollection is that there are some specific conditions that must be met in order for a recognition of equality to take place, and I want to remain with this theme and to parse more precisely what is entailed in such a recognition.

Notice first that the notion of equality involves the notion of comparison.[5] Two things can be known to be equal only by holding them together—holding them *with* one another—so that they are at the same time maintained in their difference and also taken up in their sameness. To deal with equalities is already to have advanced beyond the notion of isolated atoms and to occupy a space of community, a space of which the units to be compared are members. An equality, then, involves a metaphysical universe larger than that of two isolated entities, for we must recognize the integrity of the space of comparison itself as a necessary participant within the situation of equality. A comparison is an answer to the question "How are you with respect to each other?" a question that can be asked only within the space of a "with." This "with" is the essence of a "two": The shared community is how the two make one dyad.[6]

Notice further that to deal with equalities is to introduce the _qua_. _Two_ equals are not simply the same one thing. Even if a condition for being a dyad is that it be _a_ dyad, it is equally a condition that it be a _dyad_. If comparison thus means to hold them together as the same _and different_, then it must be the case that there is a respect in which they are not the same, which means their sameness can only be in some respect; that is, they are equal _qua_ . . . : Indeed, only unequals can be equals.[7] The space of comparison is thus also necessarily the space of quality, and, since the _qua_ is precisely the route of differentiating different respects, the space of quality can only be the space of a multiplicity of qualities.[8]

Third, notice that this holding-together-_qua_, this comparison, is the space in which those held-together-_qua_ are measured—evaluated—which means held up against some standard that sets the terms of measure. The _qua_ itself—the quality—that is featured in the comparison must be a reality that both share, but that is exhausted by neither (and that, furthermore, invites further holdings-together-_qua_ with others that might be introduced into the space of comparison; that is, it is a "with" with an indeterminate horizon for possible expansion), and the evaluative comparison must involve terms of comparison, which is to say a comparison can only be effected in a space governed by the axes of greater and lesser, better and worse.[9] These pairs of comparative terms themselves are dyads of which the member terms are compared and defined correlatively with respect to some quality. With better and worse this is clearest: They answer to the question "How good?" No one who does not understand what _good_ is can ask "Better or worse?" and no one who cannot ask "Better or worse?" can compare. Comparison, we might say, is the mode of existence within the space of question and answer illuminated by the good.

Finally, notice that these comparisons—these evaluations in terms of the good—cannot be simply external. Those that differ must hold themselves apart as separate, determinate identities if they are to _be_ different; that is, to differ they must _be_. They must, then, be themselves—indeed, be equal with themselves. And it is only insofar as the things themselves differ from each other that they can have differentiated identities within the space of comparison; but if they themselves differ from each other, then their very identities are already involved in relations with those from which they differ. To differ from another is already to be different within oneself, that is, to already have in oneself the relation to the other from which one is differing. In other words, then, the dyad is only possible if each member both *is* and is *different,* which means is equal with itself and is different from itself: Thus the relations of equality that hold *between* the members also hold *within* each member. This means, first, that being, sameness, and difference are inseparable[10] and, second, that to be is to set oneself into comparison with others. In other words, to differ—and, therefore, to defer the closing of one's identity to the measuring up to one's others—are intrinsic to each of the members of the comparison. The compared things themselves evoke their others and their spaces of comparison from within themselves. To be is to invite comparison, to invite imitation.[11]

To recognize equality, then, requires three things. First, it requires the ability to recognize being, sameness, and difference; to recognize the *as* or the *qua;* to recognize the greater and lesser; and to recognize the good. Second, it requires the ability to recognize these as inseparable from one another. And third, it requires the ability to recognize each member of any comparison as invoking these from within itself. In any recognition of equality we have already recognized that the things themselves define themselves as measuring up to various qualitative values in the light of the good. It seems to me, in short, that Socrates' (Plato's) choice of "equality" to make this point about recollection is not arbitrary; rather, the concept of equality is decisive because it is inseparable both from a Socratic universe and from our universe; in other words, our ability to understand equality shows we live in the world Socrates insists upon. Let this suffice as an attempt to think through the argument about recollection. Let me turn now to the argument about harmony.

The Soul as *Harmoniē*

The arguments about why the soul cannot be a harmony are quite bad. This is not Socrates' fault, of course. It is Simmias's poor answers that lead the discussion astray. I want to consider the arguments about whether the soul is a harmony and to show some of their problems, especially by way of a comparison of this account of harmony with Heraclitus's account of the backturning harmony, the *palintropos harmoniē.* We will see, I think, that, contrary to the conclusion reached in the dialogue that the theory of recollection proves that the soul cannot be a harmony, the doctrine of recollection is, in fact, equally the doctrine that the soul *is* a harmony. Let us turn to the basic argument in the *Phaedo,* in order, ultimately, to harmonize the two speeches about equality and harmony, that is, to show how the two are one.

The argument about harmony is delivered in two stages, interrupted by the digression on misology with which I began above. The first part (85e–86d) introduces the challenge from Simmias, and the second (92a–95a) is the refutation. The argument about harmony is initially introduced as an argument against the immortality of the soul. The soul, Simmias suggests, could have the characteristics that their discussion so far has demanded of it while still being not an independent substance, but a state of some body—it could be what results from a harmonization of certain bodily conditions. The harmonizing of certain bodies—the strings of an instrument—allows beautiful music to be produced; and so the tuned instrument has properties that the untuned one does not. That is, there are properties—powers—which attach to the attunement itself. If the soul was thus an attunement of the body, we could agree that it is not just the body as an arbitrary lump of material. But it would be true, nonetheless, that the soul would disappear—would be destroyed—with the demise of the body. Simmias says,

> One might make the same argument about harmony, lyre, and strings, that a harmony is something invisible, without body, beautiful and divine in the attuned lyre, whereas the lyre itself and its strings are physical, bodily, composite, earthy, and akin to what is mortal. . . . If, then, the soul is a kind of harmony or attunement, clearly, when our body is relaxed or stretched without due measure by diseases and other evils, the soul must immediately be destroyed, even if it be most divine, as are the other harmonies found in music and all the works of artists. (85e–86a, 86c)

The argument against this conception of the soul as a harmony[12] has a number of specific parts, but the most important is that such a portrayal of the soul makes it derivative of body—makes it the ruled—whereas soul should be the ground and definition of the body: It should be the ruler. Consequently, it would seem, the conception of the soul as a harmony could not adequately explain the characteristics we know the soul to have.[13]

What is most decisive, I think, in the argument against the harmony theory is the claim, proposed by Socrates and endorsed by Simmias, that the harmony is the product of that which it harmonizes. Let us look at three specific ways this comes up. At 92ab Socrates describes the harmony as a composite thing and shortly thereafter asks Simmias, "Do you think it natural for a harmony, or any other composite, to be in a different state from that of the elements of which it is composed?" "Not at all," answers Simmias. Again, Socrates proposes, "Nor can it act or be acted upon in a different way than its elements?" Simmias agrees. Finally, Socrates says, "One must therefore suppose that a harmony does not direct its components, but is directed by them"(92e–93a). This portrayal of the metaphysics of harmony seems to me the opposite of the truth. Let us see why.

It is the image of the lyre that Simmias first invokes when he begins speaking about harmonies. This is not a novel correlation. Heraclitus has made the harmony which is the lyre famous: "They do not understand how differing with itself it agrees with itself: a backturning harmony like the bow or the lyre."[14] I do not want to pursue the complexities of this image (such as the exact make-up of a lyre, the type of bow Heraclitus has in mind, or why exactly he chooses the adjective *palintropos*).[15] It seems to me that a simple understanding of how a bow, differing with itself, agrees with itself will suffice for making our way through Plato's text. The key to a bow is that its two elements—the frame and the string—are set into opposition, but into an opposition that cannot be resolved. The frame of the bow is forcibly bent into a position from which it would naturally move (like an Aristotelian element) were it able; it is not allowed to move, however, because the bowstring, itself forcibly stretched to a length it would not naturally accept, holds the frame constrained to its unnatural posture. Reciprocally, the frame holds the string taut, not allowing the string to relax to its preferred posture. The bow works because each element is held by the other in an unnatural posture in such a way that the effort of either element to pursue its own course is equally its resistance to the other's pursuing its own course. An opposition between the elements is built into their relation, *and this is the feature* that lets the bow be a bow. Neither the wood by itself nor the string by itself has the potential to send an arrow hurtling through the air for great distances and with great accuracy. This capacity belongs neither to the wood and string nor to their simple combination (that is, it is not a sum); rather, this power is precisely what is brought into being *by the relation and opposition of these elements*. The institutionalized opposition is what gives the bow its distinctive—its definitive—power. The bow is not the wood plus the string, but is precisely the self-identity achieved through establishing their antagonism, through the opposition of one of its elements with the other: It is by thus differing with itself that it agrees with itself. This is what it means to call the bow a harmony: It is an identity that is not reducible to the parts, but is, rather, the space in which they are allowed—indeed, forced—to differ (which is, to recall our earlier discussion of equality, the space of their "with"). Let us reflect further on the logical dimensions of such a harmony.

According to Heraclitus, the bow is the harmony. Let us pose Socrates' questions about harmony to this harmony. Can the harmony act or be acted upon in a different way than can its elements? It seems the answer must be yes. The harmony can shoot arrows, and this is a power possessed by neither of its elements. Does the harmony direct the components, or is it directed by them? The harmony seems clearly to direct. Left to themselves, the wood and string "would do their own things," but the harmony will not allow this. The harmony defines the state and the powers of its elements: It forces them into situations they do not willingly accept, and it thereby enables them to participate in activities that would otherwise be foreign to them. Can the harmony be in a different state from that of its elements? Again, it seems the answer is yes. There may be many ways that this is so, but perhaps the most important is that the harmony is single and simple while the elements are multiple and, in the case of a laminated frame or a woven string, for instance, composite: I mark this last feature because it draws our attention to the problems introduced when Socrates—with no justification—slips from Simmias's discussion of the *harmonized* as composite, which Simmias portrays as *opposite* to the state of the harmony (85–86a), to his, Socrates' own, characterization of the *harmony* as composite (92a). We could, no doubt, take up answers to all of Socrates' questions in far more elaborate fashion, but we have already seen enough of the metaphysics of harmony to see that the discussion between Socrates and Simmias is unsatisfactory, and that in each case the wrong answer is given to Socrates' questions.

What is even more interesting, though, is that if we compare this logic of the harmony with the logic of the space of comparison revealed in the argument about recollection, we will find them to be equals. The harmony is itself not an element, but is that in terms of which the elements are given their related but differentiated roles within the identity. The frame is not the same as the piece of wood *that could be harmonized:* It is only *within the context of the backturning harmony* that the frame exists and has the properties it has. The harmony is the bringing of the two elements into a metaphysical space in which they can share an identity—an equality—in terms of which they can be seen to differ. The bow—any harmony—is an equality, an equating of two differents in terms of a quality by which they are measured. To harmonize is to equalize, to bring together into the generative tension which is the space of comparison and measure, to bring into "with."

Socrates, in accordance with Simmias's answers to his questions, reached the conclusion that, since the doctrine of recollection is true, the soul cannot be a harmony. We have seen, on the contrary, that the arguments against the soul being a harmony are based on asserting the opposite of what is true, and, in fact, precisely what is explained by recollection is harmonies. What I want to show now is that these are not just compatible logics: They are actually the same. By harmonizing these arguments with the discussion of mind, I shall maintain that this space of harmony and recollection is the space of determinateness itself.

Mind

In the third major argument in the *Phaedo,* namely, Socrates' discussion of his response to Anaxagoras's claims about mind (*nous*), one of the major points Socrates insists on is directly at odds with the claims he makes in his critique of the harmony theory and exactly corresponds with the points I am here making. This point is the distinction he insists on between the cause and the conditions without which a cause could not be cause. The cause gives the definition of a thing—the "what it is"—and the material conditions enable this cause to realize itself, to be defining. This is just the distinction Simmias would have needed in order to resist the challenges to the harmony theory that we have been discussing, for it is this relation between the defining harmony and the material conditions that make its realization possible that we have just analyzed. Just as this distinction between the cause and the conditions that allow it to function speaks directly to the preceding argument about harmony, so does Socrates' discussion of what it would take to explain mind to be the cause of all things speak to the first argument about recollection. Indeed, it seems that it is by understanding the first two arguments in the way we have here that the argument about mind becomes clear.

Let us take the theme of the cause and its conditions first. Socrates complains against what I will call a "materialist" account, which would say the cause of his sitting is his bones and sinews.[16] Socrates insists, on the contrary, that he is sitting because that seems to him the best way to spend his time in the context of living up to his belief that he should obey the laws and in the context of those laws sentencing him to imprisonment and death. The bones and sinews do not define the situation. They are the material conditions "without which not," the necessary realization the decision to sit must take—that is, it must be a disposition of bones and sinews—but they get their significance from the decision, and not vice versa. This is exactly the relationship we discovered in the harmony: The bow is a harmony that cannot be realized without wood and string, but the harmony defines them and gives them their power, not vice versa. The first point to note, then, is that this third major argument of the *Phaedo* confirms that Socrates' and Simmias's challenge to the harmony theory should be rejected: It should be rejected because it fails to make this distinction that Socrates here deems essential.

The second theme is that of mind as cause. Here, Socrates says that one would show mind to be the cause of all things by showing how they are for the good, that is, by showing that the way things are is the way that is best. Socrates claims that Anaxagoras failed to do this precisely by confusing the cause with its conditions, as Simmias and Socrates did in the harmony account. Socrates, too, speaks as if he has not produced this account either, but this seems wrong. It seems to me, rather, that his account of recollection was exactly the correction of Anaxagoras's error. Let us first reconsider the discussions of form and matter here.

To claim that equals get their identity by equality rather than vice versa is rightly to invert the materialist account and recognize the primacy of the cause, of the defining form. This is repeatedly stressed for us in the argument that 2 is 2 by twoness, greater is greater by greatness, and so on.[17] This discussion shows us the logical and metaphysical primacy of the form, of the definition, the harmony. This discussion also shows us how such an account could be empty (because on their own such forms are empty abstractions), and why, therefore, we must see that the defining forms also necessarily specify conditions of realization. This is the side that is emphasized in the harmony arguments. The way the harmony argument is explicitly treated does not make clear how it can avoid a materialist reduction and be reconciled with the argument for the primacy of form, but the argument concerning the distinction between cause and condition has shown us how to reconcile the role of form discerned in the argument from recollection and the role of matter discerned in the argument about harmony. In sum, it is by seeing both the recognition of equality and the harmony as characterized by the same logical relations—differing with itself, agreeing with itself—that we assign the proper roles to defining form and realizing elements.

But, in putting form in the proper position in the recollection account, we also found that we were operating in the space of the good; that is, we found comparison—the recognition of equality—to be the invoking of the good as the highest cause. Let me make this point by taking us back through some of the themes we developed in our study of the recognition of equality.

When we first considered equality, we considered the comparison of two different things with respect to some quality. Let us now take up this issue where the quality with respect to which they are compared is precisely difference as such. Let us ask how we make the equation of two things in which we say "They are different."

What does it take to recognize difference? What does it take, that is, not to discriminate this or that quality, but to be able to recognize difference as such, and thus to recognize differences as differences? My claim is that the one who can so recognize must be recognizing in light of the good itself. We have already seen that to *recognize* difference is to recognize comparability: For differents to differ they must be able to be spoken of *together* as differing. This comparability—that is, their mutually being the kinds of things which can differ from each other—is, therefore, a sameness. To compare is to measure, to find a common term—what Aristotle would call a *mean*—which sets the standard for marking the identity of each. To thus measure is to evaluate, for the standard is a grade, a value invoked (rightly or wrongly) to set the terms of importance for judging the relation of the differents. To thus evaluate is, then, to invoke a good: not the good as such, but some good relative to the terms compared. But to be able to recognize any good—like the ability to recognize any equality—depends on being able to operate with the very notion of goodness. Differing is thus possible only in light of the good. The good, we might say, is the ultimate defining form of all differences, for it is the ground of the possibility of difference as such: The good exists as giving light to differences.[18] This lesson of the argument about recollection puts us well on our way to giving an account of mind as the cause of all things. Let us pursue further this theme of difference.

Any recognition of difference, which is to say, any recognition of determinateness, will be a recognition of that determinateness within a field constituted as differings, as negations, as non-beings, and this space of the *not* is the space of the *good;* that is, any recognition of determinateness will be the recognition of a differing which invokes from out of itself a field of values and comparabilities by virtue of its refusal of others. To be a determinateness, then, is to situate oneself both in terms of finite others and in terms of overarching standards of evaluation. The determinateness of the determinateness is precisely how, as a specific *not,* this one differing marks out that from which it differs and to which it defers—both its finite others and the values it invokes with which it is not identical. Any determinateness can thus only exist in a double harmonious tension. It is at odds with others from which it cannot separate its identity. It is at odds with a value which it itself projects. To be a determinateness is thus to be a striving—a striving to be *this* and not *that,*[19] and this striving to be *not that* is thus a pursuit of itself, which means it projects a good in terms of which it is to be measured—what Aristotle would call its *telos.* To recognize difference is thus to recognize this double striving, and our philosophical question is just whether we acknowledge this in our account of difference. Typically the answer is no. Whether it is in the direction of the Eleatic Stranger or of David Hume, our philosophies have typically tried to sever difference from its others—sameness and the good—and have, thereby, lost the ability to let differing differ. "To be" only is *as* "to differ"—from others (with which one is the same) and from oneself (as actual from ideal, as "is" from "to be")—and we need to acknowledge the primacy of this double strife if we are to do to difference the justice it demands of us. It demands this of us, for it and we are differents to each other and we therefore have each other as our standards, our measures. Let me explain this last point.

Our argument shows that what *is* is a field of differences striving after their own goods, where this striving takes the form of a struggle for place within this field—a mutual opposing which is inseparable from a striving after mutual integration—and this field is the field *of the human psyche itself:* For us, to be is to be recognizing this differing, this striving. Our soul differs—is determinate—as the ability to differ from the whole sphere of differences *as differences*. It is our soul which is the space of universal differing—the *chōra*—or, as Aristotle says of mind (which he describes as Timaeus describes the *chōra*), the place of all forms. Mind is the cause of all things being able to be what they are, because it is the space of recognition—the space of comparison in terms of forms, that is, in terms of the good as such.

Differences appear to us as strivings to live up to values. This is because we are beings for whom there are values, for whom things matter. To be a being living in light of the good is to be a being who cares, and that means to be a being who is already *with* those things in their struggles. The things that differ from us impinge on us because to differ means not to be able to let them alone. As minds—as mindful—we are the being of the with, the being whose difference is marked as the universal inability to separate ourselves. To differ is to be with: The greater the difference, the greater the "with," and, as mind, our difference—or at least the difference we can participate in—is the greatest, the absolutely comprehensive. The good is the differing of all from the good, and mind is the space of this differing: It is as mind that the good can be as the being of difference, for the mind is the experience of difference as the call to responsibility, as the demand that we strive for the good together. Giving thought to the good together, we give space to the good together—we give space to determinateness.[20]

Seeing and Reading

I think this whole argument is contained in the single claim that gives the title to this paper: In the course of his argument about recollection, Socrates makes the pivotal empirical claim that "we sense that things strive." I take this claim to be phenomenologically sound: The experience of determinate others striving to realize goods is empirically immediate. If I understand my own argument of the last section, it is this character of *aisthēsis* that is the presence of *nous* in us. To have a mind is no different than to be a being who senses determinate strivings, and we are this being. Again, if I am right in my reasoning, it would follow from the fact that we immediately recognize things as striving that the good is the ultimate cause, and it exists as the universal differing of which mind is the space. In answer to the question "Do we sense that things strive?" I have said that I believe the answer to be yes. Indeed, I believe this is obviously so; in fact, I think this is the very structure of obviousness. Let me discuss this a bit.

Aristotle makes this point in his *Physics.* In Book 2, Chapter 1, of the *Physics,* he says of *phusis*—of nature—that its reality is manifest and that anyone who would try to prove its existence rather than simply recognize it would evince a singular inability to distinguish what is clear from what is not. This *phusis* of which we seem to be immediately aware is exactly the field within which forms—entities—are distinguished in terms of their pursuit of goals. I think I could defend Aristotle here, and make my point by reference to the perception of nature, but I think there is a place other than nature where we can notice this, and this site is perhaps more pivotal for the reading of Plato, and perhaps more convincing for our generation, which takes literary criticism over the observation of nature as its paradigm for experience. This other site is precisely the experience of reading.

To read is to attend to determinateness. We have built this volume around the ideal of reading: the ideal of careful attention to Plato as a text to which we must be responsible. Holding this ideal is requiring of ourselves that the determinations dictate to us what we can say. To read is to make ourselves open to letting the determination that confronts us become our determination.[21] Reading is letting the text tell us what it has to say. To attend to this determinateness requires of us two virtues. It requires, first, the *sophrosune*—the "humility" or knowledge of our own limits—to let ourselves be shown the way by the determinateness despite what we might have thought on our own. It requires, second, the *andreia,* the courage, to stand by what we have found.[22] Reading means taking a stand with a readiness to engage with the demands of the determinacy we have yet to face, which is to say, reading means letting difference call us to responsibility.[23]

Notice further the attitude that one must bring to the text. What it takes to read is to come to the text looking for what it has to say. A text is not ink on paper, but is something to-be-read: A text only exists as an element in a harmony, that is, it only exists for one who is looking for what it has to say, for one who would be with it. It is within this project of reading that the differences that make up the text can make a difference. And how do they make a difference? By our asking what they are trying to say. We only read when we experience the differences as striving, by differing in precise ways from the precise others that make up the text, to constitute an integrated field that is the space in which the meaning can show itself. To read is to let oneself be led by the determinations—by the differences—but to be thus led is to read in light of certain specific values. To look for how there is difference (already a value) means to read so as to integrate—to look for sameness—and to look for what the text is trying to say, that is, to see it as striving, as directed toward the good. To read is, in other words, to read the determinations as invoking the world of meaning of which they are the imitations, the images, the traces. The theory of the forms—the theory that mind is the cause of all things—is the theory we all endorse whenever we read.

But this reading, this making a space for difference, does not just describe what we do with books and essays. The logic we are studying is the logic of recognition *simpliciter.* What we have identified is the logic of all our dealings with those from whom we differ. The mind—this space of the "with"—is the space of universal dialogue. We are called out of ourselves to ourselves by those who differ, and it is only through them that we can fulfill our own striving. To be a being who recognizes differences is to be a mind, which is to be a sensing that is immediately sensitive to other things as values, which is to be a being defined by dialogue, by the space of question and answer illuminated by the good. It is in our dialogue that we create the space—the harmony—of recognition in which, by recalling the good, we bring things into meaningfulness.[24] It is by bringing things into the space of the "with" that we allow them to be meaningful by allowing them space to differ. To deal with others—which is the life of mind, the life of reading—is a life of engagement, a life of courage and *sophrosune.* Having minds—being rational—is the determinateness which sets upon us the demand that we be humble and courageous in making space for difference. This is how to read the theory of the forms.[25]

Notes

1. Crooks makes this point in his contribution to this volume, chapter 10, "Writing Conversion: Notes on the Structure of *Phaedo.*" On Theseus, see especially Claude Calame, *The Craft of Poetic Speech in Ancient Greece* (Ithaca: Cornell

University Press, 1995), chapter 8. This fear of argument could equally be expressed as the fear of death, the fear of the body, or the fear of indeterminateness.

2. It requires other things, as well, of course: an openness to serendipity, playful curiosity, time, money, and more.

3. It does not follow from the fact that we do recognize equality that all our experiences conform to the pattern of such a recognition. See Maurice Merleau-Ponty, *Phenomenology of Perception,* trans. Colin Smith (New York: Humanities Press, 1962), 6, for a phenomenon in which the issue of equality cannot be raised. Merleau-Ponty here identifies a necessary and primary layer of experience in which indeterminacy and noncomparability are the ruling characteristics: It is an arena governed by the logic of the *chōra,* as described by John Sallis in "Traces of the *Chōra,"* chapter 5 above in this volume. This is a sphere of experience, however, that carries within itself a tension that calls for, or at least "motivates," resolution into recognizable determinacy; see *Phenomenology of Perception,* 17. Inasmuch as we do recognize equality and inasmuch as this is a form of experiencing through which we respond to the very tension within the indeterminacy of perceptual life—its "striving"—we cannot shake off the compulsions imposed on us by the logical demands of the recognition of equality as I will articulate them in this study. Compare Merleau-Ponty's discussion of the "decisive moment in perception" and the "tacit thesis of perception" (*Phenomenology of Perception,* 53–54). As we shall see, the demands that the logic of the recognition of equality puts upon us will precisely lead us to return to the recognition of the strivings that characterize the differential character of our perceptual life.

4. Of anything about which we can really say "itself," it seems we cannot produce the understanding empirically. On the contrary, the ability to recognize it is the precondition for having experiences of it. This is the conclusion of the argument about equality in *Phaedo* 72e–77a. For this notion of "itself," compare Aristotle's discussion of *ousia* in *Metaphysics* Z.1–3 and *Categories* 5.

5. Indeed, the Latin roots of *com-pare* suggest holding together as equals. See *Theaetetus* 184–186.

6. See *Phaedo* 96e–97b, 101b–c.

7. It is only by recognizing this difference from the form—the absence of the form—that we can recognize the presence of the form. The standing apart is a standing together—a *sustasis,* as in *Timaeus* 48a.

8. *Sophist* 237b–238c reminds us that this space of multiple qualities is, therefore, also the space of number—the space where we address the abstract difference of qualities without reference to the specificity of their qualities—but I am not concerned to pursue this here. See also *Sophist* 251a–b.

9. This is especially clear in the Greek political conception of equality as *isonomia:* The "equal distribution" of *demokratia* is division according to rank. See C. W. Fornara and L. J. Samons, *Athens from Cleisthenes to Pericles* (Berkeley: University of California Press, 1991), chapter 2. Compare *Laws* 6.757b–c.

10. Compare *Sophist* 252c–255e.

11. They are *with* each other in the sense of being already *inside* each other.

12. Compare Aristotle, *On the Soul* 1.4.

13. See *Phaedo* 79c–84b.

14. Fragment 51 (Diels-Kranz numbering). Plato shows he knows this saying at *Sophist* 242e.

15. These themes are all pursued carefully by Abraham Schoener in "Heraclitus on War" (Ph.D. diss., University of Toronto, 1993).

16. Note, incidentally, that these "bones and sinews" he picks are precisely the body parts that he earlier marked as deathless, that is, as having the same character, apparently, as soul.

17. *Phaedo* 100d–101d. Our study of equality and harmony has explicitly answered Socrates' questions about what happens to the two ones that become two. It is the metaphysics of the "with" that has solved this.

18. Compare Aristotle's discussion of sense and difference in the opening lines of *Metaphysics* A.1.

19. For a differing, the goal of which is to avoid being engulfed or lost in another, compare Spinoza's discussion of *conatus*—a drive to self-preservation—in *Ethics,* Book 3, Propositions 6–8.

20. Recall the point that Francisco Gonzalez makes in "Giving Thought to the Good Together: Virtue in Plato's *Protagoras,*" chapter 9 of this volume, that *sunousia* is *sugchōrein* in the *Protagoras.*

21. Compare Aristotle's discussion of sense and intellect as "object driven." I have take up this theme in "Aristotle's Animative Epistemology," *Idealistic Studies* 25 (1995): 241–53; see especially 249.

22. It also requires memory; compare Abraham Schoener's discussion of *chthes,* "yesterday," in chapter 4, "Not the Sophist," in this volume.

23. See *Apology* 28b–29a.

24. Kenneth Cheung has pointed out to me that Plato shows this with the wind—the threatening wind that might blow Cebes' soul away, but that made possible this philosophical dialogue by allowing Socrates some extra time. The wind became the ground for Socrates' ability to differ. It allowed the fragility of his caring to care longer, and this caring reciprocally invested the wind with a place in light of the good. This is soul: It is the fragile harmony that allows us to recollect the values in light of which differences can differ.

25. The soul is the space of value, the space of the "with." It is where differences differ, where things stand compared and measured, where questions are asked and answered, where we can read together, where the good can manifest itself. Socrates says something very revealing at the end of the *Phaedo:* His corpse is not him. When he is dead, he will not be with us anymore. This is what death is: the end of the "with." A mark of Plato's gift is his ability to leave us writings in which Socrates is again alive for us, but this "with" is one-sided: We still have a score of "cloaks" woven and worn by Socrates that let us have a chance to experience the presence of Socrates, but Socrates can never experience our presence. What we can never do again is see the soul of Socrates dancing in his eyes. Death is the end of the "with," but only the being that dies—the being for whom things matter, the being who can take a stand even in the face of death, the being who can manifest rationality as courage and *sophrosune*—can let the "with" be.

7

The Idea and Mixture
of the Good

Günter Figal
Translated from the German by Michael McGettigan and Cara Gendel Ryan

T he Idea of the Good is the key to understanding Plato's philosophy.
For many commentators, however, to admit this is tantamount to
forfeiting any possibility of a consistent and plausible interpretation
of Plato's dialogues. Even Aristotle, the very first to take on the bewilder-
ing thoughts at the center of the *Republic,* voices his incomprehension
in terms often suggesting he suspects Plato's notions to be bordering
on senselessness. In the well-known passage from the *Nicomachean Ethics*
where the Platonic "Universal Good" is put on trial, Aristotle objects
that the Good is spoken of in too many irreducible ways, and that a
common idea cannot do justice to the plurality of things it is meant to
subsume (1096a 19–28).[1] More serious is the objection that if the Good
is understood as one, that is, as "a unity or something existing separately
and absolutely," then it cannot be realized by human action (1096b 32–
35). But that is precisely the point: For the Good, according to Aristotle,
is what we strive for and seek to realize. It is, in fact, what we experience
as the reality of human life.

Aristotle's objections mark out the basic possibilities for further
interpretations. We can decide to reinforce, and then perhaps defend,
the ideal nature of the Good, though this option marginalizes Aristotle's praxis-oriented approach and ultimately amounts to nothing more
than the bare assurance of the "axiological" dimension of Plato's central
thought.[2] Alternatively, with a plea for the Aristotelian perspective we
can link the claim that Plato basically meant the same thing as his former

student—or at least something similar—so that Aristotle's critique, while certainly understandable in terms of its motivations, in the final analysis, misses the mark. This last option, however, puts to the margins everything Plato intended when he characterized the Good as an idea.[3]

But both lines of interpretation have something important to say. Both are right in a way, but each is incapable of integrating the other into its respective approach. This, however, does not necessarily have to be the fault of the interpretations. It would be a relief, in this case, to realize that the Idea of the Good, as discussed in Plato's text, is nothing but a chimera, or as one commentator observed, a "hybrid of distinctly different domains."[4] If we did not try to bring together what does not belong together, problems of interpretation would be solved in one stroke.

In the end, this approach would prove Aristotle right. If the domains are so strictly distinguished from each other that philosophical reflection cannot grasp them as a unity, then the only appropriate solution to Plato's problem would be to divide philosophy into separate disciplines. What Plato wanted to hold together, what he wanted to see as being derived from one single thought—namely, a philosophy of ideas (as theory) and a discussion of the good life (as praxis)—is thus divided into separate disciplines in order to do justice to the respective objects of inquiry. And if there is something left over, something that cannot be simply classified on the one side or on the other, then this could be what is of true interest for retaining the original nucleus from the overloaded conception of the Idea of the Good.

But perhaps things are not quite like that. Perhaps the overloading supposed here is really demanded by the nature of the conception itself, and what we call the "Good" can only be adequately discussed when the different elements are seen as belonging together. If this is so, then the solution of "distinct domains" may not be the final word on the subject. And, perhaps, to understand the Good in this way is not just one of philosophy's many tasks, but rather it is philosophy's only real central task. To complete it will demonstrate the possibility of philosophy and provide justification for it.

Philosophy's division into disciplines cannot and should not be disputed. After it has become a fait accompli, it cannot simply be forgotten or reversed. But the division does not preclude philosophy having a structure made up of different questions which are only really meaningful taken together. This can be made clearer by taking a step back to a form of thinking which is still simply philosophy—to Plato's philosophy. Where Plato's texts speak of the Good, of the Idea of the Good, we find traces of philosophy's variegated structure.

The first succinct definition of the Good revolves entirely around human action, and, in retrospect, we can say it falls within the purview of practical philosophy. "When it comes to the Good," according to Socrates in the *Republic*, "no one is content with only the appearance, but all men seek the reality, and the semblance satisfies nobody"(505e).[5] In explanation, Socrates adds:

> That, then, which every soul pursues and for its own sake does all that
> it does, with an intuition of its reality, but yet baffled and unable to
> apprehend its nature adequately, or to attain to any stable belief about it
> as about other things. (505e)

In this passage, as well as corresponding passages in the *Gorgias*, Plato points clearly to the teleological structure of the Good in the way Aristotle will later develop it. The Good is the true end of human action; it is what we desire, and if it did not determine how we act and what we want, there would be no such thing as either action or desire. For we certainly cannot desire anything without being convinced that what we desire is good. Otherwise, we would desire something else and only would have been driven or compelled to do what we did. Even when we play along with the pretenses of social convention and do what is considered right by others without knowing or bothering to ask ourselves whether it is truly right in itself, we must in fact be pursuing an end the whole time, for without some end in mind we cannot act deliberately at all. No one desires the pretense of an appearance of something; at best, they will disguise their real goal in their actions. This, however, is the crux of the matter: Anyone who inquires into the Good has already stepped beyond the realm of mere appearance and opinion.

As Socrates explicitly states, however, this step falls short of giving direction to our desires and actions. When we see through mere appearance, or simply intuit that something only seems to be what it is, when we ask ourselves what we really want, and insecurity sets in, an uneasiness and a vague presentiment warns us that there must be something more to know here. We feel our way about in the half-light of a certainty only now awakened. We must make decisions, take our lives in our hands, but without really knowing how. So we vacillate between the two basic alternative possibilities Socrates suggests in the *Gorgias*. We do not know whether we are doing what seems to be the best, or whether we are really doing what we desire (366e).

It seems obvious to suppose that in order to resolve this problem we must elucidate the nature of action. The solution comes into view as soon as we are clear about the nature of what can and cannot be desired.

Once we know this, we will be able to zero in on the appropriate goal for our actions, and we will also recognize that there are goals which we would like to pursue but that because of their unstable and volatile nature will always elude us, like shades or phantoms which briefly hover in our thoughts and then vanish into thin air.

In fact, many of Plato's considerations go in this direction. He is often interested in showing that attempts to make pleasure or power the basis of our actions are doomed to failure; in connection with power, two examples are the wish to be stronger and the wish to wield greater influence. In these and other cases, we would also have to desire the opposite of our original wish. The desire for power implies the desire for weakness in order that power can be increased. Likewise, the desire for pleasure entails the desire that the pleasure must before remain unsatisfied in order for it to be experienced at all. According to this logic, we achieve by our actions not only what we want, but also what we do not want. We cannot even really desire pure and simple, for it is always a matter of desiring and not desiring at the same time. On the basis of this, Plato shows that only what promises order and consistency can give direction to our actions. It is what we "look to" that creates order and consistency in our actions (*Gorgias* 503d–e).

This notion of "looking to" marks a shift, a change in perspective. What was seen before as the immanent goal that gives direction and form to human action has been transformed into an idea. In the *Gorgias*, Plato makes it particularly clear how we should think about this transformation. With regard to human life, we must, in principle, proceed like someone who has mastered a *technē*. The soul (*psychē*), which animates all human life, is similar to something produced by a skill or a craft, in that it only has worth when it functions in an orderly and consistent way. Those who have mastered a *technē* do not "employ means and material at random," but rather have a "definite object in view" in order to give a "definite form" (*eidos*) to the thing they are fashioning (503d–504d).

In the case of *technē*, it is obvious what we "look to" in producing an object. We look to the idea of the object to be produced, its "look," not in the sense of its superficial appearance, but rather its structure, or what we might call its "blueprint." After this is clearly apprehended, a unified picture of the projected object in the order of its parts comes into view and then is realized in the process of production. When it is a question of the *psychē*, however, Socrates does not say what the "look" would be that would give us direction. This is probably because Socrates' dialogue partner in this passage, Callicles, would not know what to do with such an insight, anyway. In the later dialogue, the *Republic*, Socrates openly states what he seems only to have thought in his exchange with Callicles: Namely, the greatest and most important thing to learn and to know is the Idea of the Good (*megiston mathēma,* 505a).

The implications are troublesome and helpful at the same time: troublesome because Socrates obviously understands life to be analogous to a *technē,* and helpful because of the light it sheds on Plato's text. It goes a long way to solving the notorious problems involved in understanding the Idea of the Good. Socrates pictures life as a product and, accordingly, the way we conduct our lives as a form of production. And apparently the "look" of a blueprint is to provide direction for producing the appropriate form of life.

Perhaps we are reluctant to attribute to Plato's Socrates such a simplistic and problematical analogy, and we would have grounds for our reluctance. After all, elsewhere Socrates rejects in no uncertain terms the consequences of the analogy drawn between *technē* and life. In the *Protagoras,* for example, Plato has Socrates deny the possibility that there could be specialists in the concerns of life, and especially of political life, regardless of whether this means knowledge possessed by qualified experts or expert knowledge possessed by all citizens. In equally adamant terms, Socrates refuses to accept the further sophistical claim that the best disposition for life—virtue—can be taught.

The orientation toward the *technē* model appears in a particularly ambivalent light. It seems to have arisen from an uncertainty concerning the structures of human action. Perhaps it can be viewed as the first attempt to gain a purchase on a problem whose main concern was to emphasize that true action must be guided by knowledge. Every now and then, however, Socrates manages to go beyond this model and to arrive at the first fundamental definitions for what action really is. This is where Aristotle had only to pick up the thread in order to work out in a more explicit way the structures of action and then drop what remained of the *technē* model and, along with it, the Idea of the Good.

Abandoning the *technē* model comes with a price, however. It is much more difficult to make out now what sort of experience will give rise to the question of how life as a whole should be conducted. As Plato implies in the passage from the *Gorgias* quoted above, to produce something of value, artisans must take a step back from what is immediately before them and not simply "employ means and material at random." Only in this way can they achieve the necessary perspective for understanding what will be the best means for fashioning the material immediately before them and giving it the appropriate order and form. If Plato is right, then the way artisans approach the task of creating things will give us insight into how we should best conduct our lives. This means we must find the right distance from the turmoil of immediate desires, as well as emancipate ourselves from the logic of detachment and conformity, of self-preservation and self-advancement, a logic which often finds itself at the beck-and-call of our desires. We need to get free of ourselves so we can take a cool look at ourselves from a different perspective and thus give more meaningful shape to our lives in the light of this new, hard-won understanding. Understanding is never immediate, but only possible when we create a distance between ourselves and whatever it is we want to know more about. We understand something only by recourse to something else.

It is not difficult to see that this thought lies at the heart of Plato's conception in the *Republic.* What I have in mind is the myth of the cave, designed to show that the experience of understanding depends on creating distance. Plato makes this point so plausible that it would be almost impossible to misinterpret the meaning of the myth. New distance and understanding are achieved at every stage of the ascent out of the cave. Plato portrays the beginning of the ascent so vividly that no doubt can arise as to what Plato means: Understanding begins with the end of imprisonment, with the removal of the chains binding the dwellers of the cave to what lies immediately before them. The narrative of understanding, or as Plato would put it, of *paideia,* is the narrative of freedom. By formulating the Good as an idea, Plato creates a horizon from which life and action can be viewed from an all-important distance. Because the Good as Idea guarantees this distance, it also marks the beginning of freedom.

This brings us to the question of how life is to be understood from the perspective of freedom. The way in which Plato portrays the earliest stages through the cave, gives the impression that the outlook for freedom is bleak indeed, as if it were not possible at all. According to the myth, the experience of freedom at this point is so diffuse that it still cannot be said to be perceived as freedom. Plato's description of the soul's relation to the Good, which I quoted earlier, is in this context also apropos, namely, that the soul is "baffled and unable to apprehend its nature adequately, or to attain to any stable belief about it as about other things" (*Republic* 505e). This will change only when the soul is able to catch sight of the Idea of the Good, that is, after we complete the ascent from the cave and experience what lies beyond it. According to the myth's logic, the experiences outside the cave are the necessary prerequisites for "seeing" the Good. And because the ascent from the cave is a process of learning to distinguish the ideas from appearances and thus also coming to know what the ideas are, the experience of the Idea of the Good is first and foremost a philosophical experience. As such it comes at the end with the completion of philosophy's own *paideia*.

This seems to go against the grain of the crucial interpretation of the cave myth that Socrates makes later on in the dialogue. He says in this passage "that anyone who is to act wisely in private or public must have caught sight of the Good" (517c). But if Socrates means that only the philosopher has the ability to catch sight of the Good, then his interpretation here is in keeping with the earlier telling of the myth. Once we try to make some sense of all this, we are led straight to the notion that philosophers should be rulers, as it is explored in the *Republic*. For many, the implications of a philosopher-king is probably reason enough to maintain an extreme skeptical attitude toward the thesis that it is part of the philosophical character to act wisely.

All the same, the notion that only a philosopher can rule wisely is neither absurd nor elitist, at least not when we are willing to admit that those who act wisely only do so on the basis of their knowledge of the form of life in which such conduct is realized. This knowledge of life, however, should not be understood as empirical, nor should it be understood as consisting in the sum of life experiences. Rather, it consists in the ability to see into the structure of life, the way, for example, insight into grammatical structure makes us more aware of our own language in our everyday linguistic transactions with each other.

In the *Republic*, Plato thinks of philosophical insight as nothing other than insight into the structure of life. He means, in this case, that we learn to see beyond what we once always took for granted, including the presupposition of knowledge. Plato explains this in terms of the difference between mathematics and philosophy, or, more precisely, the difference between how mathematics and philosophy experience or know ideas. Mathematicians are also aware that there are ideas. It is certainly characteristic of their type of knowledge that, for example, circles, angles, and lines are distinguished from their respective representations. Mathematicians know what an idea is and what its representation is. Yet, ideas function for them as the unquestioned assumptions (*hypotheseis*) of their science. As a consequence, mathematicians lack distance from the ideas around which their inquiries turn.

Distance, however, is precisely what distinguishes philosophical knowledge from all other forms of knowledge. In philosophy, ideas do not function, as they do, for example, in geometry, as assumptions or postulates from which demonstrations are constructed. Rather, for philosophy, as Socrates says in the *Republic*, an idea functions as access to the "*pantos archē*" of everything else, and thus ideas are the "springboards" which enable philosophy "to rise to that which requires no assumption and is the starting point of all" (511b). In this way, philosophy frees itself from the bond tying all knowledge of things to ideas by reaching up to the Idea of the Good and "touching it" (511b).

If we want to understand what this experience means, we must turn back to the comparison of the sun with the Idea of the Good which Socrates has already drawn a little earlier in the dialogue. Here he says, just as the sun acts as "yoke" to bind sight with objects of sight, there is also a "more worthy yoke" which binds knowledge to the objects of knowledge (508a). According to the logic of this famous simile, the Idea of the Good is the *pantos archē*, that is, the cause and the beginning of all *epistēmē* and *alētheia,* understood here not simply as truth, but as the way knowledge discloses the accessibility of what is knowable. The Idea of the Good thus turns out to be synonymous with the freedom to comport ourselves in relation to knowledge. It is the point of reference which allows us to understand knowledge and everything that reveals itself in knowledge.

We can still ask ourselves, however, why this point of reference, in which are rooted *epistēmē* and *alētheia,* should actually be understood as the Good. In the course of our examination, the meaning of the Good has shifted so much, that it now seems almost impossible to pin down how it should relate to human action at all. Is it possible to desire the whole's cause and ground? This question, in turn, brings us back to our original problem of whether we overload the Idea of the Good when we understand it as final principle and point of reference of praxis.

To formulate the problem in this way, however, exposes Plato's thought to the danger of being distorted. Once we find ourselves trapped in the dualism of the suggested alternative of the two-realm theory, we could perhaps then look for possible ways to connect the realms or to translate one into the other. But no one asks the question anymore as to whether there might be an inner unity of the two aspects or moments. If we formulate the question more concretely, it would read, "How do our basic experiences of freedom and the way we conduct our lives belong together?"

Plato's texts offer us an answer to this question. The freedom that arises from the philosopher's *paideia,* as it is described in the *Republic,* is not a matter of a highest science. Therefore, it is not in opposition to life's constraints. Rather, it leads straight through knowledge to freedom, and, at the same time, it retains a positive relation to knowledge. Even those discussions in the *Gorgias,* which are based upon the *technē* model, are intended to show that life can only be consistent and ordered if it is conducted according to knowledge and insight, not for the sake of knowledge, but rather for the sake of an ordered life. Only a life lived in this way can be "good," and not the self-evident, self-contained pursuit of a skill or a science.

To put it another way: Because life is guided by knowledge, knowledge must belong to life. And, therefore, it is necessary to have distance from knowledge and to be able to move freely in its context. Only by virtue of this distance can we ask if our insight or knowledge discloses what is appropriate to each of life's situations and its particular aspects, that is, if our insight is insight into the "Good" (*Republic* 505b). Considered in this way, the Idea of the Good turns out to be the principle regulating what Wolfgang Wieland calls "the operation of judgment."[6] To put the point more sharply, we can say that the Good is the principle from which anything like the ability to judge first arises. The Good is the freedom of judgment.

Such a definition, however, does not in any way preclude what was said before in regard to the Idea of the Good being the "cause and the ground of the whole." Paradoxically, we understand this at first glance because of the meaning the Idea of the Good has for praxis and life. If it is important not only to have knowledge or insights but, above all, to act, then the possibility of having an effect at all must lie in the freedom-giving experience of the Good. The freedom of the Good must also be action's freedom and, therefore, must also disclose what action really is—as it is performed within the structure of life.

The solution to this problem can be found in the *Philebus*. The dialogue is concerned with the connection between insight or knowledge and the way we carry out our lives. Life thus consists in a mixture of insights and other stirrings or articulations of the soul's animating principle. This is demonstrated in a series of subtle analyses carried out on ever-new aspects of the problem. The analyses culminate finally in the notion of the Beautiful. The Beautiful here is understood as the perceivable unity of dynamic life and the harmony of form. It is the shining forth of "measure and proportion," the only possible way measure and proportion can be experienced as such.

This can be understood in terms of the discussion in the *Gorgias* where order and consistency were the conditions for producing an object. Yet it is crucial to situate the Beautiful in the context of the *Philebus*. Here it is shown to be a "mixture" of limit and limitlessness, of *peras* and *apeiron*. This allows us to see Plato's thinking in the *Gorgias*, which was still mired in the *technē* model, to be an anticipation of the ideas presented in the *Philebus*. We can further see in *peras* and *apeiron* those two principles from Plato's doctrine of first principles, which according to Aristotle were described as the One (*hen*) and the Indefinite Dyad (*ahoristos duas*).

This is central for our understanding of the Good. For the Good cannot be the One, in the sense of the first principle, as was concluded by Aristoxenos (in one of the fragments we have of his later work). And once this is accepted, then it will be quite difficult to read an argument for the Good into the discussion of the One in the first and second hypotheses of the *Parmenides*. As we learn from the *Philebus*, "the power of the Good has taken refuge in the nature of the Beautiful" (64e). If we go on to situate this last statement within the context of our interpretation, then the Good is the unity of *peras* and *apeiron*. This unity can only be the fortunate coincidence of the two principles in which form retains its harmonious proportions in the midst of becoming, and the ephemeral nature of becoming comes to anchor in form. The Good would be this unity, if only we did not have to speak of it as the Beautiful. Nevertheless, every time the Beautiful is made manifest, it is still possible to predicate "good" to the fortuitous unity of *peras* and *apeiron*. Thus, in calling this unity "good," we are actually referring to the power of the Good, which makes itself felt, precisely at the moment it eludes us and takes refuge in the Beautiful. This is why the power of the "Good" is beyond all being and can thus serve as the horizon from which it is possible to recognize that something in the realm of being has succeeded in becoming beautiful. This is the form of freedom in which our lives come together in such a way that we are convinced they have turned out well.

In the *Nicomachean Ethics*, Aristotle writes "someone willing to engage in politics . . . must study the nature of the soul, though he will do so as an aid to politics, and only so far as is requisite for the objects of inquiry that he has in view" (1102a 23–25). As we can infer from this passage, in limiting practical philosophy's interest in the soul to matters necessary for a statesman to know, Aristotle, in a distant way, echoes Plato, for whom praxis and theory stand in a closer but more strained relation to each other. As soon as we are able to distinguish two forms of life, one which is built around action, the other around philosophical contemplation, then the relation of praxis and theory can only be understood as a reciprocal mirroring relation, in which one is reflected in the other and both remain exactly what they are.

In this mirror relation, however, something of Plato's discussion of the Good survives. For retained in this relation is the insight that if we are to gain a clear idea of the nature of action as well as continuing to see philosophy as one of life's most fundamental possibilities, then action and understanding must not be closed off from each other. When Aristotle concludes the *Nicomachean Ethics* with a depiction of philosophy, he is suggesting that the *vita activa* points beyond itself and that the *vita contemplativa* clarifies our actions. Yet both are forms of life in themselves, each with its own different experiences of freedom. If it is to be otherwise, then the actual end of action must become the point of reference for understanding, and by breaking free from its place in action, it first establishes action's freedom. A life which is thoroughly consistent with freedom must be able to be at home elsewhere and at the same time remain itself.

Notes

1. Quotations from the *Nicomachean Ethics* follow the edition by I. Bywater, *Aristotelis Ethica Nicomachea* (Oxford: Oxford University Press, 1894).

2. Compare G. Figal, "Riesenschlacht? Überlegungen zur Platoninterpretation," *Internationale Zeitschrift für Philosophie* 1 (1994): 150–62; H. J. Krämer, *Plato and the Foundation of Metaphysics* (New York, 1990); G. Reale, *Per una nuova interpretazione di Platone* (Milano: Vita e pensiero, 1995); and T. A. Szlézak, *Platon lesen* (Stuttgart: 1993).

3. Compare Hans-Georg Gadamer, "Die Idee des Guten zwischen Plato und Aristoteles" (1978), in *Gesammelte Werke*, vol. 7 (Tübingen: Mohr, 1991), 128–227; and W. Wieland, *Platon und die Formen des Wissens* (Göttingen: Vandenhoeck and Ruprecht, 1982).

4. R. Ferber, *Platons Idee des Guten* (Sankt Augustin: H. Richarz, 1984), 149.

5. Quotations from Plato's works follow the edition by J. Burnet, *Platonis Opera* (Oxford: Oxford University Press, 1900–1907).

6. Wieland, *Platon und die Formen des Wissens*, 164.

PART III

PLATO'S
OTHER SOCRATES

...ophanes in the Platonic Text

Bernard Freydberg

> "The question you are asking," I said, "needs an answer given through an image."
>
> "And you, in particular," he said, "I suppose, aren't used to speaking through images."
>
> "All right," I said. "Are you making fun of me after having involved me in an argument so hard to prove? At all events, listen to the image so you can see still more how greedy I am for images."
>
> —*Republic*

No one with the desire to do so will have any trouble tracing Homer and Aristophanes in the Platonic text. This ease is due not only to their at least occasional prominence (and perpetual presence) in the body of the dialogues, but also to the many tracings already undertaken by accomplished Plato scholars. My retracing, undertaken in the spirit of John Sallis's *Being and Logos: Reading the Platonic Dialogues*[1] on a topic not treated extensively in that work, makes some trouble for the widely transmitted and accepted view but, I hope, ends some trouble and opens the dialogues up for an approach which allows the dialogues to speak from themselves on this issue.

Contrary to the received wisdom on Plato and Homer (a wisdom which, happily, is receding more and more),[2] the Platonic dialogues do not advocate censorship, nor are they "against" poetry. It is one purpose of this essay to contribute to the ultimate decisive defeat of the received wisdom on this issue, doing so not so much by engaging opponents, but far more by showing how thoroughly and how positively poetry and philosophy nourish and belong to one another in Plato and, by extension, in philosophy.

The text which best served to frame and locate Homer in the Platonic corpus is not the *Republic* (although the *Republic* offers the most provocative encounter), but the *Ion.* Ion is celebrated as the rhapsode who best brings the music of Homer to his hearers. But he does not know the meaning of what he sings, as Socrates' questioning discloses, nor does Homer, whose work Ion sings. The principal point is not Ion's or Homer's obtuseness. It is that the work of the god can get done without any knowledge on the part of the poet, the rhapsode, or the audience. The accomplishment of the god's work is imaged by the stone of Herakleia, which binds the god to the people in a chain whose rings extend from the god to the Muse to the inspired poet to and through (it turns out) the rhapsode and, finally, to the audience, the spectators (533c9–535a1). Absent are good sense (*emphrones*), intellect (*nous*), and skill (*technē*). Present are inspiration (*entheōs*), possession (*embōsin*), and divine power (*theia dunamei*). The blindness and senselessness of the poet has the function of introducing measure into the bacchic transport inspired by the poem. The infirmity of the poet reminds us that it is the god and not the human being who is the source of the poem, that is, that human insight had nothing to do with the creation of the poem in its beauty (534c7–d4). In light of Socratic ignorance, the charge of the ignorance of the poet and rhapsode loses much of its sting. There is no mention of the danger to souls of Homeric poetry in the *Ion,* but merely a reminder of its nonrationality. In the divinely inspired poems of Homer, more than any other poet, "the god himself is the one speaking" (534d4). And Socrates confidently and playfully cites the Homeric epics—to show that Ion does not know what he's talking about.[3]

The philosopher as playful, thoughtful interpreter of such poetry is the voice of the *Republic,* not some poetry-censoring would-be tyrant. The kinship and the conflict of poetry and philosophy in Plato's *Republic* cannot be properly appraised unless the manner in which these two ways of *logos* perform the same function is understood. Both address the individual human soul in the deepest way, attending to its most fundamental concerns and touching it where it is both most vulnerable and most hopeful: its pleasure and pain, its knowledge and ignorance, and its goodness and badness. In so doing, both poetry and philosophy contest the claims, which are just claims, of the actual city. Thus both open up a distance which disengages them, at least in *logos,* from the city's opinions and practices.

This disengagement in speech from the realm of the actual city takes place on an engagement with philosophy, with poetry, or with both. This is the threat to the actual city: that this disengagement in speech might provoke a disengagement in deed. It is in this light that the objection raised by Socrates in the second and third books of the *Republic*, against permitting certain kinds of poetry in the city precisely because such poetry threatens the stability of the bonds of absolute identification of human being and city, must be understood. More precisely, certain poetry threatens the preservation of the opinion of what is terrible, a preservation which is central to the guardians' bearing (429b8–d1). That is, by presenting heroes as fearful of death, or by singing of the gods as acting against their ruler, Zeus, certain poetical passages and rhythms disrupt the bond of guardian and city, provoke the guardians to call the prevailing opinion into question, and thereby introduce distrust of this opinion into the soul of the guardian. This distrust endangers the city, as certain shared opinions form the basis of its existence and preservation.

But philosophy introduces the same distrust. Namely, philosophy provokes the one in whose soul it has taken hold to call prevailing opinions, indeed all opinions, into question. In so doing, it introduces doubt in the soul where previously there was assurance. This likeness of function, namely of challenging the bond of opinion and in so doing of breaking the bond of complete identification of human being and city, constitutes the core of both the kinship and the quarrel. The kinship concerns this common deed, the quarrel concerns the way the deed occurs, that is, the direction which is both taken and prescribed in the performance of the deed. In other words, the quarrel concerns the measure of the deed. So poetry measures philosophy and finds it empty. Philosophy measures poetry and finds it ignorant (*Republic* 607b1–c2). Philosophy lacks beautiful images; poetry lacks reasoned accounts.

The quarrel and kinship (and these are not ultimately separable) can be seen clearly in the contrast between the two contexts within the *Republic* in which the "Achilles in Hades" passage from Book 11 of the *Odyssey* appears: "I would rather be on the soil, a serf to another, to a man without lot whose means of life are not great, than rule over all of the dead who have perished" (*Republic* 386c5–7; *Odyssey* 11.489–491). The passage first appears at the beginning of Book 3, where Socrates seems to profess the most unambiguous disapproval. He is concerned that hearing Homer's words would introduce a dangerous fear of death into the souls of the guardians. In fact, it is the first such passage he would ban from his city (386c4). Its next appearance is shortly after Book 7 opens and occurs after the human being who has been liberated from the cave has had a taste of life on the earth. Socrates notes that such a man would have no desire for the honors bestowed by the men who live among the shadows and would rather " 'be on the soil, a serf to another man, to a portionless man' than to opine those things and live that way" (516d5–7).

Several matters should be noted about this apparent reversal of sentiment. First, only when considered from the standpoint of the total identification of human being and city does the passage in question become dangerous, for in this context the hero is interpreted straightforwardly as one who should in all aspects be imitated. When freed from the bond to the city (when freed from the bond to convention and to opinion), another possibility of interpreting the hero arises: No longer is the hero a kind of "original" to be imitated, but, rather, the hero functions as a vicarious image of a human life properly lived. In this context, the words of Achilles are heard to say not that death is fearful and that even the most sniveling life on earth is preferable. Rather, they are interpreted to say that to live among shadows without being, that is, to live holding blind opinions—even to be named king in the realm where blind opinions are honored—is worth nothing to the one who has come to see more clearly. Anything, even the greatest suffering or the greatest dishonor, is preferable to such a life.

Second, since the Homeric passage is the same one cited in Book 3 and Book 7, the crucial factor cannot be the poetical passage. The framework of its interpretation, and not the image created by the poet, is the issue. Poetry does not come complete with its own interpretation, and every interpretation of poetry occurs within a certain framework; we have considered two divergent ones. At the least, this says that poetry by itself is not a culprit. Any harm it may do, as we indicated earlier, does not belong to its nature, but occurs as a result of where and how it is employed. It cannot be held accountable for being interpreted in certain, perhaps subversive, ways.

Third, only the one who has been liberated from the cave, who has been liberated in some way from the condition (*pathei*) of the city and its education, that is, only the one who has seen the shadows as shadows and knows that they are not real being, is able to hear the poem in a thoughtful way. To such a one, the poem images his condition as a human being seeking a life governed by love of truth, as opposed to one in which political opinions are accepted without serious question. This says: Only someone in whom *philosophy* has begun to take hold (for the task of seeing opinions as opinions, that is, of recognizing one's own ignorance and the partiality of one's insight, is among philosophy's most basic tasks) can interpret the poem in a healthy manner, one which does not subvert the proper humanity of the soul. In this sense, philosophy is required in order for poetry to be properly heard. So poetry needs philosophy as its measure, not of the poetic art itself but as work to be received appropriately by human beings.

With these considerations in mind, the role of Homer in *Republic* 10 is recast. The apparent condemnation of Homer might not be one at all.[4] The charges against Homer of ignorance, and of his inability to found a school or an enduring tradition of disciples which would make men better, are unconvincing because—as Socrates knows—the same charges could be levelled against *him,* if indeed they are charges. That they are not serious charges is clearly indicated by Socrates' selection of certain sophists (600c1–d4) as examples of men who, unlike Homer, know how to make citizens better and who have built an enduring following. In distinguishing Homer from the same sophists from whom he also distinguishes himself, Socrates subtly affirms his positive kinship with Homer. So, then, is the positive kinship of philosophy and poetry in which thoughtful questioning and inspired images encounter one another.

In this light, the *Hippias Minor* occurs primarily as an encounter of human beings with Homeric heroes, not another encounter between philosophy and sophistry. The dialogue begins with a silence, the silence of Socrates after hearing Hippias's discourse upon Homer, and its turning point is another silence threatened by Hippias after Socrates' *elenchos* of the former's distinction between the willing (*hekonti*) and the unwilling (*akonti,* 371e9–372d1). Both are mediated by Eudikos, and this mediation of the silences is his sole and crucial function.[5] Hippias is presented as the one who knows and can do all things, a caricature of a sophist. Socrates is presented as the most ignorant of all (and unable even to distinguish goodness from power), a caricature of himself as philosopher.

By contrast, Homer's heroes Achilles and Odysseus, who can be seen as poetic enlargements (and, in that sense, caricatures) of men, appear in their full humanity. Both Achilles and Odysseus are shown to tell the truth at some times and to lie at others; yet their stature never suffers: Socrates and Hippias regard them both as excellent men, although from different sides.

Hippias's speech (not itself presented) treats the famous embassy of Odysseus, Aias, and Peleus to Achilles in Book 9 of the *Iliad.* Hippias argues that Achilles is superior to Odysseus as a "kind of man" because the former is true (*alēthēs*) and simple (*haplous*), while the latter is "many-wayed" (*polutropos*) and false (*pseudēs*) (365b3–5). Socrates, citing Achilles' many conflicting accounts of his plans and Odysseus's simple trust of the account given to him by Achilles, argues instead for Odysseus's honesty and Achilles' guile. Hippias then maintains that Achilles lies unwillingly, while the lies of Odysseus are willing. But Socrates leads Hippias to agree that the one who acts willingly is always better than the unwilling. The runner who can run both rapidly and slowly, for example, is better than the one who has no choice but to run slowly (373c1–374a1). The reasoning is similar for other arts, for sciences, and ultimately for justice. Surprisingly and preposterously, this line of reasoning leads to the conclusion that the man who voluntarily does disgraceful (*aischra*) and unjust things is good.

This ending is unsatisfactory to both Hippias and Socrates, and one is tempted to call it aporetic. Socrates, assuming the role of the perplexed innocent, chides the "wise" Hippias for not giving him guidance. We are brought before our ignorance, are called to begin again, and are presumably in better condition to philosophize by virtue of the exercise. There is no denying this. But things look somewhat different from the point of view of the playful inversion, according to which the interlocutors are caricatured in the dialogue and the heroes are reduced to ordinary mortals.

Retracing the path to the aporetic ending in terms of the role of poetic imagery in the *Hippias Minor*, we should notice that Socrates presumably leaves Homer behind near the beginning of the inquiry "since we are incapable of asking him his thoughts (*noon*) on the verses he has made" (365c9–d1). Near the end, he says that his perplexity—confirmed by the bad result of the inquiry—causes Socrates, causes other ordinary people like him, and causes even the "wise" sophists like Hippias *to wander* (*planasthai*, 367c3).[6] The word "wander" is used four times in the last four lines and is the last word in the dialogue. In terms of the poetic elements of the dialogue, *Odysseus* is the famous wanderer in Homeric poetry.

In the *Odyssey*, Odysseus reclaims his home in the guise of an ordinary beggar after wandering in search of great fame (*mega kleos*) for twenty years. In the myth which concludes another dialogue, Plato's *Republic*, Odysseus the wanderer is said to have been purified of love of honor and seeks the life of a private man who minds his own business (620c1–d3). In this way, muddling about honestly in mere confusion on the level of argument is presented as a heroic journey home on the level of poetic imagery.

So Homer's poetry, said earlier to be left behind, playfully returns and frames the discourse, which at its conclusion is shadowed by the image of wandering Odysseus.[7] At the close of the *Hippias Minor*, the poetic travels of Odysseus intertwine with the philosophical forays of Socrates and are joined in the image of wandering to which the falsely confident Hippias has been playfully invited. Taken together with the role of Achilles in the ascent out of the cave, the great Homeric heroes belong to philosophy as vicarious images of fearlessness toward truth and toward disdaining unexamined opinion (shadows) and of willingness to wander in confusion rather than profess something unworthy until a way (home) to wisdom is found. In this way, the dialogues weave the inspired poetry of Homer and the thoughtful questioning of Socrates such that neither determines the other, leaving both at play.

Socrates proclaimed a hunger for images at *Republic* 487e4–488a2, but declared no such hunger in his defense as presented in the *Apology*. The image he craves least of all is the one of himself fashioned by the only one of his old accusers whose name he knows, and "who happens to be a certain comic poet" (18d1–2). In his defense before his fellow Athenians, Socrates seems to expel the playfulness that characterizes his activity in other contexts: "Perhaps it will seem to some of you that I am playing, but be assured that I will tell you the whole truth" (20d4–6). But the deeper movement of the dialogue reasserts this play.

The mutual nourishing and belonging together of philosophy and poetry, discussed above in connection with Homer, receives its greatest challenge in the life of Socrates from the images of *comedy*, not in the confrontation of philosophy with Homer and tragedy. The complementarity of philosophy and Homeric poetry in the *Ion*, the *Republic*, and *Hippias Minor* is also present in the *Apology*, where Socrates employs Homeric images in his defense.[8] But no such employment is possible in the case of Aristophanic imagery. Nevertheless, the battle of Socrates to overcome his comic caricature by Aristophanes in *Clouds* serves as a mask for the deep bond also shared by philosophy and comedy.

On one level, the poetic gift of Aristophanes gives the stock charges against the philosopher a vividness and a comic richness which would make them all the more difficult to shake: a lizard defecates into the open mouth of a heavenward-gazing Socrates (169–174); the philosopher's disciples bend over the more closely to survey with their eyes what is beneath the ground, as their rumps are aimed at the heavens which would so pointedly mark their master (186–194); weaker *logos* defeats stronger *logos* largely through recourse to buggery (1088–1104).[9]

In the *Apology*, Socrates notes the great difficulty he will have in fighting shadows (*skiamachein*). What shadows these are! He complains that there is no cross-examination possible with no one to cross-examine. On the one hand there is the clear and obvious reason for this impossibility: The prejudices begotten through such powerful imagery are too deeply rooted to excise, and its originator(s) are long gone and probably forgotten. But the more subtle reason in the case of Aristophanes, as in the case of Homer, is the paradox in the comportment of the philosopher toward images, which consists of an ever-present need for them and an equally present need to transcend them. This paradox is experienced most sharply when great artists like Homer and Aristophanes are their inspired makers.

The pointedness of this case arises from the fact that the principal shadow with which Socrates must contend is no mere general accusation about philosophers whispered out of his earshot to innocent ears, but a powerfully specific and vivid image of Socrates himself created by precisely such an artist and presented to his fellow citizens at the Dionysian festival in 423 B.C. Against this image and its impact (as well as against the more general and ethereal shadows), Socrates will try to present the truth about himself in 399 B.C. to the judges he will not call true judges, but merely "men of Athens" (17a1).

But it quickly becomes clear that it is not so much a contest between the true Socrates and his image as it is a contest between *two images* of Socrates, with his provocative words and deeds in the *Apology* fashioning the competing image. Despite his apparent insistence upon presenting the true Socrates in opposition to a comic image of him, it should hardly be any surprise that Socrates is engaged with images in the *Apology:* He is always engaged with them, even as he endeavors at times to transcend them. The special circumstance here is that he must contend with *his own* image. The nature of this contest shapes the self-image he presents.

Next to the babbler and evasive fraud of *Clouds,* the *Apology* juxtaposes an aggressive, direct attacker who instructs his judges on the meaning of their oath (18a2–6), who likens his behavior in Athens to that of Achilles in Troy (28b9–28d5), and who proposes a reward for himself rather than a penalty upon his conviction (36d1–d9). Just as no one had ever encountered a Socrates resembling the one seen in *Clouds,* no Socratic behavior which approaches such continuous stridency and anger occurs anywhere else in the Platonic corpus. To maintain that both images are poetic in the same sense would be excessive. But it seems clear, in light of the early and pointed reference to Aristophanes, that the Aristophanic Socrates in *Clouds* called forth the Platonic Socrates of the *Apology.*

So a comic image has called forth a philosophical image; philosophy is in some way appropriated to comedy in the Platonic dialogues. In a straightforward sense, it appears that the distortions of comic poetry call forth the measure-providing corrective *logos* of philosophy as *pharmakon,* just as in the case of Homer and the tragedians. But as we have seen, the image of Socrates in the *Apology* is unusual in its stridency and humorlessness. This stridency and absence of play cannot be explained by the seriousness of the trial: In the *Phaedo,* in the face of death, Socrates exudes playfulness and good cheer.

This inner relation of comedy and philosophy is the crucial issue in the effort to understand the strange image of Socrates and his uncharacteristically serious tone in the *Apology,* quite apart from the issues which tend to dominate the scholarship.[10] Whatever the conscious purposes of Aristophanes and whatever the actual historical and cultural circumstances might have been, the battle in Plato's *Apology* over the image of Socrates does not have much to do with the intentions and larger purpose of individual actors on certain stages—not, at least, in terms of its philosophical significance. At issue is the ancient quarrel, which we treated earlier with respect to Homer. Here the quarrel occurs with respect to comedy, which results in a different but kindred reconciliation.

There is no doubt that although the Aristophanic image (or at least what it represents to Socrates as the source of the old accusations) proved too powerful to overcome at the actual trial, the philosophical image of Socrates presented by Plato has triumphed since. While the old accusations against philosophers still surface and thus are, in a sense, still influential, the defense of Socrates as a defense of philosophy and philosophers who are worthy of the name is widely if not near universally regarded as entirely successful. It is obvious that the Socratic image in the *Apology* is closer to an accurate representation of philosophical activity than the image of the sophistical natterer in *Clouds,* even if the most generous allowance is made and if Aristophanes' intention is interpreted as entirely friendly. Nevertheless, the image of Socrates in the *Apology* is also distorted as well as incomplete.

Perhaps surprisingly, the most likely candidate for an appropriate complement to the partial image in the *Apology* is that same Aristophanic image in *Clouds* with which Socrates must fight for his life and which he would expel from the atmosphere of his trial. The fight on the level of history, with this image powerfully in the background, resulted in the successful prosecution of Socrates by Meletus and Anytus which led to his death. On the level of the ancient quarrel, however, the serious and sober image of Socrates rejoins with its playful and liberated counterpart. On the former level, the images of honorable and serious servant and subversive and frivolous fraud opposed one another; there could be no compromise. On the latter level, a seriousness which excluded all play (Socrates of *Apology*) opposed a playfulness which excluded all seriousness (Socrates of *Clouds*). On this level, the two partial images merge, and the Socrates of the other dialogues, who both argues and plays, is genuinely re-encountered. The comic image provided by Aristophanes in *Clouds* fills out the serious one presented in Plato's *Apology.* In another formulation, the opposition which occurs as serious on the level of history and which led to the conviction of Socrates[11] occurs as playful on the level of the quarrel between philosophy and poetry.

The attempted expulsion of playfulness can be attributed to Socrates' need to suppress both the poetic in general and the Aristophanic-comic in particular in order to present his defense to the "men of Athens," a defense which is commanded by the obligations of citizenship. He will "tell the truth," which is his obligation in his position as speaker (*rhētoros*, 18a5–6), and, in so doing, attempt to answer the charges of the comic poet *as if they were not playful but only serious.* The charges are treated as detached from their specific location in the poem of *Clouds* and in the sacred setting of the Dionysian festival: They are treated as if they were actual accusations.

In defending himself against the charges of professing arcane knowledge and making the weaker argument appear stronger, Socrates finds himself defending philosophy "against" poetry in the setting of the city at its most "political." The poets "say things many and beautiful, but know none of the things they say" (22c3–4), although they thought they were wise. They lack the recognition of ignorance necessary for genuine philosophical activity and even for gaining knowledge generally. They proceeded "by nature and inspiration, like prophets and the givers of oracles" (22c1–2). Their difference presents itself sharply: To travel the path of the philosopher requires great seriousness, involving perpetual self-reflection and self-criticism. The path of the poet, even of the tragic poet, seems more playful and innocent, involving the mere discharge of one's nature or gift.

The Socrates of other dialogues does not so radically oppose the poetical, as we have seen. Recourses to nonrational sources abound. To cite just a few cases, he allows the authority of dreams in the *Phaedo* to lead him to practice music on his final day (60e4–8). In the *Symposium*, he strongly implies that the poets beget the worthiest children of all (209c9–d4). In the *Apology*, he is instructed not only by his divine sign (*tou theos sēmion*, 40b1), but also by "oracles and dreams and every way" (33c5–6). Even in the *Meno*, where center stage seems to be held entirely by Socratic *elenchos*, he invokes the authority of certain priests and priestesses (81a5–c4) and declares the source of virtue as divine dispensation in his final hypothesis (99e6). And the *Republic* calls for poetry, with its nonrational origin, to give an account of itself in order to be admitted to the city, while arguments (*logoi*) are to be chanted (607b–608b).

This call, which would bring together rational and nonrational sources, has already been answered both in poetry and in the dialogues. The *Mēnin aeide, thea, Pēlēiadēo Achilēos* ("Sing, goddess, the rage of Peleus's son, Achilles") of Homer's *Iliad* (1.1.1) and the *Mousasōn He-*

likōniadōn archōmeth' aeidein ("From the Helikonian Muses begin to sing") of Hesiod's *Theogony* (l.1), and even the *iou, iou: ō Zeu basileu* ("Oh oh king Zeus") which opens *Clouds* may all be seen as providing apologies in meter. In so doing, they wholly satisfy the requirements for admission to the city. While they are surely terse when compared with their philosophical counterparts, they acknowledge the inspiration spoken of by Socrates in the *Apology* and with it the nonrational origin of their work. In this way, their measure is enacted in the poem itself.

From the side of philosophy, the Platonic dialogues themselves may be seen as chanted *logoi* on account of their playfulness and their often inspired speech. In this sense, they are instances of a certain music which charmingly fends off the charm of the beautiful images of the poets, which would otherwise overcome the reasoning powers of their entranced hearers. Measured by philosophical *logos*, these beautiful images serve as occasions for reflection upon and celebration of the most basic matters confronting human life—including the issue of how to deal with beautiful images! By Homeric or Hesiodic standards, the dialogues are musically moribund, but they are rich with myths, jests, sudden twists, and, in general, the drama and playfulness one finds in the poetry Socrates putatively criticizes. This odd complementarity, united by the common bond of philosophy and poetry to imagery, provides the condition for the surprising view that only when the Aristophanic image of Socrates in *Clouds* is added to the Platonic image in the *Apology* do we arrive at an image from which Socratic philosophizing, with its peculiar synthesis of seriousness and playfulness, can be discerned.

There is a symmetry to the treatment of (Aristophanic) comic and (Homeric) tragic themes. Both can be injurious to souls if they are interpreted as actual proposals issuing from the identification of individual soul and city, rather than as playful and often profound possibilities for the liberated human soul. Both the damage in speech done by Achilles' words from Hades to the guardians-in-training in their city and the actual damage done by Aristophanes' play to the reputation of Socrates in his city issue from the city-based literal interpretation these works of art were given. According to such literalism, death makes the bravest one tremble, and Socrates is a money-seeking fraud. And in both cases, the poetic images disclose the real possibility of a philosophical life when they are interpreted as free creations of and for the wisdom-seeking soul, which is capable of honoring the obligations of citizenship, but which is also capable of discerning other obligations and, while mindful of the dangers, engaged in other possibilities, seeing which are appropriate and nourishing to one's humanity.

In tracing their presence in the Platonic text by means of some of their most inspired images and in attending to the precise Socratic response to those images—by which I mean, by paying an attention which does not fit poetry into a predetermined rationalist schema or a predetermined characterization which is negative, but which allows the Homeric and Aristophanic images themselves to interact with Socratic practice as they do in the dialogue—the poetry of Homer and of Aristophanes serve the philosophical interest as they impel Socrates both to take their measure in his questioning and to allow them *their* own measuring function in accord with the nature of *their* activity. Such a friendly interpretation, though it seems to run counter to many passages taken in their isolation, is faithful to the dialogues read thoughtfully—as the ongoing interaction of *logos, muthos,* and *ergon,* in Sallis's terms.[12] I'll close with a suggestion from an early footnote in *Being and Logos* where Sallis, in a characteristic mixture of careful reticence and outrageous boldness, writes—in an apparent aside—on the issue of translating Plato:

> It is perhaps not too much of an exaggeration to say that the "real translations" are to be found in the interpretations and that the translations given of the actual Greek texts are intended primarily to "hold open" the "space" for the interpretation, that is, to prevent closing off of the questioning.[13]

In light of the interpretive liberation effected by this holding open of the space which makes it possible to allow the Platonic text to speak to us from itself, with at least fewer sedimented preconceptions, it is perhaps not too much of an exaggeration to retrace Homer and Aristophanes into the Platonic text in the shape not merely of problems for but also and primarily of friends of the philosopher and the philosophic enterprise.

Notes

The ideas in this essay comprise part of my larger study of Platonic play entitled *The Play of the Platonic Dialogues* (New York: Peter Lang, 1997).

　　1. John Sallis, *Being and Logos: Reading the Platonic Dialogues,* 3rd ed. (Bloomington: Indiana University Press, 1996).

　　2. Here are two samples of the conventional wisdom. A. E. Taylor, writing in *Plato: The Man and His Work* (London: Methuen, 1952), 279–80, maintained:

> [Socrates] is seriously proposing to censure just what we consider to be the imperishable contributions of Athens to the art and literature of the world,

because he holds that they have tendencies which are unfavorable to the development of the highest development of moral personality.

Even the astute Friedländer wrote: "[T]here is no place for any mimetic art and its ancestor Homer . . . This, to begin with, must be taken quite seriously." See Paul Friedländer, *Plato*, 3 vols. (New York: Pantheon; London: Routledge; 1958–66), 1: 121–2.

Two examples may represent the harbingers of the demise of this error. Julius Elias writes in *Plato's Defense of Poetry* (Albany: SUNY Press, 1984), 1: "Plato's writings contain and imply an acknowledgement of the indispensability of poetry." Elias's book emphasizes the positive contribution of myths to the pursuit of truth and of a good society. Jean-François Mattei also grants intrinsic centrality to myth in "The Theater of Myth in Plato," from *Platonic Writings: Platonic Readings*, ed. C. L. Griswold (New York: Routledge, 1988), 66–83.

3. For an analogous treatment of the *Ion*, see John Russon, "Hermeneutics and Plato's *Ion*," *Clio* 24(1995): 399–418.

4. See also *Gorgias* 523a2–3, where Socrates invokes Homer's authority to prove that he is speaking "the real truth" (*hōs alēthē gar onta*) in his myth, and, with somewhat less import, 524d7, where Homer is appealed to as an authority on Hades. (See also chapter 11 of my *Play of Platonic Dialogues*.) Further, Socrates remarks that only poetry which celebrates gods and heroes and good men in songs of praise should be admitted into the city (607a3–8). But this proscription excludes no poetry at all by Homer and the tragedians.

5. Three telling silences occur in the *Hippias Minor*: first, the silence in the face of the uninterrupted assault of Hippias's confident speech at the dialogue's outset; second, the silence at the end in the face of the wandering, which is the fate of human beings and which precludes too much confidence; and third, the threatened silence of Hippias in the middle, which Socrates and his philosophical "embassy" interrupts.

The silences occur, first, after what seems to have been a long rhetorical onslaught from Hippias; second, after a long ironic and philosophical piece of rhetoric from Socrates; and, third, after the discussion leads to a conclusion that neither can accept. In all cases, the soul seeks to step back and redirect itself. These telling silences which interrupt the flow of noise and/or confusion also belong to the play of philosophy and poetry as granting a space which makes this play possible.

6. *Plagchthe*, from *plazō*, the epic form of *planasthai*, belongs to the description of Odysseus which opens the *Odyssey* (Book 1, line 2).

7. After praising Achilles in argument, Socrates wins a playful victory over proud Hippias—using the image of Odysseus originally championed by the latter. Socrates' thoughtful and playful relation to poetic matters shows itself here once again.

8. See *Apology* 28d1–5, where Socrates cites *Iliad* (18,1.96f.), and 34d3–4, where he quotes *Odyssey* (19.1.163).

9. The references to Aristophanes' *Clouds* are to the edition by Kenneth Dover (Oxford: Clarendon Press, 1968).

10. One such issue concerns the meaning and intention of the Aristophanic parody and the role of the historical circumstances surrounding the production of *Clouds* and the trial of Socrates some two decades later. Whether Aristophanes' intention was benign and the meaning playful or the reverse—and whether, as Gilbert Murray, in *Aristophanes* (New York: Russell & Russell, 1964), maintains, "the whole trouble and danger came from the change in atmosphere. In 423 these charges (that is, the old accusations) were jokes. In 399 they were not jokes at all" (99)—or whether some less innocent explanation accounts for Aristophanes' status as an old accuser, the *Apology* shows Socrates fighting with this image as he fights for his life. But how can one fight with an image?

It is not unusual to view this battle as having Aristophanes on one side and Plato and Xenophon on the other, with the reputation of Socrates at stake and with one or the other position having more justice on its side; there are also variants within this scenario, such as *Clouds* being a friendly but misunderstood satire, or Socrates having changed from a sophist to a sage in the intervening twenty-four years. (Compare Kenneth Dover, "Socrates in the Clouds," in *The Philosophy of Socrates: A Collection of Critical Essays,* ed. Gregory Vlastos [Garden City, NY: Anchor Books, 1971], 67–68.)

11. The conviction of Socrates is "avenged" not long after by the prosecution and death of Meletus and Anytus.

12. For a treatment of the interplay of *muthos, logos,* and *ergon* in their dialogical context, see my *Play of the Platonic Dialogues.*

13. Sallis, *Being and Logos,* 5n.

9

Giving Thought to the Good Together: Virtue in Plato's *Protagoras*

Francisco J. Gonzalez

Socrates' claim in the *Phaedrus* (264c) that a *logos* must, like a living creature, possess both a middle and extremities suiting both one another and the whole is as true of the *Protagoras* as it is of any other dialogue. Yet a common tendency among interpretations of this complex body of text is to amputate one limb or another (for example, the arguments for the unity of virtue or the account of the "science of measurement") and examine it in isolation, while ignoring that "middle" from which these extremities derive their life and meaning. Plato makes clear the identity of this "middle" by putting it literally at the center of the dialogue and flagging it with a crisis that threatens to dissolve the discussion. I am, of course, referring to the dispute concerning method, including the contest in poetic interpretation. The goal of the present reading of the dialogue is to interpret its different parts from this, its philosophical center or heart. The dialogue will thereby be shown not only to be a truly unified organic whole, but also to communicate a positive conception of human goodness or virtue.

Socrates Tests Hippocrates' Desire for the Wisdom of Protagoras

Socrates narrates his discussion with Protagoras, from which he has just returned, to an unnamed friend. Their opening exchange highlights

Socrates' erotic drive (initially understood by the friend as restricted to the pursuit of Alcibiades, but explained by Socrates to be in reality directed at the wisdom others claim to find in Protagoras).[1] Though *erōs* is not made an explicit topic in this dialogue, it is an implicit issue throughout. Socrates surprisingly begins his narrative, not with the main discussion, but with an earlier one between himself and a young man named Hippocrates. Socrates clearly considers this earlier discussion indispensable to an understanding of the encounter with the Sophist.

Having learned the previous evening that Protagoras is in town, Hippocrates ardently desires to be accepted as his pupil and awakens Socrates before dawn in the hope that he will intercede. Unwilling simply to pander to Hippocrates' passion, Socrates uses the earliness of the hour as an excuse to engage him in a discussion and thereby *test* his passion (310a8–311a7). The outcome is predictable: Hippocrates is shown to have no idea of what he will learn from Protagoras. But why need he know this *before* becoming Protagoras's student? Will he not find out *afterward*? Socrates sees a great danger here and severely upbraids Hippocrates for his willingness to risk his soul in this way. His own description of the Sophist as "a kind of merchant who peddles provisions upon which the soul is nourished" (313c4–6)[2] is meant to show that the Sophist no more knows which of the teachings he sells are harmful or beneficial for the soul than the grocer knows which of the foods he sells are harmful or beneficial for the body. But in this way Socrates shows Hippocrates that he is in need of a specific kind of knowledge perhaps much more important than that which the sophists have to offer: a knowledge of how to *evaluate* their teachings with regard to their benefit or harm (313e2–5).

The questions provoked by the reference to this knowledge are crucial for an understanding of the rest of the dialogue. First, if the physician of the body is the one who can evaluate the benefit and harm of the grocer's wares, who is the analogous "physician of the soul" (*peri tēn psuchēn iatrikos*, 313e2)? The Sophist is ruled out by what Socrates says.[3] It is instead Socrates himself who, in testing and evaluating for Hippocrates Protagoras's teachings, assumes the role of such a physician.[4] But this answer in turn raises two more questions. First, what is the nature of the knowledge that enables Socrates to act as a physician of the soul? Is it a *technē*, like medicine for the body? Second, how is this knowledge related to the "wisdom" the sophists claim to teach? It might at first appear simply propaedeutic: While it can determine whether or not a certain teaching is beneficial, one must go to the sophists for the teaching itself. But there is a strange circularity here. How can I know that a certain piece of knowledge will benefit me before I learn it? Socrates points out that teachings, unlike food and drink, cannot be taken away in a container in order to be evaluated later: Because they benefit or harm us as soon as they are taken into the soul, we must be able to evaluate them prior to having them (314a–b). But how is this possible?[5] How can we evaluate Protagoras's claim that his teachings will benefit us unless we already know both his teachings and what will benefit us? And in that case, why do we need Protagoras? These questions suggest a possibility which, I will argue, is confirmed especially by the dialogue's "middle": that Socrates' higher-order knowledge of how to evaluate what the sophists teach is not simply a propaedeutic to sophistic teaching, but its rival. In that case, Hippocrates' mistake is that he uses Socrates only as a means of gaining access to Protagoras, rather than remaining in conversation with Socrates himself (see 310e2–3). His *erōs* is misdirected.

On their way to Callias's house to meet Protagoras, Socrates and Hippocrates do something significant: Unwilling to leave incomplete (*atelēs*) a discussion they have pursued along the way, they stand before the door to Callias's house until agreement is reached (314c3–7).[6] We see here what Socrates has to offer Hippocrates prior to, and perhaps in place of, the teachings of Protagoras: engagement in dialectic with the goal of arriving at a common understanding. This passage thus suggests what will be confirmed later: The quasi-medical skill that enables Socrates to improve the "health" of Hippocrates and to evaluate the "foods for the soul" sold by the merchant Protagoras is nothing other than *dialectic*. But then the questions raised above can be reformulated. Is Socrates' dialectic merely a propaedeutic to teachings of the kind offered by Protagoras, or is it a rival to such teachings, indeed, an alternative to the very idea of "teaching" as understood by Protagoras? Specified in terms of what will prove to be the relevant subject matter, the question is: Does Socrates' dialectic only clear the way for the positive teaching of virtue, or does it itself already understand virtue in its ability to evaluate the benefit and harm of teachings about virtue? That the dialogue is meant to address this question explains why Socrates will not immediately focus on the content of Protagoras's teachings, but will instead ask the more fundamental question of whether or not the virtue Protagoras claims to teach can be taught at all. It also begins to explain why the central portion of this dialogue on virtue focuses on the opposition between the *methods* of Socrates and of Protagoras.

Socrates Tests Protagoras's Wisdom

When Socrates finally meets Protagoras and describes his mission, he offers the sophist the choice of conversing alone or before the others. Protagoras thanks Socrates for his forethought, since

> Caution is in order for a foreigner who goes into the great cities and
> tries to persuade the best of the young men in them to abandon their
> associations with others, relatives and acquaintances, young and old
> alike, and to associate with him instead on the grounds that they will be
> improved by this association. Jealously, hostility, and intrigue on a large
> scale are aroused by such activity. (316c5–d3)

Here we get a clear indication of the deep antagonism that exists between
Protagoras and the people: The latter believe that the traditional associations of family and state provide a sufficient education in goodness, while
Protagoras claims that the young need a complete outsider like himself
in order to become good. Protagoras proceeds to explain that, unlike
the concealed sophists of old, he has decided that the best precaution
against the hostility of the masses is to ply his trade in the open, though
he has also discovered other precautions in case this one fails (317b5–7).
This final provocative comment must make us wonder what other means
of safety Protagoras has devised.[7]

When asked what Hippocrates will learn by studying with him,
Protagoras claims the knowledge which, according to Socrates' earlier
warning, a sophist as such does not have: "The very day you start, you
will go home a better man, and the same thing will happen the day after.
Every day, day after day, you will get better and better" (318a6–9). Asking
questions similar to those he asked Hippocrates earlier, Socrates tries to
get Protagoras to demarcate his *technē* from other *technai* that also claim
to make people better in one respect or another. Protagoras complies,
defining what he teaches as follows: "Good deliberation [*euboulia*], both
in domestic matters—how best to manage one's household, and in public
affairs—how to realize one's maximum potential for success in political
debate and action" (318e5–319a2). As soon as Protagoras agrees to call
this "the political art" (*politikē technē*), Socrates questions its existence.
What Socrates explicitly questions, of course, is that this subject can be
taught; but since any *technē*, as a *technē*, is teachable, Socrates is also thereby
questioning the very existence of a *technē* in this subject. The two reasons
Socrates gives for his doubt are well known. First, when questions of civic
virtue arise in the Assembly, the Athenians recognize no experts, but
allow all an equal voice in the debate, something they do not allow in
the case of subjects they consider technical. Second, in private life, the
best and wisest citizens seem incapable of passing on their virtue to their
children. There is a good reason for why Socrates here, counter to his
usual custom, appeals to the actions and beliefs *of the people* to support
his view: He wishes to highlight and exacerbate that antagonism between
Protagoras and the people to which Protagoras himself alluded earlier.

In this way, a great onus is placed on the sophist to explain and justify the art by which he claims to be better able than the society as a whole to make people good. This use of majority opinion against Protagoras does not, however, imply that the view Socrates defends here is in no way his own.[8] Both before (319b2–3) and after (328e1–3) Protagoras's reply, Socrates mentions his real reason for doubting that virtue can be taught: He does not think that good people become good through any purely human care or practice (*anthrōpinē epimeleia*). Unexplained at this point, however, is the nature of the "care" that *does* make us good.

Protagoras's Precautionary Myth and Logos

Protagoras decides to defend the teachability of virtue by means of a story (*muthos*), to which he ends up appending a long argument or *logos*. To understand this defense (often referred to as the "Great Speech"), it is first important to note what Protagoras does *not* do. Given his pretensions as a sophist, we would expect from him the following replies to Socrates' objections. First, the Athenians give equal weight in the Assembly to what anyone says about virtue because they are all equally ignorant about virtue and, therefore, do not even know that they should consult Protagoras. Second, the best and wisest citizens cannot pass on their virtue to their sons because they lack the sophist's art; that is why their sons should go to Protagoras. These replies, however, would have required Protagoras to demonstrate that he has a knowledge of virtue that mere laymen do not possess. Protagoras therefore avoids this onus that Socrates has tried to place on him by adopting the opposite strategy: He *defends* the actions of the Athenian people and argues, contrary to his own claim earlier, that there is absolutely no disagreement between their views and his.

Protagoras attempts to explain and justify the actions of the Athenian Assembly by telling the following story (320c8–323a4). At the time when mortal creatures first came to be, the brothers Prometheus and Epimetheus were put in charge of assigning to each its special powers. Epimetheus begged his brother to be allowed to carry out this task by himself. His request granted, he proceeded to provide each animal with what it needed to survive: speed for some, great size for others, strength for yet others, and so on. After all the powers had been distributed, however, Epimetheus realized that he had overlooked human beings, who were therefore left naked and defenseless. Desperate to remedy this grievous oversight, Prometheus stole fire and the technical arts from Athena and Hephaestus and gave them to the needy humans. Equipped with these

---

arts, humans were able to provide for their own clothing, housing, and nourishment. Because they lacked political wisdom, however, they could not band together without wronging each other and were, therefore, at the mercy of wild animals. At this point Zeus intervened, commanding Hermes to distribute justice and shame (*aidōs* and *dikē*, 322c2) to *all* humans, since cities could not arise if only a few specialists possessed these things, as in the case of the technical arts. The moral is clear: The existence of community depends on *everyone* possessing virtue, and this is precisely what distinguishes virtue from a technical expertise that is possessed only by a few.

The myth, however, appears to have the unfortunate consequence of undermining Protagoras's own claim to special expertise in virtue. Protagoras, therefore, leaves the myth at this point to argue that the Athenians do not see themselves as possessing virtue *by nature,* but believe that it is acquired through teaching (323c5–324d1). But how is this view to be reconciled with the moral of the myth? Protagoras attempts to do so by characterizing virtue as a teachable *technē* that differs from other *technai* only in that it is possessed and taught by *everyone.* Thus the main idea of the concluding part of Protagoras's speech is that no Athenian is a layman in virtue; *everyone* is an expert (see especially 326e8–327a2).

But what does this mean? Protagoras uses his rhetorical skills to ensure that it does not mean anything, since any clear meaning would be disastrous for his purpose. If the meaning is that all Athenians have equal knowledge of virtue, then Protagoras is putting himself out of a job, as well as rendering meaningless the very claim that virtue needs to be taught, a claim that presupposes both the existence of people who are not yet knowledgeable and, most importantly, different levels of achievement in learning; where everyone is equally a teacher, no one is. If, on the other hand, the meaning is only that all Athenians have more knowledge of virtue than the uncivilized savage, then Protagoras's argument still allows for some Athenians to be much more knowledgeable about virtue than others and therefore cannot justify the actions of the Athenian Assembly.[9] Since either interpretation is fatal if consistently adopted, Protagoras's strategy is to use the vagueness of the idea of universal expertise to move back and forth between them as suits his purpose.[10] The first interpretation is suggested by the myth and by Protagoras's claim at the very end of the speech that the reason why it is hard to find a single teacher of virtue is that everyone teaches it: Such a search is as futile, he explains, as looking for someone who will teach the sons of craftsmen the craft they have already learned from their fathers (327e1–328a8). The second interpretation is suggested by Protagoras's explanation of why the best citizens of Athens cannot impart their virtue to their sons:

Just as some people have a greater natural aptitude (*euphuestatos*) for flute-playing than others, so do some people have a greater natural aptitude for virtue (326e6–327c3).[11] This interpretation is also supported by Protagoras's attempt to reconcile these differences in aptitude with his claim that all Athenians are experts in virtue: Even the most unjust citizen is a "craftsman of justice," compared to uneducated and undisciplined savages (327c3–e1). Finally, Protagoras must obviously rely on the second interpretation in order to conclude that he is "a little ahead" of others in his knowledge of virtue (328a8–b5). Thus Protagoras's trick is exposed: He appeals to an idea of universal expertise vague enough to encompass both sides of the antagonism between himself and the people; he then interprets this idea now in favor of the people, now in favor of himself.[12]

But Protagoras's opposition to the people, and therefore his dissimulation, may go even deeper than yet suspected, since an important question remains to be addressed: What does the speech reveal about the *nature* of the virtue Protagoras claims to teach? Protagoras explicitly mentions three different virtues: justice, temperance, and piety, and even appears to equate them with the whole of virtue at 325a1–2. Two virtues conspicuously neglected in the speech are courage and wisdom: Courage is at most alluded to in the reference to the art of war as a part of the art of politics (322b5) and in the suggestion that a lack of physical training may result in cowardice (326b6–c3); wisdom is not mentioned at all. This is an odd oversight in itself, but is made only more inexplicable by the prominence Protagoras will later give to these two virtues. When he first mentions courage and wisdom in the discussion following his speech, Socrates asks if he considers them, too, to be parts of virtue (a question that calls to our attention the fact that Protagoras's speech failed to mention them). Protagoras responds: "Absolutely, and wisdom is the greatest part" (330a1–2). But then why did Protagoras neglect this greatest part of virtue in his speech?[13] The answer is simple: While Protagoras can grant the people justice, temperance, and piety, he does not think they possess courage or wisdom. We do not need to guess that this is Protagoras's view, since in moments of candor he states it clearly enough. Several times in this dialogue Protagoras characterizes the people as ignorant (317a4–6, 352e3–4, 353a7–8).[14] When the discussion later turns to courage, Protagoras characterizes the courageous man as "ready to go where the many fear to go" (349e3). In thus denying the people wisdom and courage, Protagoras must consider these two virtues the subject of his own special expertise. They are what put him "a little ahead."

But is there no relation between the two sets of virtues? Can one possess justice and piety without courage and wisdom, and vice versa? When Protagoras first mentions courage and wisdom in the passage cited above, it is to disassociate them from justice: He asserts that "many [people] are courageous but unjust, and many again are just but not wise" (329e5–6). Thus there is a complete divorce between the virtues he considers most important and the virtues he attributes to the people. But then, if the courage and wisdom Protagoras teaches have nothing to do with the justice valued by the people, could they not conceivably be used in the pursuit of *injustice*? This is Protagoras's darkest secret, what he most seeks to hide behind his rhetoric.[15] Socrates will later attempt to expose Protagoras by questioning him precisely on the *unity* of the virtues. There is, however, a very odd passage in Protagoras's speech itself that provides a window into his "esoteric" doctrine. Immediately following the myth, Protagoras attempts to provide further support for his claim that everyone has a share of virtue by pointing out the following difference between justice and flute-playing: Someone who is not a good flute player is considered mad if he pretends to be one, but is commended for his *sophrosunē* if he confesses his lack of skill; on the other hand, an unjust person who confesses to being unjust is thought *not* to possess *sophrosunē*, but to be mad (323a5–c2). This point, of course, does not at all support Protagoras's thesis: Rather than showing that everyone has a share of justice, it shows only that everyone has an interest in *pretending* to be just. Its real significance becomes apparent only when its implications are examined.[16] The first obvious implication is that it is *sophrosunē* to feign justice when one is unjust. Since Protagoras, however, explicitly states that his point also applies to the other political virtues (323b2), that is, to piety and temperance (*sophrosunē*), the other implications are that it is *sophrosunē* to feign piety and, strangest of all, that it is *sophrosunē* to feign *sophrosunē*. What this could mean becomes clear when the word *sophrosunē* is recognized to have two distinct meanings in Protagoras's speech.[17] In the present passage, it is contrasted to madness and, therefore, essentially identified with wisdom. Elsewhere in the speech, however, it has the conventional sense of shame, self-restraint, temperance (for example, 326a4–5). The overall implication of the present passage can therefore be stated as follows: It is *wisdom* to feign justice, piety, and temperance, while it is madness to confess one's lack of these virtues.

But is there any other indication that Protagoras values and commends only the *appearance* of the "political virtues"? One such indication is his reduction of these virtues throughout the speech to the purely external and conventional.[18] This is most evident in his account of how virtue is taught. If a child does not obey what his parents tell him, "they straighten him out with threats and blows as if he were a twisted, bent piece of wood" (325d5–7). At school, the children are required to read poetry describing good men of old, are made gentler through instruction in music, and receive the physical training they need to avoid acting cowardly out of weakness. Once they leave school, the city compels them to follow the laws and punishes them if they do not. This account thus tends to reduce virtue to mere lawfulness or obedience. Ostensible obedience to the laws and traditions of society is, of course, compatible with real injustice and impiety, given sufficient cleverness. Another even more important indication is Protagoras's focus on *consequences* in explaining why anyone would seek to be virtuous. He argues, for example, that parents do everything possible to teach their children virtue in order to avoid "not only death but confiscation of property and, practically speaking, complete familial catastrophe" (325c1–3). One need only be successful at *feigning* virtue, of course, to escape these consequences.

It is hard not to suspect that the wisdom and courage Protagoras teaches are nothing but the precaution and prudence that enable one to further one's own interests through injustice while at the same time maintaining the appearance of justice. The "Great Speech" itself appears to be a model instance of such precaution and prudence in its use of rhetoric to make Protagoras's claim to expertise in virtue appear in perfect harmony with the views and values of a democracy. In other words, it is an example of one of those "other precautions" Protagoras claims to have discovered against the hostility of the masses. Though openly confessing to being a sophist, he conceals what he *does* and *teaches* as a sophist. This suspicion, as will be seen, is shared by Socrates; it is what motivates his questioning of Protagoras on the unity of the virtues.

The Origin of the Crisis

As already indicated, Protagoras, in response to Socrates' probing, insists on the distinctness and separability of the different virtues. To bring out the implications of this position, Socrates argues for the opposite thesis: that the virtues are in some sense one. The present reading must pass over the first two arguments to focus on the one that precipitates the central crisis of the dialogue: Socrates' attempt to demonstrate the identity of *sophrosunē* and justice (333b7–334a2) immediately after having identified *sophrosunē* with wisdom. Protagoras finds this argument so threatening that he cannot allow it to be completed. The primary task of any interpretation must be to explain why. Socrates begins by asking if someone can *sōphronein* in acting unjustly (333b8–c1). Protagoras replies that, while this is the view of most people, he himself would be ashamed to maintain it. Yet he already has, in suggesting that it is *sophrosunē*, not madness, to feign justice when acting unjustly! Furthermore, Protagoras's anger at Socrates' attempt to refute this view (see 333e2–4) shows that it is his own, not that of the many, as he absurdly pretends.[19]

Socrates' argument begins by equating *sophrosunē* with "good judgment" (*eu bouleuesthai*, 333d4–6), so that the view under examination becomes the view that it is possible to exhibit good judgment in acting unjustly. Protagoras must be getting very uneasy at this point, since "good judgment" (*euboulia*) is precisely what he earlier claimed to be able to teach the young Hippocrates (318e5).[20] Thus, the argument is exposing the possibility of using the "good judgment" Protagoras teaches for injustice. Socrates proceeds to point out that good judgment is "good" only if it has good results and then tries to identify "good" with what is "advantageous to us" (333d7–e1). It is at this point that Protagoras derails the argument by giving a speech on the relative character of the good: What is good for some animals is not good for others; what is good for some parts of the human body is not good for other parts (334a3–334c6). What is happening here? Clearly what Socrates is trying to show is that the view that one can exhibit good judgment in acting unjustly depends on the assumption that injustice is good (in the sense of "advantageous").[21] While this assumption has been seen to explain much of what Protagoras says, he obviously would not want it exposed. He must therefore prevent at all costs any discussion of the good. And what better way to do so than to give a speech maintaining that the good is "variable and manifold" (*houtō de poikilon ti estin to agathon kai pantodapon*, 334b6–7) and therefore resists any objective characterization?[22]

Crisis: The Good and the Question of Method

We thus arrive at the central crisis of the dialogue. Socrates, claiming to be forgetful and therefore unable to follow long speeches, insists on short answers. Protagoras protests that his answers should not be shorter than necessary (*ē dei*). Socrates, of course, agrees. It immediately becomes apparent, however, that Protagoras is not assuming here *an objective standard of appropriate length,* since he proceeds to ask: "Should I answer at the length that seems necessary *to you* or at the length that seems necessary *to me*?" (334e2–3; my translation). This question does not allow that one of them might be right and the other wrong: What *seems* necessary to each *is* necessary for him. We have here an application of the relativism expressed in Protagoras's speech on the good: What is good for Socrates is simply not the same as what is good for Protagoras.[23]

But given two different views concerning what is appropriate or necessary (*to deon*) in a discussion and no objective standard by which to evaluate these views, how do we decide between them? What Protagoras proceeds to say (335a) shows that he sees in the discussion nothing but a "contest of words" and that his strategy for winning such contests is *not* to converse (*dialegesthai*) in the way *his opponent* considers necessary or appropriate. But as Socrates indicates in both word (335a–c) and deed (he gets up to leave the discussion), Protagoras's view is nothing less than a *refusal* to *dialegesthai*, since dialogue depends on a genuine "being together" (*sunousia*).[24] Here emerges what will be the major theme of the entire central portion of the dialogue: the preconditions of genuine *sunousia*.[25] That this is not simply a "methodological" issue representing a digression from the central topic of virtue[26] will be confirmed by what follows, but is already suggested here: What prevents Protagoras from engaging in genuine dialogue is his relativism concerning the good and the combative understanding of human interaction that goes with it.

When Callias forcefully prevents him from leaving the discussion, Socrates defends his view that genuine dialogue is incompatible with Protagoras's competitiveness and his consequent refusal to *give way* (*sugchōrein*, 335c2) to his interlocutor. Using an analogy (335e2–336a5) that serves to reveal the *disanalogy* between genuine dialogue and a competitive sport, Socrates claims that he can no more converse with Protagoras than he could run with the Olympic champion Crison. Since Socrates cannot run as fast as Crison, they could *run together* only if Crison were to slow down to Socrates' speed. The very idea of such cooperation is, of course, absurd in a competitive sport; such cooperation is, however, essential to dialogue, precisely because it is characterized by give-and-take in a *shared* pursuit.[27] Since Protagoras sees no distinction here between dialogue and competition, he is no more likely than Crison to "give way" to his "opponent." But then how, as Socrates asks, is the dialogue to proceed (336b1)?

Callias completely misses the point due to his own commitment to Protagorean relativism, a commitment he reveals when he defends Protagoras to Socrates as follows: "Protagoras appears to say what is just [*dikaia dokei legein*] when he judges that he is entitled to converse in whatever way he wishes while you too are entitled to converse in whatever way you wish" (336b4–6; my translation). Such a principle would, of course, result not in dialogue, but in two monologues spoken past each other. Particularly important in what Callias says is the reference to justice. On his view, and, clearly, in Protagoras's, "justice" is allowing the individual to do what seems best to him or her: It is "just" for Protagoras to converse in whatever way seems best to him. Yet there is clearly nothing "just" about this. This kind of relativism, by making the individual the standard, undermines all genuine cooperation and community and therefore can result only in injustice. Protagoras's ambivalent attitude toward justice thus begins to receive an explanation: In the arena of competing perceptions of the good, only the appearance of justice can have any value; the good judgment needed to promote one's own good can often recommend injustice. Protagoras's rejection of dialogue also starts showing itself to be more than the rejection of a "method"; it is also a rejection of virtue. The distinction Socrates makes in this context between "being together in dialogue" and "giving speeches" (336b1–3) is, therefore, not ethically neutral. Dialogue, as a coming-together in the shared pursuit of a common good, is the necessary, and perhaps even sufficient condition of justice. On the other hand, the use of rhetoric to promote a purely subjective good, something that is necessarily monological, is, at its core, an act of injustice. Here a playful remark of Hippocrates early in the dialogue acquires special significance: Asked by Socrates if Protagoras has done him an injustice, Hippocrates replies that he has by not sharing his wisdom (310d4–6).

Just as Callias's defense of Protagoras misses what is fundamentally at issue in the present crisis, so does Alcibiades' defense of Socrates. Alcibiades sees the conversation as a *contest* over who is the better speaker and, therefore, wrongly assumes that Socrates would be satisfied if Protagoras were simply to confess to being the inferior dialectician (336c2–4).[28] For Alcibiades, you engage in dialectic in order to prove yourself better at it than your interlocutor. For Socrates, this view represents a complete misunderstanding of dialectic. Nevertheless, Alcibiades rightly sees that Socrates' feigned "forgetfulness" is really a comment on Protagoras's use of speeches to make his audience forget the issue under discussion (336c4–d4).[29] He also recognizes that Socrates is the one person on whom this strategy does not work. Indeed, not even the complexity and ambiguity of Protagoras's "Great Speech" could make Socrates forget the central issue: the nature of virtue.

Critias is the first speaker to try to get away from seeing the discussion between Socrates and Protagoras as a competition. He criticizes Alcibiades for always loving a fight (*aei philonikos esti,* 336e1) and suggests that instead of fighting for (*sumphilonikein*) Protagoras or Socrates, as Callias and Alcibiades have done, they all join together (*koinēi*) in encouraging both men not to dissolve their *xunousia* half way through. Critias, however, has no specific suggestion for how the *xunousia* is to be preserved. The same is true of Prodicus, who yet provides further support to what Critias has said by means of some important verbal distinctions.[30] Perhaps the most important is that between *sharing* our attention with both interlocutors (what Critias recommended) and *giving equal weight* to what each says (*koinous men einai amphoin toin dialegomenoin akroatas, isous de mē*). The word *koinos,* in its adverbial form, occurs repeatedly in this central portion of the dialogue. A genuine discussion must be held in common or shared by all the interlocutors: There is no presumed "authority," and there is no place for partiality. Everyone owns the discussion, and everyone has a right to participate in it. As seen above, Protagoras understands this to mean that what each person says has equal weight, that what appears true to one person is necessarily as true as what appears true to the other. Prodicus's distinction reveals this to be a misunderstanding. The characterization of a discussion as shared and impartial does not preclude giving greater weight to what is said by the person who proves wiser. Indeed, though Prodicus does not explicitly make this point, it is not hard to see that "equality" as understood by Protagoras actually renders genuine discussion impossible. If what appears to one interlocutor is equal to what appears to the other, if there is no standard against which they can judge their opposing views, then there is no common ground between them and therefore no possibility of genuine discussion. There could then only be a contest of competing words. The very possibility of genuine dialogue, therefore, depends on Prodicus's distinction between having something in *common* and being *equal.*

The next speaker, Hippias, addresses explicitly the issue of community that has been implicit in the discussion so far. Using the sophists' stock distinction between *phusis* and *nomos,* he rejects the conventional sense of community in favor of a "natural" sense according to which those who are alike, in the present case alike in being wise, are truly "kinsmen, family and fellow citizens" (*suggeneis te kai oikeious kai politas,* 337c–d). As has been seen, earlier Protagoras too, in a rare candid moment, expressed his contempt for the conventional sense of community he only pretends to cherish in his "Great Speech": He admitted to awakening popular hostility by telling young men that they can be improved only by abandoning their traditional associations and associating with him (316d5–c3). Hippias, now appealing to their membership in such an intellectual association and the attendant responsibility of distinguishing themselves from the ignorant "dregs of society" (*tous phaulotatous tōn anthrōpōn,* 337e1–2) who are always at odds with one another, urges Socrates and Protagoras to compromise by finding some *mean* (*to meson*) between their preferred methods of conversing. This suggestion fails to take into account what Alcibiades noted: that Protagoras's method is to evade the issue, to get out of a discussion that would put him and his views to the test. What is the "mean" between evading the issue and confronting the issue, between, to adopt Hippias's own analogy (338a4–6), sailing out into a sea of rhetoric with no land in sight and standing firmly on the ground?[31] Hippias believes that the conflict between Socrates and Protagoras simply concerns the *length* of what is said, so that if Socrates relaxes somewhat his demand for short responses and Protagoras in turn curbs somewhat the length of his responses, the conflict will be resolved in a happy medium. Length, of course, is not the real issue.[32] But what Hippias says also raises a deeper problem: Who gets to decide what the appropriate mean is? Hippias's suggestion is to choose some umpire who, watching over their discussion, will ensure that the words of both keep to a moderate length (*to metrion mēkos tōn logōn ekaterou*, 338a7–b1).

But Socrates significantly rejects this suggestion. He points out that it would be shameful to choose an umpire either inferior or equal to the interlocutors; he would need to be superior. But who, he asks, could be found wiser than Protagoras (338b4–c6)? Socrates has already made us suspect Protagoras's "wisdom," but he here uses it as a pretext to make an important point: that there is for human beings no wisdom independent of dialogue that could thus from the outside measure and judge the appropriateness of a dialogue. The unavailability of such wisdom is a point that Socrates will emphasize in his interpretation of the Simonides poem. Socrates clearly does not agree with Protagoras that there is *no* objective measure available for the appropriateness of a conversation, but his rejection of an external "umpire" suggests that this measure is to be found only *within* the conversation; it is discovered only through the process of becoming genuinely engaged with each other and with the subject matter, not prior to and independently of this process. The interlocutors test each other within the discussion or, rather, are both tested by the discussion (as Socrates states the point at 333c7–9). They take measure of each other according to how the subject matter takes measure of them. No external measure is needed, therefore, no umpire to test them from without. To make the same point from a different angle, an umpire would need to know the truth of the matter under discussion in order to be able to judge the appropriateness of the responses. But such knowledge, rather than guiding the discussion, would render it superfluous.

Socrates offers a countersuggestion consistent with this insight: Rather than seeking a mediator outside the discussion, he suggests that he and Protagoras switch roles within the discussion. Socrates will answer Protagoras's questions on the condition that Protagoras will then answer his (338c6–d5). Here we have a conception of justice or fairness as the interlocutors' shared responsibility of submitting their beliefs to examination, of exposing them to common scrutiny. Justice is here the recognition that the good is common and that we all have an equal responsibility of submitting ourselves to examination in its pursuit. This conception of justice is the opposite of the one that was seen to arise from Protagorean relativism: justice as an alleged right *not* to submit what appears to one to the judgment of others.[33]

To preserve the community of shared responsibility in inquiry, we do not, as Socrates remarks, need an umpire, since all of us can be umpires together (*koinēi*, 338d5–e2). The reemergence of the adverb *koinēi* in this passage is of extreme importance. Socrates is attempting to create a real community of inquirers who share the responsibility of testing each other and keeping each other focused on the issue. If Protagoras refuses to respond when it is his turn, Socrates observes, we will together (*koinēi*) urge him to respond; we will supervise the discussion together (*koinēi*).[34]

The important achievement of this section of the dialogue cannot be overestimated. Socrates has pointed to a "dialogical" sense of "togetherness" or "community" that avoids *both* the "equality" of Protagorean relativism (which would render genuine dialogue impossible) *and* subjection to some external, nondialogical, absolute standard (knowledge of which, as wisdom, would render dialogue superfluous). This has also been seen to be the kind of community in which genuine justice is realized.

The Simonides Interpretation: The Impossibility of Being Good

Protagoras's inability to engage in dialogue is only confirmed when he is given the opportunity to ask questions. He uses this opportunity, not to examine Socrates' views on virtue, but rather to get Socrates committed to the excellence of a poem by Simonides. This enables him to humiliate Socrates, not by directly refuting his words, but by simply producing a prepared refutation of the poem. Thus Protagoras once again avoids conversing with Socrates. Just as earlier he used speeches to avoid responding directly to Socrates' questions, so now he uses a poem to avoid directly *questioning* Socrates. To treat the present section as only a comic interlude, however,[35] is to fail to notice that Socrates insists on pursuing here his substantive debate with Protagoras, even at the cost of doing great violence to the words of the poem through which Protagoras has forced him to speak.[36]

While Protagoras points out that Simonides' poem is about virtue and, therefore, relevant to the present discussion, his refutation, by focusing on a purely *formal* contradiction, manages to avoid any engagement with the nature of virtue. The formal contradiction is this: Simonides begins the poem by asserting "For a man to become good truly is hard,"

FRANCISCO J. GONZALEZ

but then later in the poem he criticizes Pittacus for his saying "Hard it is to be good." Thus Simonides is contradicting himself by claiming that it is hard to become good and then arguing against Pittacus that it is not hard to be good. The great irony here, apparently missed by most readers, is that Protagoras is himself guilty of the contradiction with which he charges Simonides: His claim in the "Great Speech" that all Athenians are experts in virtue makes virtue something common and easy; his claim that virtue requires a special expertise that only he can provide (and for a fee) makes virtue something hard and rare.

When it is Socrates' turn to discuss the poem, he strengthens the kinship between Protagoras and Simonides by characterizing the latter as motivated to write the poem by a desire to be reputed wise (*philotimos ōn epi sophiai*, 343c1). This desire is what motivates Protagoras throughout the dialogue. At the very outset Socrates suspects that Protagoras wants to speak in front of the whole crowd assembled at Callias's house in order to show off (317c6–d1). Also revealing in this context is Protagoras's claim, during the dispute on method, that his name would not be famous among the Greeks if he had been willing to converse in the way demanded by his interlocutor (335a5–8). Protagoras has no more motive in conversing than to be reputed wise.[37]

Yet the ostensible goal of Socrates' interpretation of Simonides is to defend the poet against Protagoras's critique. How is this consistent with treating Simonides as a surrogate for Protagoras? As will be seen, Socrates can defend Simonides only by "improving" him, even at the cost of turning inside out what he says. In defending Simonides against Protagoras, Socrates is, in a sense, defending Protagoras against himself by improving and even inverting his position. The result is a consistent, truthful, virtuous Protagoras who, as such, is the opposite of the real Protagoras and thus a refutation of him. The first striking instance of Socrates' reversal of Protagoras is his parody of the latter's little speech about the disguises assumed by former sophists afraid to confess what they are (316c–317c). Socrates' parody (342a–343b) attributes such disguised wisdom to the *Spartans,* known otherwise for their martial courage and their "laconicism." In this way he identifies wisdom with both his own preferred "brevity in speech" (*brachulogia*) and courage: Protagoras has already denied the first identification and will strongly resist the second during the next stage of the dialogue.[38] Socrates also uses this parody to describe an intellectual community significantly unlike the community of sophists described earlier by Hippias. According to Socrates, the Seven Sages, inspired by the Spartan example, *came together* (*koinēi xunelthontes*) to offer to Apollo at Delphi the first fruits of their wisdom, consisting of short statements expressing human limits ("Nothing in excess," "Know thyself," and so on).[39] The nature of the piety hinted at here will be made clearer by Socrates' interpretation of the poem.

Since Protagoras earlier refused to discuss the nature of the human good, Socrates will force Simonides' poem to address this issue, in the process refuting Protagoras. In this way, Socrates roots his interpretation in a dialectical context, to the extent that this is possible. Indeed, his introductory comments insist that the poem be returned to the context of an argument between Simonides and Pittacus, motivated by Simonides' desire to make a name for himself by refuting one of the Seven Sages. Thus the importance Socrates gives to the particle *men* in the first line of the poem: Where there is a *men*, "on the one hand," there must, he insists, be a *de*, "on the other hand"; where there is a position, there must be a counterposition, and we cannot understand the one without the other (343c7–d6). In the present case, Simonides' claim that it is hard for a man to become good can be understood only in opposition to Pittacus's claim that it is hard to be good. And as we will see, this opposition parallels that between Socrates and Protagoras. Even in interpreting a poem, Socrates manages to maintain the priority of dialectic.[40]

Socrates' first act of violence to the text concerns the word "truly" (*alatheōs*) in the first line (343d6–344a6). The clear meaning of the Greek is: "For a man to become truly good is hard." Socrates insists, however, that "truly" must be taken with "hard," so that the meaning is: "For a man to become good is truly hard." Socrates' justification is that Simonides could not have said anything so simpleminded (*euēthes*, 343e2) as that something can *be* good without being *truly* good. Protagoras' own interpretation of the same line *was*, of course, that simpleminded (339d2–3). What is more, by implying that what only *appears* good in no way *is* good, Socrates is attacking the simplemindedness of Protagoras's speech on the relative character of the good, with its suggestion, made explicit by the subsequent discussion, that what *appears* good to one *is* good for one.

The real crux of Socrates' interpretation is, of course, the resolution he proceeds to offer of the contradiction Protagoras claimed to find in the poem. Socrates first suggests a formal resolution based on a distinction between *becoming* and *being*. Understood in its dialectical context, what Simonides is saying is the following: "No, Pittacus, you are wrong to say that *being* good is hard; it is *becoming* good that is hard." Unlike Protagoras, however, Socrates is no more interested in formal consistency for its own sake than he is in formal contradiction. His concern is with what Simonides could *mean* in denying that *being* good is hard. He surprisingly takes the meaning to be not that *being* good is *easy*, but that it is *impossible!* Socrates supports this interpretation by citing the next line: "God alone can have this privilege," that is, the privilege of being good. Socrates is here voicing through Simonides his own view that goodness is not a purely human achievement and that it therefore cannot be imparted from one human being to another, a view he expressed earlier in the dialogue in explanation of his denial that virtue can be taught (319b2–3, 328e1–3). Socrates is reading into the poem his own peculiar "piety."

Yet Socrates does not thereby make the good completely beyond human reach. His final solution to the contradiction Protagoras saw in Simonides' poem is that, while *being* good is impossible, *becoming* good is indeed hard, but possible. In saying that we cannot *be* good, what Socrates means is that we cannot *always remain* good (*diamenein en tautēi tēi hexei*, 344b8–c1; *diatelounta agathon*, 345c1). What prevents this is our subjection to that "incapacitating misfortune" mentioned in the next sentence of the poem (344c4–e8).

But what is the nature of this "misfortune" that repeatedly makes us bad and thus prevents us from *being*, that is, *remaining* good? Socrates' next act of violence against the obvious meaning of the text gives the answer: The misfortune of which Simonides speaks must be nothing other than *ignorance,* since this is the only misfortune that keeps us from *being* good (344e7–345c3, especially 345b5).[41] This interpretation shows the process of *becoming* good to be an intermediate state between ignorance and wisdom. Socrates points out that the state of *becoming good* is not the same as the state of *being bad,* that is, of being simply ignorant. Those who are becoming good can become bad, while those who are bad cannot *become* bad, since they already are bad. Thus, as the remainder of the interpretation will only confirm, the process of "becoming good" is to be found between the good and the bad, between wisdom and ignorance.

But what kind of ignorance and wisdom is Socrates talking about here? He uses the example of medical *technē* (345a3–b2). The use of this particular example is significant, given not only Socrates' own role as "physician of the soul," but also his characterization of the present interpretation as an attempt to "cure" the poem (340d9–e2).[42] Yet in so far as this is an example of *technical* knowledge, it appears to contradict, rather than support, Socrates' general point, since ignorance clearly is not the only thing that can turn a good doctor into a bad doctor: A doctor can become "bad" by *misusing* the knowledge he or she has. Furthermore, it clearly is *not* impossible to *be* a good doctor; the picture of a doctor periodically losing his or her knowledge is bizarre, to say the least. The next point of Socrates' interpretation only makes the incongruity of the *technē* analogy all the more striking.

Socrates turns to the lines of the third strophe: "All who do no wrong willingly I praise and love." He insists, counter to the obvious meaning of the text, that "willingly" is *not* to be taken with "who do no wrong," since Simonides could not have been so uneducated as to believe what no wise person believes, namely, that anyone would willingly do what is bad (345d3–e6).[43] But in the case of the technical knowledge to which Socrates appealed earlier, such a belief appears perfectly justified: A doctor in full possession of a knowledge of how to cure his or her patient could still choose to harm or even kill the patient. In the *technai,* knowledge of what is good and the desire to do what is good are completely extrinsic to one another. If, therefore, as Socrates implies, the mixture of ignorance and knowledge that characterizes the process of *becoming* good is inseparable from a *desire* to become good, this process must be profoundly *disanalogous* to technical knowledge.[44]

In order to disassociate the adverb "willingly" from the phrase "who do no wrong," Socrates must read it with "I praise and love." This reading requires him to make a distinction between willing praise and love and *forced* praise and love (345e6–346b8). Socrates explains the latter by claiming that good people must *force* themselves to love and praise *what is their own* (*tous heautōn,* 346b5), for example, their parents and their country, when what is their own is *bad* and thus *alien* (*allokoton*) to them. The important suggestion here is that the conventional community of family or state can be the object of only forced praise and love when it is not grounded in the community of shared goodness. A bad parent may be "one's own" on the level of convention, while at the same time *alien* to one's nature. Socrates' point is similar to Hippias's distinction between conventional community and a natural community based on similarity. The important difference, however, is that Hippias's natural community is a community of the wise, while Socrates' community of free praise and love is the community of those who are only in the process of *becoming* good and are only *searching* for wisdom.

The next point of Socrates' interpretation grounds the preceding. Rejecting as absurd the literal meaning of the final verse "All is noble in which what is shameful is not mixed," Socrates forces on it the opposite meaning: that there is an intermediate state (*ta mesa*) between the good and the bad, the noble and the shameful.[45] Socrates' willingness to use such force against the text is explained by his desire to make explicit the principle which has been seen to guide the whole of his interpretation: the existence of an intermediate state in which is to be found that process of *becoming* that constitutes our unique goodness as human beings; the state of *being* good is reserved for the gods.[46] The people in this intermediate state, according to Socrates, are the ones whom Simonides *freely* loves and praises.

On the other hand, Socrates concludes, Simonides did not praise Pittacus, because the old Sage, in claiming that being good is *hard,* did not say something even moderately (*mesōs*) true and good. This conclusion at first seems odd: Is not the claim that being good is *hard* a "moderate" approximation to the truth that being good is *impossible*? Yet the point Socrates wishes to stress here is that, in confusing *becoming* good with *being* good, Pittacus does in fact *completely* misconstrue the nature of human goodness. But then is this not also true of Protagoras? Is not the criticism of Pittacus with which Socrates concludes a disguised criticism of the sophist?[47] "While giving the appearance of telling the truth, you have in fact been completely deceptive concerning the most important matters, and for this reason I blame you" (347a2–3; my translation).

Socrates' interpretation of Simonides indeed constitutes a refutation of Protagoras's claim to teach virtue, a presumption Socrates rubs into the sophist's face in the little pep talk at 348c–349a, with which he tries to motivate him to continue the inquiry: "You yourself are good, and you are able to make others good" (348e4–5; my translation). Protagoras not only claims to be in that state of *being* good which Socrates has just declared to be the prerogative of the gods, but also claims to be able to put others in that state! This reference to Protagoras's claim to be good and to make others good also recalls an important aspect of the earlier discussion between Socrates and Hippocrates. When Socrates attempts to get Hippocrates to specify who Protagoras is and what he teaches by appealing to examples of *technai* such as medicine and sculpture, the form of his questions is always the following: one goes to the teacher *as being what* (*tini onti*) and for the sake of oneself *becoming what* (*tis genēsomenos*)? Socrates thus characterizes the teacher/student relation in terms of the being/becoming distinction: The teacher *is* what the student seeks to *become*.[48] Therefore, in concluding now that no humans are capable of simply *being* good or virtuous, Socrates is showing that there can be no teachers of goodness or virtue, as there are teachers of the *technai*. Having goodness as a firm possession that can be passed on to others is the prerogative of the gods. Socrates' claim that we humans are capable of no more than *becoming* good makes us *all* students.[49]

Though Socrates does everything possible to make his interpretation dialogical, both placing Simonides' poem in a dialectical context and carrying out his own refutation of Protagoras through the violent interpretation of Simonides' words, the result is still not a genuine dialogue. Socrates' concluding critique of the interpretation of poetry therefore returns us to the question of what constitutes genuine "being together" or *sunousia*. Those who spend their time together interpreting poetry, Socrates asserts, are like those uneducated symposiasts who, unable to entertain themselves through their own voices in conversation, require the extraneous noise of a flute. What Socrates dismisses here as an uneducated *sunousia,* is precisely what Protagoras earlier claimed to be the pinnacle of human *paideia* (338e7–339a1). For Socrates, a true, educated *sunousia* is one in which the participants *come together through themselves,* not through some external voice. "Coming together through themselves" means "*in their own words testing and being-tested by each other*" (*en tois heautōn logois peiran allēlōn lambanontes kai didontes,* 348a1–2). This testing of one another is at the same time a testing of *the truth* (*tēs alētheias kai hēmōn autōn peiran lambanontes,* 348a5–6). Socrates is once again re-jecting the existence of an external authority to which the dialogue can appeal in favor of the *mutual testing* carried out *within* dialogue. The little pep talk mentioned earlier again emphasizes the importance of this *sunousia* as the only way of getting at the truth. Stating that his only motive in the discussion is to examine what perplexes him (348c6–7), Socrates stresses, quoting Homer, the importance of *joint* inquiry in discovering and securing the truth (348d4–5). In this *sunousia* of joint inquiry and mutual testing, we clearly find the community of *free* love and praise that is to be contrasted to the conventional community of *forced* love and praise that Socrates describes in his interpretation of the poem.

The so-called digression, which is really a climax, has led us to two conclusions: first, that genuine community or "being together" is to be found in the dialectical inquiry Socrates practices and describes; and second, that human "goodness," unlike that of the gods, is a process of *becoming* rather than a state of *being.* Yet the most important "lesson" to be learned from the "digression" is that these two conclusions are not talking about different things: The process of *becoming* good is realized in the community of philosophical dialogue. The good is not something hu-mans *possess* independently of, or at the conclusion of, dialectical inquiry and which they could pass on to others in some form of monological teaching. As a process of becoming, our goodness consists of joining others in the search for the good. The community of dialectical inquiry has itself been seen to realize specific virtues: In demanding cooperation and shared responsibility, it realizes justice; in recognizing the limits of human knowledge and human goodness, it realizes piety; in testing our beliefs and exposing our ignorance it realizes specifically human wisdom and temperance. Here begins to emerge the truly Socratic "unity of the virtues." Courage has not yet been discussed and will form the major theme of the last part of the dialogue: It, too, however, will prove to be a characteristic of Socratic inquiry. To *become* good *is* to *dialegesthai,* and humans are capable of achieving no greater good.

Given what has been said, Protagoras's failure to engage in gen-uine dialectic does not simply show him to be "methodologically chal-lenged," but exposes a lack of *goodness.* This point is nicely brought out by something else Socrates says in his little pep talk at 348c–349a. In "forced" praise of Protagoras, Socrates describes him as "the best at investigating the things that a good person [*ton epieikē*] ought to investigate, especially virtue" (348d7–e1). Since it is obvious that Protagoras has no desire to investigate such things, Socrates' implication is that Protagoras, therefore, is *not* a good person. Even now Protagoras is *only with great difficulty* turned toward dialogue (*mogis proutrapeto eis to dialegesthai*, 348c3–4), and only because he feels ashamed before the other sophists. Alcibiades' observation that Protagoras in his resistance is not "acting well" (*kalōs poiein*, 348b3–5) is exactly right.[50]

It should now be evident that the dispute about method is not a digression from the main topic of virtue. The middle portion of the dialogue is truly its philosophical center. It is not only the culmination of all that precedes, but also the explanation of all that follows it. The second part of this claim is what remains to be defended.

Critique of the Sophists: The Impossibility of Scientifically Measuring the Good

When Socrates returns to the question of the unity of the virtues, it turns out that Protagoras has modified his position: he now allows that the other virtues are "somewhat similar," but insists that courage and wisdom are completely distinct.[51] Socrates' first attempt to prove their identity is derailed when Protagoras makes an objection to the argument's logic that entirely misses its point.[52] Now Socrates suddenly changes tack. He first tries to commit Protagoras to hedonism. When the sophist as usual proves unwilling to openly contradict majority opinion, Socrates asks a question that will finally force him to do so: Is knowledge a powerful force in human actions or is it something weak that is dragged around by desires and emotions? Protagoras replies that it would be shameful for him above all people to say that wisdom and knowledge are not *the most powerful* forces in human action (352c8–d3). When Socrates observes that most people do not believe this, Protagoras replies contemptuously that people are ignorant about many other things (352e3–4). When Socrates suggests that he and Protagoras attempt to convince them of the power of knowledge, Protagoras asks: "What need, Socrates, is there to examine the opinion of the majority, who just say whatever happens to come into their heads?" (353a7–8; my translation). These are surprising comments coming from a man who has maintained that all Athenians are experts in virtue. Socrates spots here his chance to drive a wedge between the views of the people and the pretensions of Protagoras. He therefore gives the ensuing discussion, up to 357e, the form of a dispute between "the many," on one side, and Protagoras and himself, on the other. Protagoras will soon become very uncomfortable with this position.

Socrates begins by getting the many to agree that when they say that something is pleasant, and yet bad, what they mean is that, while immediately pleasant, it will result in great pain in the future. The claim that something is good and yet painful is to be explained in the same way. Thus Socrates shows that the many, counter to what they say, are committed to the view that pleasure=good and pain=bad (353c1–355a5). This should already disconcert Protagoras, since his relativism is opposed to any definite characterization of the good, either as what is advantageous or as what is pleasant. And, as already noted, he rejects the view that pleasure=good immediately prior to the present dialogue with the many. But what Socrates seeks to show is that Protagoras has no more grounds than do most people for such a rejection. Before proceeding with the argument, Socrates asks repeatedly if the many have any other criterion by which to judge things good or bad besides pleasure and pain (354b5–c2, 354d1–3, 354d7–e2, 354e8–355a5). Protagoras can name none. This is not simply because he is speaking for the many; his acceptance, along with the other sophists, of the identity of the good with pleasure at 358a–b shows that he has no other criterion of his own to offer.[53]

Socrates now proceeds to show an important consequence of this identification: When we act badly by choosing to do something that, while immediately pleasant, will in the long run bring more pain than pleasure, the reason is that our perception of the true quantities of the pleasure and of the pain is distorted by the proximity of the one and the remoteness of the other. In other words, because the pain is far away in the future, it seems smaller than it really is; because the pleasure is near at hand, it seems greater than it really is. Therefore, the cause of our doing what is bad is simply *ignorance*. What is needed to eliminate this ignorance is a science of measurement, that is, a *technē* that will enable us to measure *objectively* the true quantities of pain and pleasure resulting from an action. In possession of such a *technē*, we could never do what is bad and thus would be guaranteed a perfectly good life (355a5–357e1).

What is Socrates' objective in describing this science of measurement which he claims will save our lives (*hē sōtēria tou biou*, 357a6–7)? The answer is made clear when he proceeds to use this description as an advertisement for the sophists. He upbraids the many as follows:

So this is what "being overcome by pleasure" is—ignorance in the highest degree, and it is this which Protagoras and Prodicus and Hippias claim to cure. But you, thinking it to be something other than ignorance, do not yourselves go to the sophists, nor do you send your children to them for instruction, believing as you do that we are dealing with something unteachable. By worrying about your money and not giving it to them, you all do badly in both private and public life. (357e2–8)

Socrates even goes to the trouble of committing the sophists present to every step of the argument, so that it becomes *their* argument. Is not Socrates' strategy obvious? In his description of the science of measurement, he is giving the sophists a *technē* that suits their pretensions. He is saying to them: "If you possess a *technē* of virtue, clearly it must, like any other *technē*, have a determinate object. What could this be besides pleasure and pain? Furthermore, your *technē* of virtue must, like any other *technē*, be capable of making objective and universal claims about its object. What then could it be besides a science of objectively measuring pain and pleasure? So there is your *technē*. Go ahead and teach it to the masses!" The irony, of course, is that the sophists can teach no such thing. Their professed *technē* is thus exposed for what it is: a sham.[54] Those scholars[55] who ascribe the science of measurement to Socrates can do so only by ignoring both the rhetorical dimension of the argument and the entire middle portion of the dialogue that is its necessary foil.

What Socrates says through the Simonides interpretation shows that he himself considers the science of measurement an impossibility. Such a science would enable us to *be* good in the strongest sense of the word, that is, in the sense of always avoiding what is bad and thus always remaining good, but Socrates has denied that humans can *be* good in this sense.[56] Furthermore, Socrates' characterization of dialogical *sunousia* was seen to deny any measure of the good external to such *sunousia* and capable of arbitrating over it. Stated simply, the existence of the science of measurement would render Socratic dialogue entirely superfluous. It is no accident that Socrates leaves the exact nature and identity of the science of measurement unexamined (357b): No such science could ever be developed by mere mortals like ourselves, for whom becoming good through dialogue is the greatest good attainable.

Yet, one might object, must we not take as sincere Socrates' defense of the power of knowledge against the view of the many that it is impotent and ruled by our desires and emotions? Indeed, even in the Simonides interpretation Socrates insists on making knowledge central to *becoming* good, even at the cost of doing great violence to the text. The irony, however, is that the science of measurement, rather than vindicating the power of knowledge, makes it extrinsic and subservient to the desire for pleasure, since this science does no more than calculate the means of achieving a good that is already defined by this desire. Knowledge is here the instrument of the desires, not something capable of transforming them.[57] Yet it is clearly the latter possibility that Socrates has in mind when he claims that someone who knows what is good will desire what is good. Engagement in dialogical *sunousia,* which has been seen to be the form taken by the process of *becoming* good, is an engagement of the entire person that, in continually questioning and transforming our understanding of a good we can never fully attain, transforms *both* our knowledge *and* our desire. Socrates' word for this inseparability of knowledge and desire in dialectical inquiry is *erōs,* which is as much *cognitive* as it is *conative.* The science of measurement, like Lysias's utilitarian calculations in the *Phaedrus,* is the complete antithesis to such *erōs.*

There is another way in which the pursuit of pleasure with the help of a *technē* of measurement stands opposed to the dialogical process of *becoming* good described in the so-called digression: It does not take place in a context of "being together" with others and is clearly compatible with injustice and impiety.[58] But in describing such a *technē,* Socrates is simply making explicit Protagoras's "esoteric" conception of virtue. There have already been plenty of indications that Protagoras appears to value no more than the *appearance* of justice and piety, and that the wisdom he professes to teach his pupils is in reality a knowledge of how they can get the better of others in pursuing and satisfying their own individual desires. Recall that what derails the discussion of the unity of the virtues and necessitates the long "digression" is Socrates' insistence on questioning Protagoras about the relation between the "good judgment" he teaches and injustice. By now attributing the science of measurement to Protagoras and the other sophists, Socrates makes clear that the wisdom they profess to teach has everything to do with promoting the subjective good of pleasure and nothing to do with the virtues Protagoras ostensibly commends in his "Great Speech." He thus exposes not only the arrogance of Protagoras's claim to teach goodness, but also the moral mendaciousness of his claim to be good. In the words of Simonides' poem, Protagoras is not someone "who knows the justice that benefits cities."

It is significant that Socrates begins this discussion of the role knowledge plays in human action by comparing his questioning of Protagoras to a doctor's examination of a patient. Just as the doctor, after looking at the face and the extremities of his patient's body, wishes to look at the chest and the back so as to make a more thorough examination, so Socrates wishes to expose Protagoras's true thought concerning knowledge (352a1–b2). His success in doing precisely this shows that he is the true "physician of the soul," while the sophists are the quacks. (Socrates himself suggests this contrast by calling the sophists *iatroi*, 357e3.)[59] And yet his "medical knowledge" consists of nothing more than dialectic. As for Protagoras and his teachings, the diagnosis, as has been seen, is not good.

Courage as the Maximization of Pleasure?

After getting Protagoras and the other sophists to commit themselves to the premises of the argument that what is called "being overcome by pleasure" is nothing but ignorance, Socrates proceeds to demonstrate the identity of courage and wisdom. He draws out the argument at some length (359c2–360e5), but its gist is simple. Going to war is honorable and good and, therefore, given the hedonistic premise accepted by all the sophists present, pleasurable. But then why does the coward fear going to war? The only possible explanation is that the coward *does not know* that going to war is pleasurable and should, therefore, inspire confidence, not fear. The courageous person, on the other hand, knows precisely this. Thus, courage turns out to be knowledge of what is and is not to be feared (*hē sophia tōn deinōn kai mē deinōn*), while cowardice is ignorance of the same. It is hard not to suspect that the purpose of this argument is to show the *absurdity* of the hedonistic calculus.[60] Are we really expected to believe that the coward runs away from battle because he does not realize just how incredibly pleasurable it is? Socrates, of course, is no more committed to this argument than he is to hedonism. This is not to say that Socrates does not in some sense believe courage to be "knowledge of *ta deina*." But Socrates interprets this knowledge in terms of the *technē* he has just induced the sophists to profess in order to expose the absurdity of such a *technē*. To teach me to be courageous without changing my desires (and central to the argument is the view that the courageous and the cowardly desire or *go toward* [*itas*] the same things, 359b7–e1), the sophists would have to teach me that the same pleasure I seek in running away from the battle is, in fact, to be found in greater quantity by running into the battle. The sophists would truly be in possession of a remarkable skill if they could do that!

To determine in what sense the conclusion is true for Socrates, we must ask: What things does *he* consider *deinos*? He maintained in the Simonides interpretation that the only true misfortune is *ignorance*. Ignorance, therefore, and not pain, is the most *deinos*. Courage for Socrates accordingly involves confronting and struggling with this ignorance, considering all else, such as poverty, physical pain, even death, as less to be feared. There is a striking display of this courage at the end of the dialogue. Referring to the baffling reversal of positions with which the dialogue ends, Socrates says the following:

> Seeing the present matters tossed up and down in terrifying [*deinōs*] confusion, I experience the strongest desire [*prothumia*] to have them cleared up. I would like to follow what we have said with a determined attack on virtue itself and its essential nature and then again take up the question of whether it can be taught. (361c2–6; my translation, with some of the wording borrowed from Guthrie)

It is in this willingness and determination to take on the nature of virtue in the face of the terrifying darkness of ignorance that we find genuine courage. Courage is not to be found in the knowledge and possession of the good (which, in addition to being impossible for human beings, would render courage unnecessary), but rather in the willingness to risk all in its pursuit. Thus courage, along with the other virtues, is realized in the community of shared inquiry.

This conception of courage, manifested by what Socrates does, is, of course, completely opposed to the conception defended by the argument described above, according to which courage is the avoidance of what inspires fear or dread in favor of what inspires confidence. But there Socrates is describing not his own conception of courage, but that of *Protagoras*. Protagoras is depicted as obsessed with his personal *safety*. As has been seen, he openly confesses to being a sophist only because he considers this a better precaution (*eulabeia*) against the hatred of the people than denial (317b3–6). He claims at the same time to have discovered other precautions (317b6–7), without saying what they are. Yet the "Great Speech" as a whole was seen to be a model instance of such precaution. When it comes to responding to Socrates' questions, safety rather than truth appears to be Protagoras's main concern. This is most evident in the passage where Socrates asks him if pleasure as pleasure is good. Protagoras replies that pleasure and good are distinct, not because he considers this the truer response (as noted above, he proves completely unable to defend it), but because it is a *safer* (*asphalesteron*) response, with regard both to the present question and to his whole life (351d). It is, therefore, with perfect "poetic justice" that Socrates proceeds to identify the wisdom Protagoras professes to teach with a science of measurement that will save our lives (*hē sōteria tou biou*, 357a6–7) by insuring that we never make a mistake. And it is again with perfect "poetic justice" that Socrates gets Protagoras to agree to an identification of courage with the purely prudent pursuit of what inspires confidence in being pleasurable.[61]

FRANCISCO J. GONZALEZ

On the other hand, Protagoras has already demonstrated his lack of the kind of courage Socrates possesses and he will do so again at the end of the dialogue.

Facing the Terrifying Reversal of Positions

Faced with the silence and thinly veiled hostility of Protagoras, Socrates insists that his sole motive in asking questions is a desire to investigate the nature of virtue and suggests that the only reason why they have been unable to agree on whether or not virtue is teachable is that the nature of virtue is not yet clear (360e6–361a3). This confession of *aporia* is further and definitive confirmation that Socrates does not accept as his own the view that virtue is the maximization of pleasure by means of a teachable science of measurement.[62] In fact, in contradiction to this view he has just been ostensibly defending, Socrates still maintains that virtue cannot be taught.[63] It is to this contradiction that Socrates now turns. He imagines the *logos* laughing at Protagoras and himself for having switched positions at the cost of contradicting themselves. He began by claiming that virtue cannot be taught, but now has been arguing that it is identical to knowledge, in which case it must be teachable. Protagoras began by claiming that virtue can be taught, but lately has been resisting in every way possible the conclusion that virtue is knowledge. If virtue is not knowledge, how could it be taught?

We have seen the reason for Protagoras's contradiction: On the one hand, he wishes to side with the views of the many in order to avoid their hostility; on the other hand, he professes to teach a kind of virtue which the many do not possess and which, in fact, undermines their traditional values. Socrates' contradiction, however, results from a desire completely opposed to that of Protagoras: Rather than endorsing *both* the views of the many *and* the views of the sophists, he *rejects* both.

In thus reversing Protagoras's contradiction, Socrates *solves* it. The solution is the same as the one Socrates offered to the supposed contradiction in Simonides, a contradiction that was seen to be Protagoras's own. Recall that that solution depended on a distinction between *being* good and *becoming* good. According to Socrates' interpretation, *being* good is *impossible.* On this view, there are no "experts" in goodness who can teach or impart it in the way in which the sophists claim to. Since, however, the process of *becoming* good is described by Socrates as intermediate between ignorance and wisdom, it requires a knowledge that transcends the ignorant opinions of the many (recall that Socrates distinguished becoming good from being bad). While *becoming* good is possible, it is also *hard*. As has been seen, the knowledge involved in the process of becoming good is not *technical* knowledge: unlike a *technē*, it is inseparable from ignorance and is essentially conative. Socratic *erōs* and Socratic ignorance, rather than being merely preliminary to some technical and sophistic wisdom, themselves form a different sort of wisdom. Virtue is not to be identified with the unattainable state of *being* good; virtue is instead that very process of *becoming* good that unites *erōs*, ignorance, and knowledge.

Prometheus vs. Epimetheus: Giving Thought to the Good Together

But how exactly do we *become* good, if not by being taught? As the so-called digression already revealed, and as the concluding words of the dialogue confirm, to *become* good is to *care for the good by becoming engaged in that dialogical sunousia to which Socrates has devoted his entire life*. Immediately following the exhibition of courage cited above, Socrates makes clear what virtue is for him. Referring to the myth of Protagoras's "Great Speech," he asserts himself to be following the lead of Prometheus, whose name means forethought, taking thought, care: "I liked Prometheus in the myth better than Epimetheus; so I follow his lead and spend my time on all these matters as a means of taking forethought [*promēthoumenos*] for my whole life" (361d2–5; Guthrie translation). The means, of course, by which Socrates takes forethought for his whole life is shared inquiry or dialogue. It is precisely this forethought that characterizes the process of *becoming* good. This forethought is not simply a preliminary stage to *being* good; it is our only and distinctive goodness. The claim that goodness just *is* giving thought to the good in shared inquiry, or that virtue just *is* the determined search for virtue, seems, of course, extremely paradoxical.[64] This is why Socrates, when he expresses precisely this view in the *Apology*, describes it as the one his fellow citizens are least willing to believe:

> And when again I say that *the greatest good for human beings is to spend every day discussing virtue* and the other topics about which you hear me conversing and examining both myself and others, and that the unexamined life is not worth living for human beings, you believe what I say even less. (38a1–7)

To understand virtue we must be able to contrast it with vice. Where there is a Prometheus, there must also be an Epimetheus, someone who is careless, who takes no forethought. If Socrates is the Prometheus here, it should by now be clear who is Epimetheus.[65] In his persistent unwillingness and inability to engage in genuine dialogue with Socrates, Protagoras has exhibited the lack of precisely that care for the good and that forethought for the whole of one's life that characterize Socrates. This is not to say that Protagoras takes *no* kind of forethought for his life. At the very beginning of the discussion Protagoras recognizes fore-thought (*orthōs promēthēi*) in Socrates' offer of a choice between convers-ing alone or in front of others (316b5). He interprets this forethought as mere concern for his own safety, however, and, as noted above, this is his own concern throughout the dialogue.[66] This cowardly prudence is diametrically opposed to that care for the good that will risk all in its pursuit. When Socrates expresses his preference for Prometheus, he significantly describes Epimetheus as threatening to trip up the inquiry through deception (361c7–d2). This is a thinly veiled description of Protagoras. As has already been seen and as should be even more evi-dent now, Protagoras's rejection of dialogue is not simply the rejection of a method, but of a way of life, of the good and virtuous life. The dispute about "method" in the so-called digression is the central dispute of the dialogue.[67]

This is confirmed by the dialogue's closing words. After Socrates' description of his own Promethean way of life, he once again invites Protagoras to share the inquiry with him (*meta sou an hēdista tauta sun-diaskopoiēn*, 361d6). In reply, Protagoras tries to demonstrate his unbe-grudging nature by "praising"[68] Socrates' eagerness and predicting that he will one day be among those "renowned for wisdom." This little speech reveals two important things: first, that what matters to Protagoras, what he cares about, is a *reputation* for wisdom, and second, that he sees Socrates as simply on the way to the wisdom he himself already possesses (compare 335a4–8 with 361e4–5). This view of Socrates as a mere "go-between" the aspirant to wisdom (Hippocrates) and the possessor of wisdom (Protagoras), and of his dialectic as a mere propaedeutic, has been completely overturned in the course of the dialogue. If Socrates is "on the way," it is only in the sense in which human life is itself never more than "on the way," "in between" the bad and the good, the shameful and the noble, ignorance and wisdom.

It should already be clear that Protagoras's "praise" for Socrates does *not* express a new willingness to join Socrates in inquiry.[69] He concludes his little speech by saying that he and Socrates can discuss these matters some other time, but that it is now time to turn to something else (*nun d'hōra ēdē kai ep'allo ti trepesthai*). It is time to turn to something else? Socrates has just characterized the dialectical inquiry in which he wishes to engage Protagoras as a matter of taking forethought for *one's whole life.*

What else is there to turn to? Presumably, Protagoras will simply go back to *not* taking forethought for the goodness of his life, instead securing his reputation and safety by means of deceitful and flashy rhetoric. "So be it," Socrates replies, "if that is your wish."[70]

Conclusion

My conclusion is my title. The colon is meant to express identity: Giving thought to the good together *is* virtue in Plato's *Protagoras*.

Notes

1. Most scholars make nothing of this introductory frame dialogue and therefore do not see the theme of *erōs* as having any bearing on the rest of the dialogue. An important exception is Friedländer, who sees *erōs* as central to the contrast between sophistic and Socratic education; see Paul Friedländer, *Plato*, 3 vols., trans. Hans Meyerhoff (New York: Pantheon, 1964), 2:5–6 (hereafter cited as Friedländer 1964).

2. Except where otherwise specified, I use the translation of Stanley Lombardo and Karen Bell, *Plato: Protagoras* (Indianapolis: Hackett, 1992).

3. Contra Martha Nussbaum, *The Fragility of Goodness* (Cambridge: Cambridge University Press, 1986), 93 (hereafter cited as Nussbaum 1986), and M. Gagarin, "The Purpose of Plato's *Protagoras*," *Transactions of the American Philological Association* 100 (1969): 133–64, 137 (hereafter cited as Gagarin 1969). It is true that at 313d7 Socrates claims only that "probably some" of the sophists lack knowledge of what is harmful and beneficial for the soul. Yet the point of Socrates' analogy in the passage as a whole is the following: The grocer *as a grocer* has no knowledge of what harms or benefits the body; if he has this knowledge, it is only because he is *also* a doctor. Analogously, the sophist *as a sophist* has no knowledge of what harms or benefits the soul; if he has this knowledge, it is only because he is *also* a "physician of the soul." In short, just as being a grocer is not the same as being a doctor, so being a sophist is not the same as being a "physician of the soul." Therefore, the only possibility left open by 313d7, and ironically so, as the dialogue will show, is the possibility that some sophists are more than sophists.

4. Compare Eugenio Benitez, "Argument, Rhetoric, and Philosophic Method: Plato's *Protagoras*," *Philosophy and Rhetoric* 25 (1992): 222–52, 230 (hereafter cited as Benitez 1992): "Socrates is such a doctor: Given the view he has just expressed, could he allow Hippocrates to meet Protagoras under any other condition?" Landy inexplicably sees Socrates as implying that the notion of such a doctor is preposterous; see Tucker Landy, "Virtue, Art, and the Good Life in

Plato's *Protagoras*," *Interpretation* 21 (1994): 287–308, 290 (hereafter cited as Landy 1994).

5. Compare Larry Goldberg, *A Commentary on Plato's Protagoras* (New York, Bern, and Frankfurt am Main: Peter Lang, 1983), 85 (hereafter cited as Goldberg 1983).

6. On the significance of this scene, compare Malcolm Schofield, "Socrates versus Protagoras," in *Socratic Questions: New Essays on the Philosophy of Socrates and its Significance*, ed. Barry S. Gower and Michael C. Stokes (New York: Routledge, 1992), 122–36, 126–27 (hereafter cited as Schofield 1992); Rudolph H. Weingartner, *The Unity of the Platonic Dialogue* (Indianapolis: Bobbs-Merrill, 1973), 50–51 (hereafter cited as Weingartner 1973); Friedländer 1964, 18; and R. B. Rutherford, *The Art of Plato* (Cambridge, MA: Harvard University Press, 1995), 125–26, 140 (hereafter cited as Rutherford 1995). Goldberg rightly suggests that Hippocrates' engagement in dialogue "ultimately constitutes the truest form of dissuasion from associating with Protagoras" (1983, 76).

7. Compare Goldberg 1983, 34–35.

8. As Michael C. Stokes appears to assume in *Plato's Socratic Conversations: Drama and Dialectic in Three Dialogues* (Baltimore: Johns Hopkins University Press, 1986), 203–6, 384–87, 439 (hereafter cited as Stokes 1986).

9. Compare C. C. W. Taylor, *Plato: Protagoras*, rev. ed. (Oxford: Clarendon Press, 1991), 83 (hereafter cited as Taylor 1991).

10. For thorough documentation of the confusion in Protagoras's speech concerning the relation between goodness and technical expertise, see Stokes 1986, 229–36. Stokes also gives an accurate diagnosis of the source of the confusion:

> One factor making Protagoras's position uneasy is his wish to combine the democratic notion that everybody is skilled in, and qualified to teach, political goodness with the fundamentally élitist idea of an "art" with special or specially effective teachers such as himself. (235)

Yet Stokes does not appear to recognize the extent to which this confusion is deliberate. On the other hand, David Roochnik, in *Of Art and Wisdom: Plato's Understanding of Technē* (University Park: Pennsylvania State University, 1996), 218–27 (hereafter cited as Roochnik 1996), does, although he still appears to regard Protagoras's motives as nobler than they really are. See also Patrick Coby, "The Education of a Sophist: Aspects of Plato's *Protagoras*," *Interpretation* 10 (1982): 139–58, 145 (hereafter cited as Coby 1982).

11. "But, since this single capacity produces in reality such a wide range of endowment, it is hard to see why all men should be allowed to speak to the assembly when those who know something about fortifications but far less than master builders are not granted permission" (Goldberg 1983, 44; see also 43). Protagoras actually turns to Socrates' second objection at 324d2, but what he says in the very long digression between 324d2 and 326e5, as showing only that Athenians put great effort into teaching virtue, appears beside the point; the

recognition, however, that some people do *not* share in virtue and, therefore, need instruction and punishment (325a5–7) supports the second interpretation.

12. According to Gagarin, the speech successfully answers Socrates' objections by demonstrating "that *aretē* is similar to the other *technai* in that it is taught, but different from them in that it should be possessed to some degree by all" (1969, 144). But this is no solution unless both claims can be made consistent. All Protagoras does is hide the inconsistency by covertly shifting from one claim to the other.

13. Goldberg (1983, 40) and Scott R. Hemmenway, "Sophistry Exposed: Socrates on the Unity of Virtue in the *Protagoras*," *Ancient Philosophy* 16 (1996): 1–23, 14 (hereafter cited as Hemmenway 1996), also note this omission and consider it important.

14. This rules out Taylor's suggestion that Protagoras does not mention *sophia* only because he assumes that every fully adult, responsible member of the community must already possess it (1991, 81–82).

15. This thesis has been defended by Hemmenway, who distinguishes between "demotic virtue," or "simple-minded restraint and law-abidingness," and "elite virtue," which "is the instrument of political success and . . . is primarily associated with courage and wisdom" (1996, 2). He characterizes Protagoras's strategy in the "Great Speech" as one of openly defending demotic virtue before the many while covertly offering elite virtue to his prospective students (4). This interpretation appears to provide a solution to a problem raised much earlier by Adkins (though oddly Hemmenway does not cite him). Adkins sees Protagoras's speech as confusing "cooperative excellences" and the "competitive excellences" required for success in politics; see, especially, page 7 of A. W. H. Adkins, "Arete, Techne, Democracy, and Sophists: *Protagoras* 316b–328d," *Journal of Hellenic Studies* 93 (1973): 3–12 (hereafter cited as Adkins 1973). Adkins attributes the confusion not only to the ambiguity of the word *aretē* at this period (4), but also to Protagoras's prudent desire "to reassure the mass of citizens that what he was doing was 'democratic,' and essentially the same as they did everyday . . ." (12). Adkins therefore calls the speech a "smoke-screen" (12). Hemmenway's interpretation is also suggested, but not as well developed, by C. L. Miller, "The Prometheus Story in Plato's *Protagoras*," *Interpretation* 7 (1978): 22–32, 27 (hereafter cited as Miller 1978); Coby 1982, 146; Goldberg 1983, 48–52; and Landy 1994, 293–99. Stokes argues at length against Adkins's distinction (210–29), an argument that could apply to Hemmenway's own version. Stokes's main contention is that the Athenians of this period tended to believe that justice and success go hand in hand (225–26). This may well be true of Protagoras's *audience:* a young aristocrat such as Hippocrates may well believe that he can pursue his own advantage within the boundaries of the conventional virtues. Stokes may, therefore, also be right in his contention, contra Adkins and presumably Hemmenway, that Protagoras's speech is not aimed at two different audiences (see 210 and following): Protagoras's prospective students are themselves part of the many and can be expected to share the beliefs of the many. What is true of Protagoras's audience, however, is not necessarily true of *Protagoras:* Apparently, what puts

him "a little ahead" of others in virtue is precisely the kind of distinction Adkins and Hemmenway describe. Others who fail to see through Protagoras's feigned conservatism are George Grote, *Plato and the Other Companions of Socrates,* 2 vols. (London: J. Murray, 1888), 2: 300 (hereafter cited as Grote 1888); Paul Shorey, *What Plato Said* (Chicago: University of Chicago Press, 1933), 125 (hereafter cited as Shorey 1933); Gregory Vlastos, Introduction to *Plato: Protagoras,* ed. Martin Ostwald (New York: Library of Liberal Arts, 1956), xxiii (hereafter cited as Vlastos 1956); Weingartner 1973, 47; Nussbaum 1986, 105 and 447 n.34, for a critique of Adkins; and Joseph Cropsey, "Virtue and Knowledge: On Plato's *Protagoras,*" *Interpretation* 19 (1991–92): 137–55, 143 (hereafter cited as Cropsey 1991). Irwin recognizes that the speech leaves open the possibility of cultivating the "self-regarding virtues" at the expense of the "other-regarding virtues," but assumes that Protagoras does not intend this and is simply confused. See Terence Irwin, *Plato's Ethics* (New York: Oxford University Press, 1995), 79, 81, 94 (hereafter cited as Irwin 1995).

16. The significance of this passage has also been recognized by Coby (1982, 146), Goldberg (1983, 45–48), and Hemmenway (1996, 11). This passage and the others cited below contradict Nussbaum's claim that Protagoras's speech characterizes social excellence, including justice, as an *intrinsic, non-instrumental* good (1986, 102–3).

17. For evidence that *sophrosunē* was not simply a cooperative value but could also (as soundness of mind) refer to rational self-interest, see Stokes 1986, 227–28.

18. Coby observes that the virtue of which all partake, according to Protagoras, "amounts to little more than the citizen's habit of rendering obedience to the law" (1982, 144). This interpretation is quite thoroughly defended by Hemmenway (1996, 11–12), who concludes, "Obedience and conformity seem to be all that is required to have learned political or demotic virtue" (2). See also Vlastos 1956, xix.

19. Both Weingartner (1973, 91–92) and Goldberg (1983, 123–26) rightly draw attention to the need to explain Protagoras's anger here.

20. This important connection between 333d4–6 and 318e5 is seen by Stokes (1986, 307–8) and Hemmenway (1996, 18). Only Hemmenway, however, recognizes that Socrates is here uncovering Protagoras's true view.

21. Socrates would have reached the desired conclusion by forcing Protagoras to admit that injustice is bad and that it therefore cannot be the result of good judgment. See Weingartner 1973, 91.

22. S. Moser and G. L. Kustas, "A Comment on the 'Relativism' of the *Protagoras,*" *Phoenix* 20 (1966): 111–15, 114–15 (hereafter cited as Moser and Kustas 1966), as well as Taylor (1991, 133–35), rightly deny that anything Protagoras says here about the good commits him to strict relativism. More revealing than what he says, however, is *why* he says it: His intention is clearly to derail any attempt at an objective characterization of the human good. Nothing he says, in fact, stands in the way of such a characterization, and, therefore, nothing he says is really relevant to Socrates' argument. Protagoras's aim, however, is to promote

relativism, not by explicitly defending it, but by throwing into confusion and refusing to enter any inquiry into the good.

23. For the same view, see Cropsey 1991, 146. One can also see here an application of Protagoras's *homo mensura* doctrine. Though that doctrine is nowhere mentioned in this dialogue, Benitez (1992) sees it as explaining three points. First, it explains why Protagoras understands association as essentially competitive— if the good is relative to the individual, one person's good can conflict with another's (233–34). Second, it shows why "Protagoras has no particular concern for an investigation of excellence; he already assumes that excellence is whatever a person takes it to be" (234). And third, it explains why for Protagoras ethical argumentation is only a means of enhancing reputation and shaping public opinion (234–35).

24. Klosko characterizes the dialogue as an eristic contest between Protagoras and Socrates, apparently for no other reason than that this is how *Protagoras* sees it; see George Klosko, "Toward a Consistent Interpretation of the *Protagoras*," *Archiv für Geschichte der Philosophie* 61 (1979): 125–42, 126–29 (hereafter cited as Klosko 1979). As even Gagarin, who defends Protagoras's words and actions in the dispute concerning method, acknowledges, "Socrates is making every effort to remove competition from the discussion and make it instead a cooperative venture" (1969, 149). While Schofield agrees that this is Socrates' aim (1992, 128), he nevertheless sees Socrates as purely competitive in the interlude and in much of the rest of the dialogue (128–31). As I show later in this essay, while Socrates must to some extent play the sophists' game, he does so in such a way as to subvert it. See also Benitez 1992, 243–45.

25. This word already occurs four times just in the present short passage. Benitez provides the following significant statistics:

> *Sunousia* appears more times in the *Protagoras* (15) than in any dialogue except the *Laws* (18), a dialogue seven times its size. The frequency per page is far greater than in any other dialogue—*Protagoras*, .294, *Symposium*, .196, *Phaedrus*, .096—and the number of uses of *sunousia* in the section presently under discussion (the interlude) is double that of any comparable section in the Platonic corpus. (1992, 252 n.96)

26. While the Simonides interpretation is finally being considered by some scholars to play an important role in the dialogue as a whole (see the references below), the dispute on method that precedes it is still much neglected. Stokes, for example, devotes to it less than two full pages out of 256 (1986, 311–13). Three exceptions are C. L. Miller, "Two Midpoints in Plato's *Protagoras*," *Modern Schoolman* 55 (1977): 71–79 (hereafter cited as Miller 1977), Benitez (1992), and Goldberg (1983, 128–55); of these three, Goldberg provides by far the most detailed account currently available.

27. Compare Benitez 1992, 244, and Gagarin 1969, 149.

28. Compare Goldberg 1983, 34. Grote (1888, 2: 282) appears to accept Alcibiades' characterization of the conversation as a contest over who is the better dialectician.

29. Compare Goldberg 1983, 128, and Miller 1977, 72–73.

30. On the virtues and limitations of the speeches by Critias and Prodicus, compare Goldberg 1983, 134–37. Miller (1977, 77) claims that Critias, too, sees the discussion as a contest, but with little evidence.

31. See Goldberg 1983, 139: "There can be no compromise between precision and evasion."

32. Socrates' speeches are, of course, just as long as the sophists', if not more so. But for the real differences that nevertheless exist, see Benitez 1992, 242.

33. The political dimension of this part of the dialogue is emphasized by Goldberg 1983, 144, 205.

34. I cannot agree with Miller's claim (1977, 78–79) that Socrates appoints *himself* moderator. It is true that Socrates defines how the discussion is to proceed, but this is due to the dialectical ineptitude of his interlocutors. The ideal with which he tries to inspire them is still a conversation in which all would equally be moderators. Rutherford (1995, 135) draws attention to a parallel passage from the *Republic* (348a–b) where Socrates contrasts the procedure of giving opposed speeches, in which a judge is required to decide between them, and the procedure of searching through mutual agreement, in which we ourselves are both judges and advocates.

35. It is easier to list the few scholars who see the Simonides interpretation as essential to the significance of the dialogue as a whole than it is to list the many who do not. Let four examples of the latter suffice here: for A. E. Taylor, in *Plato: The Man and His Work* (New York: Meridian, 1956; hereafter cited as Taylor 1956), the episode is "mostly fun" (255) and an "amusing skit" (256); according to Shorey 1933, "It contains little or nothing that bears on the main argument" (128); for Vlastos 1956, it is "a labored one-man charade" which turns Socrates into "a practical joker, almost a clown" (xxiv); for W. K. C. Guthrie, in *A History of Greek Philosophy*, 4 vols. (Cambridge: Cambridge University Press, 1975; hereafter cited as Guthrie 1975), it is "splendid entertainment, but hardly philosophy" (227). Dorothea Frede is one scholar who disagrees, arguing that "Already the length of Socrates' exegesis and its position right in the middle of the dialogue make it implausible that its function is only polemical"; see "The Impossibility of Perfection: Socrates' Criticism of Simonides' Poem in the *Protagoras*," *Review of Metaphysics* 39 (1985–86): 729–53, 737 (hereafter cited as D. Frede 1985–86). Yet while Frede provides a detailed account of Socrates' exegesis, she makes no attempt to integrate it into the rest of the dialogue. Instead, she argues that its "serious" part is a *later insertion*, composed and added to the dialogue at around the time the *Symposium* was written (748). Frede supports this chronology by pointing to a "textual oddity": Socrates' description of the right kind of symposium at the end of his interpretation "is not just a description of *a* symposium but of *the Symposium*" (747). She also points out that, with the exception of Aristophanes, all of the speakers of the *Symposium* are mentioned as present in the audience of the *Protagoras* (747). I fail to see why Socrates' description of an ideal symposium must refer to the *Symposium* in particular nor do I find odd the presence in the *Protagoras*

of prominent members of the Socratic and sophistic circles. Furthermore, I am not convinced that the *Protagoras* as a whole could not have been written close in time to the *Symposium*. Frede appears to have two major arguments for considering the Simonides interpretation a later insertion: First, major ideas of the interpretation, such as the skepticism concerning the stability of human knowledge, the distinction between being and becoming, and the recognition of a "middle state" between wisdom and ignorance, are not to be found in earlier dialogues (744–46); and second, these ideas are ignored by what is said in the second half of the *Protagoras* itself (749). I doubt that the first point is true, but even if it were, it would not support Frede's thesis: After all, the *Protagoras* could be the *first* dialogue in which these ideas are presented. The second point is unquestionably true, but casts doubt on Frede's interpretation, rather than confirming it: If Plato at a later date inserted new material into the Simonides interpretation, would he not at the same time have revised the second half of the dialogue to make it consistent with this new insertion? As will be shown later in this essay, this second point is explained by the dialogical context, something Frede altogether ignores in favor of fanciful speculation about Plato's "development." In short, Frede indeed takes the Simonides interpretation seriously, but only at the cost of divorcing it from the rest of the dialogue. Goldberg, on the other hand, sets out to show that it "is in fact integral to the dialogue and necessary for an overall understanding of its argument" (1983, 156). Goldberg provides many important insights, some of which are cited in later notes. His account (1983, 156–220), however, disappoints in the end: It does not make clear the true significance and the cohesion of the main ideas Socrates presents. Stokes's interpretation (1986, 313–23) characterizes the episode as *dialectical* (316): In other words, he sees Socrates here as using a method approved of by the sophists in order to deduce conclusions unpalatable to Protagoras (321–22). There is indeed this *ad hominem* dimension to the episode, but Socrates also uses this opportunity to present some of his own views, views that explain the antagonism between himself and Protagoras. Gundert sees the Simonides interpretation as forming the "middle" of the dialogue in which all of its different threads are tied together; see Hermann Gundert, "Die Simonides-Interpretation in Platons *Protagoras*," in *Platonstudien,* ed. Klaus Doring and Felix Preisshofen (Amsterdam: B. R. Gruner, 1977), 23–45, 43 (hereafter cited as Gundert 1977). He rightly argues that to see "mere play" here is to misunderstand the seriousness of Platonic play (41); the views of Taylor, Vlastos, and Guthrie cited above appear to represent precisely such a misunderstanding. For some problems in Gundert's account, however, see note 46 below.

36. Compare Goldberg 1983, 169: "If we consider that the fullest exposition of Protagoras's position is to be found in his long speech, then we may conclude that this lengthy discourse of Socrates is his most concentrated response to that speech."

37. Compare Goldberg 1983, 176–77, and Coby 1982, 152 n.8. Anne Carson, in "How Not to Read a Poem: Unmixing Simonides From Protagoras," *Classical Philology* 87, no. 4 (1992): 110–30, 112–14 (hereafter cited as Carson 1992), shows

FRANCISCO J. GONZALEZ

an important way in which the historical Simonides provides an appropriate analogue to Protagoras: He was the first poet to live by his poetry, demanding a fee for it.

38. Compare Stokes 1986, 323–24.

39. Goldberg also sees in this passage a description of a philosophical community distinct from that of the sophists (1983, 174–75; see also 217 n.10).

40. On the dialectical character of Socrates' interpretation, see Gundert 1977, especially 30–32.

41. The characterization of knowledge here as unstable and always threatened by ignorance finds a parallel in *Symposium* 207e5–208a7, as noted by D. Frede 1985–86, 743–44. Gundert observes that *being* good is denied man not only "weil die täglichen *sumphorai* auch sein Denken ändern, sondern weil dieses Denken, eben im Lernen und Vergessen, selber zeitlich und 'werdend' ist" (1977, 36).

42. Compare Goldberg 1983, 195–96. As Goldberg observes, "Protagoras makes the poem of Simonides worse than we see it to be while Socrates attempts to make it better" (195).

43. Coby (1982, 154) sees a connection between Socrates' claim that wrongdoing is unwilling and his critique of competitiveness.

44. It should not need to be pointed out that Socrates' use of the *technē* analogy does not commit him to the view that virtue is a *technē*. As D. Frede correctly observes: "Virtue is here undeniably treated as *analogous* to craft-knowledge. Absolutely nothing is said, however, about the *kind* of knowledge in the exegesis of the poem" (1985–86, 743). I would go further and claim that Socrates here makes clear the extent to which they are *not* analogous. (For this point, see also Landy 1994, 288, 299–300). And yet many scholars assume that Socrates in this dialogue considers virtue to be a technical expertise. According to Michael Frede, for example, Socrates "seems to think" that the notion of virtue is the notion of a *technē;* see his Introduction to *Plato: Protagoras,* trans. Stanley Lombardo and Karen Bell (Indianapolis: Hackett, 1992), xx (hereafter cited as M. Frede 1992). But *how* does Socrates seem to think this? Likewise Goldberg writes: "For, Socrates, unlike Protagoras, *does not appear* to separate radically technical knowledge from knowledge of virtue" (1983, 234; my emphasis). The only evidence for attributing this view to Socrates in the present dialogue is the account of the science of measurement. But, as I attempt to show later in this essay, Socrates is there drawing out the implications of *the sophists'* identification of virtue with a *technē,* rather than presenting this view as his own.

45. As D. Frede recognizes (1985–86, 745), this description of a "middle state" parallels *Symposium* 201d and following. Frede also sees a parallel to *Philebus* 22c.

46. M. Frede interprets the phrase "becoming good" as referring "to the kind of behavior a virtuous person would display, where it is left open, or even questioned, whether in the case at hand it actually is produced by virtue" (Frede finds this usage in Thucydides) and equates "being good" with "acting freely out of insight, and not out of social coercion" (1992, xiii). Yet this interpretation is clearly untenable. Since Socrates claims that "being good" is impossible for

human beings, Frede's interpretation would have him claim that it is impossible for human beings to act freely out of insight. More importantly, Socrates clearly equates "becoming good" with a process between wisdom and ignorance, not with blind obedience to convention. Gundert makes a similar mistake when he interprets the important notion of *ta mesa* as referring only to conventional virtue and goodness as opposed to philosophical (1977, 40, 42). On the other hand, Gundert, unlike M. Frede, rightly sees in "*becoming* good" the process of philosophical understanding, the striving of *erōs* and a "space" that defines man's existence as such (35–36). As Gundert admits, therefore, his interpretation makes *ta mesa* and "becoming good" two completely different things and thereby undermines the unity of Socrates' exegesis (40). But why, then, accept this interpretation, especially when it receives no support from the text?

47. This is also suggested by Stokes 1986, 320.

48. Hugh Parry, "An Interpretation of Simonides 4 (Diel)," *Transactions of the American Philological Association* 96 (1965): 297–320, 319 (hereafter cited as Parry 1965), and Landy (1994, 288) draw attention to this parallel.

49. Relevant in this context is Goldberg's important observation:

> Strictly speaking, then, the good man is the learner not the learned. And, while one can obviously teach a learner, can one teach a person to be a learner? In fact, Socrates is continuously and with little success trying to teach young men and even Protagoras to be learners . . . (What Protagoras does not know is not this or that bit of doctrine, but how to learn; and he cannot learn, in part, precisely because he considers himself so venerable and wise). (1983, 206)

50. I therefore could not disagree more with Weingartner's characterization of Protagoras as "a man of considerable nobility" (48). The main thesis of Gagarin 1969 is "that Plato is trying to present a sympathetic portrait of Protagoras in this dialogue, and that he shows great respect, not only for the man, but also for his thought" (163). This thesis rests on a number of misinterpretations criticized throughout the present paper. Gagarin even thinks that Protagoras is sometimes depicted more favorably than Socrates: see 147, 148, 151, 163.

51. Why does Protagoras insist on this distinction, especially given his implied view that courage and wisdom together, as virtues lacked by the majority, form his special expertise? In addition to seeing here a chance to win the argument, he perhaps believes that the kind of prudence he teaches presupposes a native daring he cannot teach. He could in this case still see himself as making his students *more courageous* by enabling them to make the most of this native daring. For a similar explanation, see Hemmenway 1996, 19.

52. Goldberg (1983, 228–34) shows in detail how Protagoras's objection is a misinterpretation and evasion. See also Vlastos 1956, xxxi–xxxvi, and Guthrie 1975, 229–30.

53. Gagarin denies that hedonism is the view of either Protagoras or the many (1969, 156). Donald J. Zeyl argues that Protagoras is committed to hedonism by his initial admissions (351b3–7) that a man lives badly if he lives in distress

and suffering and lives well if he lives a pleasant life to the end; see "Socrates and Hedonism: *Protagoras* 351b–358d," *Phronesis* 25 (1980): 250–69, 251–55 (hereafter cited as Zeyl 1980). Therefore, when Protagoras refuses to endorse hedonism, he is being inconsistent. Zeyl rightly characterizes this refusal as "a fainthearted concession to the unpopularity of hedonism as a theory" (254); Protagoras does not hide the fact that he is motivated here by nothing more than a desire to give the *safer* response (351d2–7). Zeyl's interpretation is also adopted by R. Weiss, in "Hedonism in the *Protagoras* and the Sophist's Guarantee," *Ancient Philosophy* 10 (1990): 17–39, 21–22 (hereafter cited as Weiss 1990), and by Hemmenway 1996, 21. A similar view is found in Weingartner 1973, 113. According to J. P. Sullivan, "The Hedonism in Plato's *Protagoras*," *Phronesis* 6 (1961): 10–28, 22–23 (hereafter cited as Sullivan 1961), and, apparently, Stokes (1986, 357, 365–67), Protagoras does not initially accept hedonism, but is convinced by the argument that he must.

54. Weiss 1990 provides a thorough defense of the thesis that Socrates' account of the science of measurement, rather than representing his own position, is simply a formulation of the conceptions of knowledge and the good that would enable the sophists to teach virtue to the many. Weiss sees Socrates as then proceeding to provide a *reductio ad absurdum* of these conceptions by showing them to lead to an absurd characterization of courage. A similar view is defended by Hemmenway 1996, 21; Coby 1982, 142, 155–58; and Tucker 1994, 287–88, 301. Many scholars have, of course, argued against ascribing the hedonistic calculus to Socrates: see especially Sullivan 1961; Zeyl 1980; Stokes 1986, 358–70, 406–7, 419; and Goldberg 1983, 260–64. Some scholars, however, think that Socrates' account of the science of measurement is separable from any commitment to hedonism: see especially Friedländer 1964, 30–32; Gagarin 1969, 55–58; Vlastos 1969, 74–88; Weingartner 1973, 115–16; Goldberg 1983, 274; and M. Frede 1992, xxviii–xxxi. Two objections can be made here: First, there is evidence, cited in this paper, that Socrates cannot be committed to the identification of virtue with a science of measurement, whether or not this science is hedonistic; and second, I agree with Weiss that "Socrates never intimates that the denial of incontinence or the definition of courage can stand apart from hedonism. On the contrary, he makes every effort to ensure that Protagoras and the reader are aware of the dependence of these doctrines on hedonism (358b–c and 360a)" (1990, 35 n.29).

55. Most prominent among those who see the whole argument as representing Socrates' own view are Grote 1888, 2: 305–6; Vlastos 1956, xxxvi–xlv; Nussbaum 1986, 109–17; and Irwin 1995, 81–94. For scholars who see Socrates as endorsing an ethical science of measurement *minus the hedonism*, see the preceding note. It is significant that Grote, Vlastos, Nussbaum, and Irwin all ignore the main thesis of Socrates' interpretation of Simonides, that is, that it is *impossible to be good*. They also pay little or no attention to the dispute about method that forms the dialogue's literal and figurative center.

56. The incompatibility of Socrates' interpretation of Simonides with the account of the science of measurement has also been noted by D. Frede 1985–86, 749, and Landy 1994, 301. Frede, however, wrongly assumes that this incompatibility can be best explained by the hypothesis that this part of the Simonides

interpretation was a *later insertion*. (For a critique of this view, see note 35 above.) Landy unfortunately jumps to the conclusion that knowledge of virtue is simply unattainable and fails even to mention Socrates' introduction of a "middle state."

57. Compare Sullivan 1961, 19 n.1, and Weiss 1990, 24–25.

58. This is recognized by Grote 1888, 2: 309. Grote, however, wrongly attributes this conception of virtue as a science of measurement to Socrates and wrongly believes that Protagoras's speech provides the needed conception of justice (309–13).

59. Compare Goldberg 1983, 245–47, 277.

60. This is the view of Weiss 1990, 30. Friedländer 1964, 31, and Goldberg 1983, 286, suggest a similar interpretation. Gagarin's view, shared by Weingartner (1973, 129–30), that "the hedonistic equation, that pleasure equals good, has no direct bearing, in fact, on the proof that courage is knowledge" (Gagarin 1969, 160) is refuted by Weiss (1990, 29).

61. As Hemmenway observes, "What the unity of courage and wisdom means for Protagoras is base calculation, prudent boldness, or Promethean stealth" (1996, 22). Protagoras's stealth, however, is not "Promethean" in Socrates' sense of the word. Goldberg (1983, 295) sees Protagoras's unwillingness to yield to the argument as itself a display of cowardice.

62. That Socrates' concluding confession of *aporia* is incompatible with his endorsement of the science of measurement and the final account of courage is also seen by Sullivan 1961, 27; D. Frede 1985–86, 735–36, 749; and Weiss 1990, 29. Frede rightly insists that the *Protagoras* be read as an *aporetic* dialogue (736).

63. And as has been seen, Socrates *is* committed to this view, especially by the conclusions of his interpretation of Simonides. Compare Landy 1994, 301. Yet a popular way of getting Socrates out of the contradiction is to deny this commitment: see Gagarin 1969, 161; Weingartner 1973, 132–33; Goldberg 1983, 316; Stokes 1986, 439; Taylor 1991, 213; and M. Frede 1992, xxxii.

64. Compare Benitez 1992, 245:

> [A]n intriguing feature of Socratic dialogue is that, when properly conducted, it fosters excellence in the interlocutors: They must show wisdom in the pursuit of truth, courage in admitting mistakes and conceits, fairness toward others, and restraint in judgment.

Unfortunately, Benitez adds:

> But it would be a mistake to think that his only aim is to foster excellence through dialogue. Rather, the possibility of real education in excellence depends, for Socrates, on the success of his inquiry into the nature of excellence. (245)

An aim of the present paper is to show that this is *not* a mistake.

65. Miller 1978 does not do justice to this contrast, characterizing *both* Socrates and Protagoras as Epimethean *and* Promethean (28–29), with only a hint

as to a possible difference (31). Coby, on the other hand, rightly observes that it is in the philosopher's question of the good "that the cautious Prometheanism of the art of measurement gives way to the erotic Prometheanism of Socratic philosophy" (1982, 158).

66. Compare Goldberg 1983, 32–33, and Hemmenway 1990, 4–5.

67. Compare Goldberg's observation:

> The true failure, however, is not in the fact that he [Socrates] does not convince Protagoras about virtue, but that he fails to engage him lastingly and wholeheartedly in discourse. *To turn away from discourse means also to turn away from virtue.* (1983, 305; my emphasis)

Unfortunately, Goldberg does not develop this point.

68. There may be some irony in Protagoras's use of the word *agamai* here, since, as Carson 1992, 127, points out, this word "can mean equally 'I am moved to wondering admiration, I praise you' or 'I am moved to envy and begrudgment, I blame you' (LSJ)."

69. Here, too, Protagoras's rhetoric manages to fool some readers: see Vlastos 1956, ix, and Gagarin 1969, 161.

70. As Taylor observes, "Socrates' silence in response to this [Protagoras's] encomium is positively deafening" (1991, 215).

Writing Conversion: Notes on the Structure of the *Phaedo*

James Crooks

At both the beginning and the end of his philosophical life, Nietzsche represents the spirit of his own work in contrast to the figure of Socrates that Plato sketches in the *Phaedo*. In *The Birth of Tragedy* (1872), the "image of the dying Socrates" is an "emblem" of the will to intelligibility which displaces and devalues the Dionysian art-instinct.[1] Higher powers may have exhorted Plato's master more than once to "practice music."[2] But to little or no effect. At best (and then only in the eleventh hour), Nietzsche imagines, Socrates becomes uneasy:

> He may have said to himself: "Have I been too ready to view what was unintelligible to me as being devoid of meaning? Perhaps there is a realm of wisdom, after all, from which the logician is excluded? Perhaps art must be seen as the complement of rational discourse?"[3]

By 1888, the critique is completely unforgiving. For Nietzsche circa *Twilight of the Idols,* any stand against art is a stand against life itself. Accordingly, like so many of the other figures celebrated by philosophy and religion, Plato's Socrates is a closet nihilist:

> In every age the wisest have passed the identical judgment on life: It is worthless. . . . Everywhere and always their mouths have uttered the same sound—a sound full of doubt, full of melancholy, full of weariness with

life, full of opposition to life. Even Socrates said as he died: "To live—that means to be a long time sick: I owe a cock to the savior Asclepius."[4]

These writings, of course, are unapologetically polemical.[5] Nietzsche makes a virtue of crossing the line between scholarly criticism and caricature. But he also plants and nurtures two questions about Plato's thought—in the *Phaedo* especially—which have since grown up in our collective philosophical imagination: Doesn't Platonism teach indifference to aesthetic experience and its representation in *mousikē* and *muthos*? Doesn't it recommend *flight* from our condition, from our existential or embodied present, under cover of the metaphysics of forms and its epistemological/ethical correlates?

In what follows, I will pursue a reading of the *Phaedo* that would permit us to answer both of these questions in the negative. My argument turns on three interdependent claims regarding the dialogue's structure. The first is that the philosophical climax of the dialogue comes in a set of three variations on the theme of moral discourse (88a–102a), culminating in Socrates' autobiography. The second is that that climax constitutes a discursive conversion, an intellectual "turn," the function of which is to invite the reader to revisit territories explored but not settled in the first part of the dialogue. The third is that Plato's return to these territories at the end of the conversation effectively stresses both the ultimate reciprocity of *muthos* and *logos* in philosophical discourse and what we might call the validation of our existential or embodied present.

These claims I will treat as hypotheses. Their viability will depend largely on the coherence and the promise of the interpretive sketch which takes them as a point of departure, that is, on the extent to which they open up and clarify the text of the *Phaedo* both in relation to other dialogues and in its own terms. Keeping this in view, I will direct my commentary to the following ends: first, placing the notion of an intellectual turn or conversion in the wider context of Plato's philosophy; second, outlining the tensions that necessitate such a conversion in the text of the *Phaedo;* third, proposing in relation to the center of that text (88d–102a) a kind of anatomy of conversion; and fourth, exploring, at least tentatively, the implications of this conversion for reading the remainder of the work.

In the past few decades, Plato's philosophical readers have recognized what those outside the discipline were for a time perhaps better able to see: that the dialogues are almost without peer in the challenge they present as literary phenomena. Above and beyond any arguments that are made, they ply us with the discourses of politics, social commentary, satire, myth, poetry, prayer, and pedagogy. Attempting to reconstruct Plato's intent and his procedure in putting these discourses together, I have found the theme of conversion increasingly useful. In advance of developing that theme in broad strokes, I would like to call to mind a familiar text in which Plato himself stresses its importance. It comes at the end of the allegory of the cave, *Republic* 7:

> Of this very thing, then, [Socrates] said, there might be an art, an art of the speediest and most effective shifting or conversion of the soul, not an art of producing vision in it, but on the assumption that it possesses vision but does not rightly direct it and does not look where it should, an art of bringing this about. (518a)[6]

This is Socrates' plain talk about education. To educate is to convert or turn the soul. But what Plato has Socrates *say* here he also has him *practice*—both in those dialogues which scholars associate with his attempt to represent Socrates' historical reality (for example, the *Charmides,* the *Crito,* the *Euthyphro,* the *Gorgias,* the *Laches,* the *Lysis,* and the *Protagoras*) and those where Socrates' voice has been appropriated and modified to suit his own philosophical concerns (for example, the *Phaedo,* the *Phaedrus,* the *Symposium,* and the *Republic*). A word is in order here concerning each of these dialogue-types with a view to setting the pattern of the *Phaedo* in an appropriate methodological context.

The works of the early period, first, contain a series of conversions orchestrated by playing the discourse of the Socratic *elenchos* against that of an irony which is sometimes explicitly Socratic, sometimes implicit in the situation or in statements made by his interlocutors. In such cases, the encounter of a theoretical limit becomes the occasion for turning around or back in the direction of the conversation that led us there, regarding that conversation, on another plain, as an instance, a demonstration or a "show," of what we are seeking.

In the *Charmides,* for example, the interlocutors seek a definition of temperance. Under the scrutiny of the *elenchos,* every hypothesis crumbles; so that at the level of theoretical argumentation, the inquiry is an abject failure. In spite of this, however, the dialogue concludes with Charmides and Critias more determined than ever to attach themselves to Socrates. They say so explicitly (176a–b). That is ironic, but also philosophically telling and perfectly in order. For if we permit ourselves to be *turned,* along with the interlocutors, in the direction this irony opens up, we see that, at the level of practice, genuine temperance is nothing but the persistence in appropriate measure, that is, in the pursuit of wisdom which is instantiated in the Socratic inquiry.

The *Laches* unfolds along similar lines. There, courage is the virtue in question. And, as in the *Charmides,* all attempts at a definition fail. Nevertheless, the dialogue ends with the suggestion that the parties concerned, all of whom have *demonstrated* their courage on the battlefield, seek courage and become educated with respect to it, that is, that they persist in the inquiry in spite of its difficulties (200e–201b). Again, that is both ironic (three experienced military men consider going "back to school" on the virtue most basic to military life) and philosophically telling. For to persist in what one already knows, to strive to recollect the essential lessons of one's education, is the very essence of courage (compare *Republic,* 429b–c). We need only permit ourselves to be turned away from the requirement of a positive theoretical result in order to see the conversation itself as an instantiation of what we are seeking.

I take this sort of turn or conversion—from the understanding of philosophy as a search for theoretical definition to the conception of it as a mode (the mode) of realizing virtue, of partaking in it—to be at the heart of Plato's writing in the Socratic or *elenchtic* dialogues. Without it, it is hard to see in that writing anything of lasting philosophical interest. The works of Plato's middle and later periods are considerably more complex. Yet, there, too, Plato is concerned with writing a conversion, and, in the works of the middle period at least, this concern becomes determinative in the elaboration of a kind of post-Socratic philosophical structure.

In the matter of articulating this structure, I have found some remarks of Robert Brumbaugh particularly helpful. His *Platonic Studies of Greek Philosophy* contains a piece on the *Republic* in which he argues that the development of themes there is symmetrical "like the design of a temple pediment."[7] The dialogue begins and ends with a treatment of religious motifs. Nested within those limits (that is, adjacent on both ends) is a consideration of poetry. Within that consideration, arguments about the soul and the character of the state: so that the basic pattern of the discussion would be something like *a b c d . . . . d c b a.* At the center of it all we find the discussion of the Good in Books 6 and 7—including, of course, the allegory of the cave which ends with the definition of education as the art of converting or turning the soul. A glance at other dialogues roughly contemporary with the *Republic* reveals a similar mirror-effect. The *Phaedo* also begins and ends with a treatment of religious themes adjacent to which we find two arguments on the relation of opposites. At the center, bounded by the brief exchanges between Phaedo and Echecrates, we find Socrates warning against misology, together with the autobiographical account of his own intellectual conversion; a kind of *a b c . . . c b a* structure. The *Phaedrus* begins and ends with the question of how one distinguishes good and bad speaking and writing, but has at its center Socrates' grand mythical account of how we are turned around in the experience of beauty (*a b . . . b a*). Brumbaugh himself mentions the *Symposium* as another instance.[8]

What he does not explore are the philosophical and pedagogical consequences of this writing to the center or to the "turn," what we might call the dynamics of the structure. Chief among these would be the possibility of reading at least some of the middle dialogues as explicit acts of recollection, as repetitions the point of which is to remind the interlocutors (and the reader) of what stands in the words that have passed between them already. I would like to suggest, in any case, that the conversation of the *Phaedo* draws us out into a certain region, past landmarks that strike us as odd or unfamiliar, to the point where we are able to recognize the peril of philosophical disorientation and the necessity of recovering our bearing. Then it takes us back, reoriented, letting us look again at what we've already seen. Exploring this suggestion, we move, as it were, in advance, against the reading of the text for which we made Nietzsche the spokesman above. For what one sees in the *Phaedo,* from the beginning, what is already there at the point of Socrates' conversion, is precisely the unresolved tensions surrounding *muthos* and *logos* in the concrete reality of a specific human situation.

Both early and later, then, Plato practices the art of converting or turning his readership. Early he does so by *pointing* from the limits of theoretical discourse back toward the act of philosophical conversation; later by *leading us explicitly* back over the terrain our conversation first opens up. This double-back or mirror-effect frames the more detailed account I would like now to offer of events in the *Phaedo.*

In a narrative/historical sense, these events are well known. The dialogue recollects the conversation between Socrates and some friends on the day of his execution. The talk turns, rather naturally, to the question of the immortality of the soul and to whether the philosopher may face death with confidence. Stories are told; arguments are made. Arguments are made; stories told. And Socrates drinks the poison. But if we probe the text, if we take it upon ourselves to wander through it with a view to understanding Plato's purpose in putting different modes of speech together, we find ourselves almost immediately in a kind of discursive labyrinth resistant to any sort of straightforward interpretation. Consider two of its substantial features.

First, there is the proximity of philosophy to the *muthos.* In the prologue to Phaedo's narrative account, he tells Echecrates that Socrates' execution was deferred by the annual mission to Delos honoring Apollo.

If that is, in fact, the case, then there is a very real sense in which ordinary piety constitutes the condition for the possibility of the entire conversation. Were it not for the interval specified in the religious rite, Socrates would be dead already. And his final hour would have been quite different.[9] That this is so becomes evident almost immediately in the exchange between Cebes and Socrates on the writing of poetry. For in the space of his temporary reprieve, Socrates has become (of all things!) a poet, a mythmaker of sorts. The explanation of this singularly odd turn of events, to be passed on to Evenus and anyone else who might be interested, becomes the point of departure for the more theoretical discussion of the status of the soul.

It is, in fact, on the path of this explanation that Socrates recounts the dream that Nietzsche presents in *The Birth of Tragedy* as evidence of belated doubt or uneasiness. Socrates says, at 60e:

> In the course of my life I have often had the same dream, appearing in different forms at different times, but always saying the same thing, "Socrates, make music and work at it." In the past, I used to think that it was impelling and exhorting me to do what I was actually doing; I mean that the dream, like a spectator encouraging a runner in a race, was urging me on to do what I was doing already, that is, making music, for philosophy is the best kind of music, and I was practicing it. But ever since my trial, while the festival of the god has been delaying my execution, I have felt that perhaps it might be this popular form of art that the dream intended me to practice, in which case I ought to practice it and not disobey. I thought it would be safer not to take my departure before I had cleared my conscience by writing poetry and so obeying the dream. I began with some verses in honor of the god whose festival it was. When I had finished my hymn, I reflected that a poet, if he is to be worthy of the name, ought to work on imaginative themes, not descriptive ones, and I was not good at inventing stories. So I availed myself of some of Aesop's fables which were ready to hand and familiar to me, and I versified the first of them that suggested themselves.[10]

The talk about philosophy and death (that is, the preface to the extended consideration of immortality) follows immediately. Socrates entrusts Cebes with the explanation of his poetic turn, but tacks on a rather disturbing postscript:

> You can tell Evenus this . . . and bid him farewell from me, and tell him, if he is wise, to follow me as quickly as he can. I shall be going today, it seems; those are my country's orders.

> What a piece of advice for Evenus, Socrates! said Simmias. I have had
> a good deal to do with him before now, and from what I know of him he
> will not be at all ready to obey you.
> Why? [Socrates] asked. Isn't Evenus a philosopher? (61bc)

And the arguments commence. But in all this it is easy to pass over
the riddle of Socrates' music, of his mythmaking. The dream from which
he derives guidance is interpreted here in two ways. On the one hand,
there is an allegorical reading in which the spirit *really* exhorts Socrates
to soldier on in philosophy. On the other, there is a literal reading in
which it exhorts him, finally, to set philosophy aside, or, at the very least,
to supplement it with the writing of the *muthos*. If we follow the path of
the first reading, it is difficult to see any point in Socrates' versifying.
For philosophy, as he has practiced it, teaches nothing positive about
Delos, Apollo, or anything of the kind. If we follow that of the second, we
must set aside the rather substantial critique of poetry Plato elsewhere
puts in Socrates' mouth and struggle with the subsequent arguments
which present themselves as sufficient. The nature of the proximity of
philosophy to the *muthos* that Plato acknowledges at the beginning of
the *Phaedo* strikes us as mysterious. And nothing in Plato's arguments
themselves assuages that sense of mystery.

But the same can be said of the relation between philosophy and
the *logos,* if, following Simmias and Cebes, we equate the *logos* more or less
exclusively with the discourses of mathematics and natural science. This
would be the second point. Gadamer, whose own hermeneutical method
developed in reaction to the "scientism" of the Marburg Neo-Kantians,
sees in the exploration of this relation, the principal thrust of *Phaedo:*

> The discussion proper takes place between Socrates and two "Pythagorean"
> friends. . . . When Plato has Socrates, in the hour of death, enter into
> conversation with "Pythagorean" representatives of contemporary science,
> that is obviously meant to show that Plato saw it as his own task to unite the
> moral introspection for which Socrates stood with the scientific knowledge
> represented by the Pythagoreans; and perhaps it will prove to be the case
> indeed that "Pythagorean" science is not without importance for the great
> human questions which Socrates would have us pause to consider.[11]

That the *logos* of science stands apart from that of Socratic moral
philosophy is evident, as Gadamer goes on to say, from the exchange
among Socrates, Simmias, and Cebes on the prohibition of suicide which
follows on the heels of Socrates' advice to hasten toward death as quickly
as possible.[12] When the question of moral sanction is introduced, both

Simmias and Cebes claim to have heard "nothing definite" (61d), admitting that such matters played no role in their education.

That Plato regards the synthesis of scientific and moral reflection as desirable seems obvious on the basis of Socrates' attempts to cater to the sensibilities of his interlocutors. The first argument for the immortality of the soul (the so-called cyclical argument on the generation of opposites, 70d–72e) is couched in the language of pre-Socratic physics. That argument is then combined with Socrates' own moral/epistemological doctrine of recollection in order to demonstrate the soul's preexistence (that is, independence) of the body (73a–77e), as if proof of the soul's immortality were a function of pooling these resources. (For purposes of convenience I shall refer to this synthesis hereafter as the *combined argument*).

The ultimate status of such a union, however, remains unclear.[13] The combined argument functions as a preface, after all, to the objections of Simmias and Cebes which lay before Socrates his real challenge. In particular, it leaves him open to the distinction Cebes makes between absolute and relative immortality (86e–88e): It may be true, in accordance with the cyclical argument, that opposites generate each other so that, in some way, one might grant that life comes from death. And it may be true, in accordance with the doctrine of recollection, that the soul has an existence that predates its association with the body, so that we need not think the two necessarily as party to a common fate. But neither these arguments nor their combination exclude the possibility of the soul's eventual death—after many incarnations—and so the possibility that the incarnation we are living out presently is our last.

This is a most serious objection. Phaedo breaks off his own narrative to acknowledge it. And when he resumes, it is to tell us how Socrates himself warned against despairing in argument (that is, against misology). Moreover, it is in response to Cebes' objection that Socrates relates the story of his intellectual conversion, the real turning point of the dialogue, if our hypotheses stand. Without speculating in detail about how things stand on the other side of that conversion (we shall arrive there in due course), it seems quite likely, given the analogy Socrates draws later on between mathematical relations and those that hold between the forms, that Plato means to propose a second, higher synthesis of scientific and Socratic discourse in his own metaphysics. But even that metaphysics, grasped as a theoretical position, is ultimately insufficient if the point of the synthesis is to *convince* us of our immortality and bolster our confidence. For when all the arguments are on the table, when both the "Pythagoreanism" of the interlocutors and Socrates' own "moral introspection" have been sublated in the doctrine of forms, Simmias says, nevertheless, "All the same, the subject is so vast, and I have such a poor opinion of our weak human nature, that I can't help still feeling some misgivings" (107b).

Simmias here speaks for the reader. We may follow the path of Socrates' arguments, even to the point of closure (should we accept their terms) and still retain misgivings. That is because the *closure* Socrates achieves at the level of argumentation is balanced by a profound and twofold *openness* or indeterminacy which seems to well up from the depths of language itself. Philosophy resides somehow in the proximity of the *muthos,* in its very space, if we take Socrates' personal situation as exemplary. But how? Philosophy is friendly to the *logos* of the scientist as surely as Socrates, Simmias and Cebes are friends. But to what end?

There is an urgency in these matters, it bears repeating, which surpasses that of the question of immortality itself (as pressing as this question is under the circumstances). The limitation of Socrates' *logos* that appears with Cebes' objection calls for a defense of argument *as such:* as if the talk about immortality were really an occasion for making the challenge of philosophical language, of what we called Plato's discursive labyrinth, thematic and explicit; as if it were really an occasion for facing down misology—a monster far worse, in Platonic terms, than the Cretan Minotaur.

In fact, there is a kinship between the stories of Theseus and Plato's Socrates that goes well beyond historical coincidence.[14] Like Theseus, the dying Socrates seems called upon to rescue his contemporaries from a (spiritually) lethal form of disorientation. And, like Theseus, he secures his own bearing along the length of a "golden braid" that runs back to the object of his desire. The nature of the philosophical "braid"—and of the philosopher's "Ariadne"—Plato indicates at the center of the *Phaedo:* the stretch that falls between 88d and 102b, following the objection of Cebes we mentioned earlier and preceding Socrates' return to the theme of opposites. The text there divides nicely into three episodes: first, Socrates' counsel against the danger of misology (89b–91c); second, his treatment of the Pythagorean concept of the soul as an attunement (91c–95a); and third, the account of his intellectual conversion (95a–102a). In each of these segments, Socrates prepares his interlocutors for their return to the constellation of the earlier discussion. And although the matters examined seem at first glance quite independent, there is a kind of progress that builds *through* them which is worthy of note.

The talk about misology, as we said before, follows Simmias's and Cebes' objections to Socrates' combined argument. For those in the prison cell, the objections seem profoundly compelling. They appear to undermine entirely the tentative union of scientific and Socratic discourse that was supposed to justify confidence in the face of death, and so to raise the question of whether and to what extent there are any discursive resources adequate to the discussion of such things. This is, of course, a fundamental question. After all, the validity of philosophy itself hangs in the balance. How does Socrates handle it?

> We must not let it enter our minds that there may be no validity in argument. On the contrary we should recognize that we ourselves are still intellectual invalids, but that we must brace ourselves and do the best we can to become healthy—you and the others partly with a view to the rest of your lives, but I directly in view of my death. (90e–91a)

The injunction against misology, cast as it is in terms of sickness, health, and the cultivation of proper character, is a moral injunction, and, in effect, the discursive repetition of a rather significant gesture Socrates makes at the outset of the dialogue. There, in the course of reminding his interlocutors of the teaching of Philolaus and others against suicide, Phaedo reports that "he [Socrates] lowered his feet to the ground, and sat like this for the rest of the discussion" (61cd). Here, too, Socrates begins simply by "putting his foot down," by insisting that the question of the viability of argument must be tied to recognition of the primacy of ethical concerns.[15]

This stand has two immediate consequences, both of which are essential to the project of conversion. First, it turns all concerned *back* to the arguments. Calculating the probability of success in inquiry, likely to be clouded by our decadence in any case, is ultimately beside the point. The capacity to endure in conversation is connected to our moral destiny, to the essential task of spiritual purification, and that alone is reason for continuing. Second, it alters the balance of parts in the combined argument. If we take seriously the terms of Socrates' counsel here, we recognize in the discourse of moral introspection—and in that alone—the philosophical "golden braid" to which we must hold fast.

The same theme is repeated and extended in the treatment of the Pythagorean concept of attunement which follows directly. Remember how things stand between our interlocutors in the wider context. Prior to Socrates' counsel against misology, both Simmias and Cebes had expressed misgivings about the combined argument. Cebes, as we said before, had worried about closing the loophole of relative immortality. For his part, Simmias had presented Socrates and the others with the popular view of the soul as a kind of harmony, an attunement predicated of the body. Insofar as one subscribes to this view (and Simmias, of course, finds it inviting), immortality seems out of the question. The soul, as a quality of the animate body, obviously perishes in bodily death.

Socrates eventually makes some arguments against the coherence of this thesis. But in trying to sort out the structure of the *Phaedo*'s center, I have come to regard his first response as more interesting. Reading at 91e:

> Well, then, [Socrates] said, do you reject all our previous arguments, or only some of them?
>
> Only some of them, they said.
>
> What is your opinion of the reasoning by which we asserted that learning is recollection, and that, if this is so, our souls must have existed somewhere else before they were confined to the body?
>
> Speaking for myself, said Cebes, I found it remarkably convincing at the time, and I stick to it still as I do no other theory.
>
> Yes, indeed, said Simmias, it is just the same with me. I should be very much surprised if I ever changed my opinion about that.
>
> But you will have to change it, my Theban friend, said Socrates, if the conception stands that an attunement is a composite thing, and that the soul is an attunement composed of our physical elements at a given tension. I imagine that you would not accept even from yourself the assertion that a composite attunement existed before the elements of which it was to be composed. Or would you?

Simmias keeps forgetting the doctrine of recollection. At 73a, on the occasion of its original appearance, he had asked Cebes to recap its "proofs." At 92ab, Socrates must remind him of its consequences: If he is willing to argue, in accordance with that doctrine, that the soul exists prior to its incarnation, then his philosophical position is already incompatible with the Pythagorean concept of attunement (that is, as a property of bodily relations). And so his objection unravels.

Here, as before, the episode turns us back to the earlier conversation. And, as before, the Socratic/Platonic "braid" is reaffirmed. On the heels of Socrates' counsel against misology, however, it also stresses the crucial point of alliance between what we might now recognize as two strands of that "braid": Socratic ethics and Platonic epistemology. Vlastos (among others) claims that the doctrine of recollection is an invention of Plato's middle period and a substantive point of departure, at least methodologically, from the historical Socrates.[16] The textual evidence for his view is compelling. But it bears notice that in both the *Meno* and the *Phaedo,* Plato's recourse to the doctrine is prompted by the threat of despair in argument, a threat the *elenchtic* procedure, operating on the presumption of faith in the possibility of genuine knowledge, is not equipped to handle. In any case, it seems to me possible to read Plato's compromise of the Socratic methodology in the middle part of the *Phaedo* as an attempt to buttress the Socratic project of moral introspection against a new kind of problem, and so to see, at least in this deployment of post-Socratic doctrine, a new orchestration of what is most basic to Socrates' position.[17]

If Socrates' insistence on the primacy of moral introspection provides his interlocutors (and Plato's readership) with a "golden braid" of sorts for navigating the labyrinth of philosophical problems, and if, in grasping that "braid" we find ourselves recognizing the doctrine of recollection as a corollary, what might we discover in following it to the end? Plato's retelling of the Theseus myth would be incomplete, surely, without some reference to the philosopher's Ariadne. Like its mythical counterpart, Socrates' "golden braid" can save us only because it is held secure at a point beyond the labyrinth. But the discovery of Ariadne is precisely what is described in the account of Socrates' intellectual conversion, his so-called autobiography. There, Plato grounds the ethical/epistemological position of the other episodes in a metaphysics, that is, a testimony concerning the genuine object of philosophical desire. It functions subsequently both as a basis for responding to Cebes' objection to the combined argument and as a compass in the mapping of those basic discursive territories, the *logos* and the *muthos,* which seemed so resistant in the first part of the dialogue.

The story begins at 96a. Socrates, having turned from the objection of Simmias to that of Cebes, claims that a proper response will involve "a full treatment of the causes of generation and destruction." He then leads his interlocutors back along the path of his own experience in that matter. Reading from the outset:

> When I was young, Cebes, I had an extraordinary passion for that branch of learning which is called natural science. I thought it would be marvelous to know the causes for which each thing comes and ceases and continues to be. I was constantly veering to and fro, puzzling primarily over this sort of question. Is it when heat and cold produce fermentation as some have said, that living creatures are bred? Is it with the blood that we think, or with the air or the fire that is in us? Or is it none of these, but the brain that supplies our senses of hearing and sight and smell, and from these memory and opinion arise, and from memory and opinion, when established, that knowledge comes? Then again, I would consider how these faculties are lost, and study celestial and terrestrial phenomena, until at last I came to the conclusion that I was uniquely unfitted for this

form of inquiry. I will give you a sufficient indication of what I mean. I had understood some things plainly before, in my own and other people's estimation, but now I was so befogged by these speculations that I unlearned even what I thought I knew. (96ac)

Here, for the third time, we are turned back to the earlier conversation. By a stroke of good fortune, Socrates' own intellectual development mirrors his dialogue with Simmias and Cebes. Like them, he was once confident in the possibility of understanding causes and causality by means of physics and the categories of becoming. And, like them, he found himself disappointed, entangled in a maze of questions, in a discourse so alarmingly labyrinthine, that perseverance in it led to the *unlearning* of things he had previously taken for granted. In recollection, Socrates attributes to his youthful state of mind a dynamism which corresponds to the booming, busting, confusion of *phusis* itself: constantly on the move but getting nowhere, wandering. It is a predicament that might well have ended in the despair of argument, had not providence (at least in Plato's literary reconstruction) seen fit to provide an alternative. Picking up at 97c:

I once heard someone reading from a book, as he said, by Anaxagoras, and asserting that it is mind that produces order and is the cause of everything. This explanation pleased me. Somehow it seemed right that mind should be the cause of everything, and I reflected that if this is so, mind in producing order sets everything in order and arranges each individual thing in the way that is best for it. Therefore, if anyone wished to discover the reason why any given thing came or ceased or continued to be, he must find out how it was best for that thing to be, or to act or to be acted upon in some other way. On this view, there was only one thing for a man to consider, with regard both to himself and to anything else, namely the best and highest good, although this would necessarily imply knowing what is less good, since both were covered by the same knowledge.

Michael Davis suggests that the encounter of Anaxagoras represents the crucial point of transition in Plato's account of Socrates' development. The recognition of *nous,* he says, introduces both "a place for something like soul in a pre-Socratic cosmos" and "what reductionist science can never give us, purposes."[18] In terms of structure, it also mirrors the shift or turn in the dialogue itself from the combined argument to the unalloyed discourse of moral introspection we saw above (90e–91) in the injunction against misology.

But in the meditative/retrospective mood of autobiography (that is, freed temporarily from the discipline of his usual modes of inquiry), Socrates permits himself a further step. He makes explicit the mature *ground* of his confidence in moral discourse, the argument behind the whole of his investigation here and elsewhere. This takes him beyond Anaxagoras. The latter's instinct for the truth notwithstanding, he remains curiously entangled in the materialism of the physicists "adduc[ing] causes like air and aether and water and many other absurdities"(98bc). That is to say, he does not see the consequences for a theory of causality implicit in his own principle: if *nous* orders things for the best, in accordance with their highest good, then that good itself, absolute and without qualification, is the only genuine cause. Ultimately, the understanding appropriate to the treatment of causes, the only understanding adequate for responding to Cebes' objection to the combined argument, regards things *sub specie aeternitatis*. Enter Ariadne. It is hardly surprising that Socrates' tale culminates in the familiar testimony of his love affair with the metaphysics of form. He seems almost embarrassed, like someone forced to repeat a story his audience has heard before:

> [T]here is nothing new about it. I have always said it, in fact I have never stopped saying it, especially in the earlier part of this discussion. . . .
> I cannot understand these other ingenuous theories of causation. If someone tells me that the reason why a given object is beautiful is that it has a gorgeous color or shape or any other such attribute, I disregard all these other explanations—I find them all confusing—and I cling simply and straightforwardly and no doubt foolishly to the explanation that the one thing that makes that object beautiful is the presence in it or association with it, in whatever way the relation comes about, of absolute beauty. I do not go so far as to insist upon the precise details—only upon the fact that it is by beauty that beautiful things are beautiful. This, I feel, is the safest answer for me or for anyone else to give, and I believe that while I hold fast to this I cannot fall; it is safe for me or for anyone else to answer that it is by beauty that beautiful things are beautiful. (100b–e)

I suggested, in the first part of this paper, that in the *Phaedo* Plato guides us out into a certain region—past landmarks that strike us as unfamiliar, to the point where we may recognize the peril of philosophical disorientation and the necessity of recovering our bearing. And that he then walks us back, reoriented, counseling us to look again at what we've already seen. Taking the affirmation of Socrates' moral introspection and its epistemological/metaphysical correlates as an Archimedean point, as one attempt at writing conversion, let us look again.

If we are right in reading the theme and variations of the *Phaedo*'s center as the performance of a discursive turn or conversion, what we ought to see in the remainder of the work is a revisitation of matters explored but not settled in earlier exchanges and arguments. In terms of the text itself, that would mean matters up to and including Simmias's and Cebes' objections to the combined argument (57a–88e). In terms of the sketch of the territories that text encompasses that we made in the second part of this paper, it means something of the truth about *logos* and *muthos*. Proceeding now, as it were, on the other side of the turn, we might expect these themes to be treated in reverse order.

And, of course, they are. In the discussion pursuant to the autobiographical episode, Socrates and Cebes return to their study of opposites, constructing a second argument, a more durable *logos,* on the immortality of the soul. Then the arguments are set aside. And Socrates spins out the tale, the *muthos,* of the afterlife. In what sense does this return resolve the indeterminacy we spoke about in relation to *muthos* and *logos* earlier?

Logos first. One might wonder, in the face of Plato's arguments on opposites, what advantage there is in constructing two separate accounts. The symmetrical repetition of themes has a certain aesthetic appeal, but philosophy almost always suffers when style dictates content. What substantive grounds are there for rejoining this discussion? I see two.

On the one hand, reviewing the relation of opposites in light of the metaphysics of form leads to the dissipation of Cebes' worry about "relative" immortality. No form, it turns out, will admit of the opposite of anything by which it is always accompanied. The form of the triple, for example, in constant conjunction with the form of oddness, cannot admit of the even. Analogously, the form of the soul, in constant conjunction with the form of life, cannot admit of death. But the opposition, in this case, is unconditional. There is no question of "relativity" in formal relations. If death is excluded from the very measure of soul, it is excluded absolutely. The loophole left in the deployment of the categories of becoming is closed at the level of being. And Cebes' objection unravels.

On the other hand, the rescue or reinvention of the combined argument at the level of being lets Socrates' interlocutors (and Plato's readers) distinguish, in the discourse of Pythagoreanism broadly defined, between natural science and mathematics. The language and procedures of the former, as Socrates' autobiographical recollection makes abundantly clear, cannot be reconciled with the demands of moral discourse and its concomitant metaphysics. Those of the latter, on the other hand, seem analogous in important respects. (I take Socrates' choice of arithmetical relations as a demonstrator of the relations of soul to life and death as evidence of this). The passage from Gadamer's analysis cited above contains the suggestion that one of the important subtexts of the *Phaedo* might be the notion "that Pythagorean science is not without importance for the great human questions which Socrates would have us pause to consider." If that is so, then the mirror-play of the arguments on opposites may be read as an attempt to rescue and purify that science's legitimate hope in the promise of mathematical thought.[19]

There is a kind of double closure, then, in the second discussion of opposites: first, at the level of argumentation, and second, in the synthesis or reconciliation of Platonic metaphysics and Pythagorean mathematics. And yet after all of this, there remain those words of Simmias we cited earlier:

> As a matter of fact . . . I have no doubts myself either now, in view of what you have been saying. All the same, the subject is so vast, and I have such a poor opinion of our weak human nature, that I can't help still feeling some misgivings. (107ab)

Simmias remains *unconvinced*—in spite of his unqualified approval of Socrates' arguments. The suggestion is that something other than, more than, theoretical argumentation is necessary for *conviction*. But what? Plato's answer is clear in what follows: the *muthos*. Socrates responds to Simmias's final misgivings with the story of the afterlife, of the true earth. At the end of that story, as if concerned above all else that his audience understand its real discursive function, he says:

> Of course, no reasonable man ought to insist that the facts are exactly as I have described them. But that either this or something very like it is a true account of our souls and their future habitations—since we have clear evidence that the soul is immortal—this, I think, is both a reasonable contention and a belief worth risking, for the risk is a noble one. We should use such accounts to inspire ourselves with confidence, and that is why I have already drawn out my tale so long. (114d)

The *muthos* supplements the *logos*. It is able to touch us, to convince us, in a way argument alone cannot. But why is that the case?

Sometimes, in describing the process of becoming convinced of something, we will say, "That really hit home!" This is a felicitous expression for our purposes. It intimates that conviction is, in a certain sense, always a property of the situation in which we find ourselves. The discourse that we take to heart is invariably the one which clarifies our place (*topos*) in the midst of things. Theoretical arguments can and do assist in this. But they are almost never self-sufficient in the consideration of fundamental issues because they are inherently nonsituational. (This would be especially true, of course, of those metaphysical arguments which labor in the light of eternity.) No discourse will "hit home," if we might put it in this way, which does not bear within it somehow an appropriate topology—an account of place or situation.

If we turn with this in mind to the final pages of the *Phaedo,* we are struck by three things. First, the myth that Socrates invents there is a topology. It describes the relation of the earth to the heavens, distinguishing the "true earth" from our present situation and from the labyrinth that threatens from below. And it suggests, albeit obliquely, that even eternal blessedness is a mode of dwelling. ("But those who are judged to have lived a life of surpassing holiness—these are they who are released and set free from the confinement in these regions of the earth, and passing upward to their pure abode, make their dwelling on the earth's surface" [114bc].) Second, this topology may be taken as a mapping of the space of dialogue itself. Socrates' description of the soul's journey after death recalls more or less explicitly the imagery of the Theseus myth in which, as we said earlier, the entire discussion is nested. And it stresses that the success or failure of that journey is a function of whether and to what extent one has cultivated the proper way of living, whether and to what extent one has grasped and followed the "golden braid" of moral introspection which is the only way of navigating the human maze. Finally, this same description permits us to see in the struggle of philosophical education, that is, in the attempt to convert the foundation of our understanding from the categories of becoming to those of being, a continuous act of purification which is itself guardianship of our immortality. In this respect, the function of myth in the *Phaedo* corresponds to that of Socratic irony in the earlier *elenchtic* conversations. It turns us from word to deed; from philosophy as theoretical knowing to philosophy as the instantiation of measure.

One hundred years ago, Nietzsche took the last words of Plato's Socrates as a prototypical statement of Western nihilism: One offers a cock to Asclepius as an acknowledgment of healing. If Socrates, on his deathbed, instructs Crito to arrange such an offering, he must have regarded life as an illness. This interpretation has some merit. Indeed, a number of scholars considerably more sympathetic than Nietzsche have endorsed it—stopping short, perhaps, of equating the devaluation of embodied life with nihilism.[20] Yet if the embrace of the disembodied afterlife were all that Socrates had in mind, it would be difficult to reconcile his final utterance with what we have now presented in outline as the dialogue's structure. The body of the *Phaedo* is undoubtedly a course of therapy.

But the patients are Simmias, Cebes, and anyone else who might find themselves beguiled by the polymathy of Pythagorean science or by some other discourse which, implicitly or explicitly, sanctions the ignorance of ethical concern—of what is proper to our human *ethos*—in its address of fundamental questions. Philosophically speaking, the dialogue leads its interlocutors continually back to the gesture with which Socrates begins. It exhorts them to "lower their feet to the ground," to take their orientation in thinking about the destiny of the soul from the challenge of dwelling in the world. In all of this, the purification we suffer in death is far less important than the purification we may win for ourselves in conversation with one another. Or we could say, coming back to the image of Asclepius, that the healing of greatest concern to Socrates in the *Phaedo* is a collective healing of the word.

An attentive rereading of Nietzsche's gloss of Plato in *Twilight of the Idols* suggests that it is just this dimension of Socrates' final request that he fails to hear. His text reads, "Even Socrates said as he died: 'To live—that means to be a long time sick: *I* owe a cock to the savior Asclepius.' " But Plato writes, "The coldness was spreading about as far as his waist when Socrates uncovered his face, for he had covered it up, and said—they were his last words—Crito, *we* ought to offer a cock to Asclepius. See to it and don't forget" (118). The last words Plato puts in the mouth of his teacher acknowledge the curative power of the shared inquiry (that is, it is *we* who are now indebted, *we* who have now been healed). And while they may well invert the popular view of death as the greatest of evils, they are, above all, a benediction of the Socratic *logos,* a final tribute.

Can there be any doubt that what Socrates calls music is central to that *logos?* The *Phaedo* turns as much upon mythmaking and story-telling as upon what we might call "argument" in isolation. And it is self-consciously embedded in the imagery and ritual of popular religion. In the end, it seems to me possible to take the entire conversation as a resolution of the hermeneutical conundrum Socrates presents at the outset in relation to his recurring dream. The *daimōn* there tells him to "make music and work at it"—leaving him to wonder whether that means soldiering on in philosophy (*logos*) or telling tales (*muthos*). Yet one need not choose when all is said and done. The expressive power of music lies in its capacity to draw us out beyond ourselves, out toward the eternal, while in the very same gesture validating the hour. In the *Phaedo,* that is the Socratic gesture as well. Socrates draws Simmias, Cebes, and the rest into the consideration of eternal things, only to open up more powerfully the space of their collective beginning, only to guide them back, in the end, to the prison cell and the hour at hand and the bond of friendship—and to the validation of what they are already doing.

Notes

1. Nietzsche, *The Birth of Tragedy and the Genealogy of Morals,* trans. Francis Golffing (Garden City, N.Y.: Doubleday, 1956), 93.

2. Ibid., 90.

3. Ibid.

4. Nietzsche, *Twilight of the Idols and the Anti-Christ,* trans. R. J. Hollingdale (Middlesex: Penguin, 1968), 29.

5. The younger Nietzsche looks into Socrates' heart of hearts and sees for a moment the intimation of Wagner; the elder appropriates and embellishes Plato's account for his own purposes, recreating Socrates as a nineteenth-century decadent.

6. From the translation by Paul Shorey in *The Collected Dialogues of Plato,* eds. Edith Hamilton and Huntington Cairns, Bollingen Series LXXI (New York: Pantheon, 1961). Subsequent references to this and other dialogues will be given in the text itself using the Stephanus pagination.

7. R. Brumbaugh, *Platonic Studies of Greek Philosophy: Form, Arts, Gadgets, and Hemlock* (Albany: State University of New York Press, 1989), 20.

8. Ibid., 22. Think of the mirror-effect in Socrates' own account of love. The story of his instruction by Diotima begins as a repetition of his interrogation of Agathon.

9. I am indebted to Lisa Guenther for bringing these points to my attention in a number of informal working papers.

10. From the translation by Hugh Tredennick in *The Collected Dialogues of Plato.* I have made one small but significant substitution. Tredennick renders *mousikēn poiei kai ergazdou* as "practice and cultivate the arts." I prefer Fowler's more literal "make music and work at it"; compare Loeb Classical Library, *Plato I* (Cambridge: Harvard University Press, 1990), 210–11. All subsequent citations of the *Phaedo* use the Tredennick translation unaltered.

11. Hans-Georg Gadamer, *Dialogue and Dialectic* (New Haven: Yale University Press, 1980), 22–23.

12. Ibid., 23–24.

13. This is a point of some controversy in the secondary literature. Some commentators see in the initial arguments material essential to the position on immortality that emerges from the dialogue as a whole. See, for example, Kenneth Dorter, "The Reciprocity Argument and the Structure of Plato's *Phaedo,*" *Journal of the History of Philosophy* 15 (1977): 1–11. Others see them as intentionally weak: a critique of pre-Socratic thinking and a preamble to the discussion of forms (100b and following). See, for example, Michael Davis, "Socrates' Pre-Socratism: Some Remarks on the Structure of the *Phaedo,*" *Review of Metaphysics* 33 (1980): 559–77.

14. See Ronna Burger, *The Phaedo: A Platonic Labyrinth* (New Haven: Yale University Press, 1984), 19–20. Also, Kenneth Dorter, *Plato's Phaedo: An Interpretation* (Toronto: University of Toronto Press, 1982), 9. Both Dorter and Burger identify the "fear of death" (the *mormolukeia* or "bogy" that Cebes mentions at 77e) as Socrates' Minotaur. Socrates himself, however, claims that the greatest of

human misfortunes consists in falling prey to misology (89cd). Where the frame of reference is the labyrinth of discourse, that seems to me the more present danger.

15. The connection is, in fact, prefigured explicitly at 89d. There, Socrates warns against "becoming misologic. . . . in the sense that people become misanthropic," claiming that "[m]isology and misanthropy arise in just the same way." Presuming that suicide is a definitive expression of misanthropy, we might expect Socrates to treat it as a symptom of the same malady that produces the misologue and to prescribe a similar course of preventive medicine.

16. See G. Vlastos, *Socrates: Ironist and Moral Philosopher* (Ithaca, N.Y.: Cornell University Press, 1991), 45–106.

17. Compare *Meno* 86bc. Socrates concludes his "demonstration" of the doctrine of recollection as follows: "I shouldn't like to take my oath on the whole story, but one thing I am ready to fight for as long as I can, in word and act—that is, we shall be better, braver, and more active men if we believe it right to look for what we don't know than if we believe there is no point in looking because what we don't know we can never discover."

18. Davis, "Socrates' Pre-Socratism," 564–65.

19. See Anders Wedberg, *Plato's Philosophy of Mathematics* (Stockholm: Almqvist and Wiksell, 1955), especially 63–84. Wedberg suggests that Plato's philosophy of arithmetic was "probably strongly influenced by the Pythagorean doctrine" (75). What he would have had to reject was the notion of numbers as "collocations" of "indivisible material particles," or, as Gadamer puts it in *Dialogue and Dialectic* (35), the mistaking of "numbers and numerical relationships for existence itself. . . . ," the inability "to think of the noetic order of existence by itself." Keeping this in view, it is worth noting that prior to the explicit introduction of the doctrine of forms at 100b, Socrates uses mathematical relations to demonstrate what he takes to be the limits of explanation in accordance with physical causality (compare 96d–97b). Immediately thereafter (100e–101e), he makes a point of showing how his doctrine surmounts those limits.

20. See Jeff Mitscherling, "*Phaedo* 118: The Last Words," *Apeiron* 19 (1985): 161–65, especially 164 n.1. Mitscherling argues that the secondary literature has yet to reconcile the irony of Socrates' final words with widespread recognition of what he calls the "Pythagorean flavor" of the dialogue. Some evidence from the doxographical tradition suggests that the sacrifice of a cock, in light of the doctrine of the transmigration of the soul, would have constituted a significant heresy for the Pythagoreans. If that is so, we may hear in the last words a final departure from those views which provide a counterpoint to the Socratic *logos* throughout.

Conclusion

On Translating Plato

Eva T. H. Brann

I imagine that Professors Sallis and Russon asked me for this essay on translating in the first instance because of some work I had done in turning German into English. First was the translation of Jacob Klein's book *Greek Mathematical Thought and the Origin of Algebra,* which was originally published by the M.I.T. Press in 1968, and, having become a sort of classic not only in the history of mathematics but also in the study of modernity, was picked up for republication by the Dover Press in 1991. I had also done an annotated version of Heidegger's essay "What Is That— Philosophy?" for the use of our seniors at St. John's College. It remains unpublished because Professor Sallis was unable to obtain reasonable terms from the Heidegger estate. Furthermore, I translated an essay written by Nietzsche when he was twenty entitled "On the Relation of the Speech of Alcibiades to the Other Speeches of the Platonic *Symposium,*" which our student journal *Energeia* published to serve not only as a model but also as an encouragement for our students who choose similar topics for their annual essay. I also did a short vignette by Hermann Hesse, called "An Evening at Home with Doctor Faustus" for the same journal; in this story, Mephistopheles invents a future-phonograph and plays for Doctor Faustus the music of our century—pretty nearly the same that sometimes wafts across our campus. The Doctor concludes that the world has gone to the devil, as he himself soon will.

In 1995, I was asked by the series adviser, Keith Whitaker, to do a first translation for the nascent Focus Philosophical Library; Plato was suggested as a possibility. The Focus Press publishes fresh translations, intended to be very reasonably priced and to be used by American students. The project was appealing to me both as a teacher in a school dependent on good and accessible translations and as a dean in need of intellectual recreation.

I had what turned out to be an inspired idea, that of seeking collaborators among my colleagues, figuring that the pleasure of becoming so really intimate with a dialogue as only a translator is would be enhanced by the close partnership of common work and that three heads could better solve the problems and detect the mistakes that would surely dog a lone translator. Peter Kalkavage and Eric Salem agreed to becoming a trio. We chose the *Sophist* because we had all three begun to recognize the dialogue as the most ontologically future-fraught of them all, and we welcomed the challenge of preserving its originary freshness.

What follows is a report, under various headings, of the things we think we learned and of the advice we might venture to give our fellow translators.

Collaboration

One feature of the Sophist is that, wherever you are, there he is not; he is forever trying to escape into trackless, impassable thickets. ("Impasse," incidentally, is one of our translations, very nearly literal, of *aporia*, "waylessness.") But those who deal in knowing also display an opposite fault in the dialogues. That is the fault of position-taking. They occupy positions in defense of which they throw up outworks (*problema* is the Greek word for such a defensive outwork) and employ various apotropaic stratagems. Evidently Socrates and Plato consider that either to have a universal escape route in all arguments or to occupy entrenched positions is unworthy of the philosopher's mission.

And so it is of the translator's task. Those who work together on transferring Greek meanings into English words have to be focused on what the Greeks call the *pragma* and what Hegel calls *die Sache*. They have to eschew both escape and entrenchment, and they must be objective—intent on the object at hand.

Yet while ego is out, there is a strong human element in a collaboration put in the service of a dialogue. It demands and develops friendship. The three of us all bring slightly different strengths: One is perhaps more alert to Greek grammar, another to the philosophical resonances of terms. All three of us, having undergone the most effective part of our education at St. John's College, are relatively fearless in the face of ignorance and fresh in our deliberate amateurism.

The way we work is that each of us presents a translation of one Stephanus page in turn every third week, which all of us together then rake over as with a fine-tooth comb, the original translator explaining but not particularly defending a choice. Often we let somewhat daring or awkwardly accurate readings stand, waiting for that reading, close to the final one, in which we attend particularly to idiom and flow while erasing false inspirations.

I think we have become persuaded that in putting a rich Greek text into English there are so many facets to be attended to that three heads are indeed better than one. We do, in fact, have grand predecessors to look to: You will recall the legend about the seventy-two scribes, six from each of Israel's twelve tribes, who produced the Septuagint, the earliest extant Greek version of the Hebrew Bible, in the third century B.C. They worked in separate cells and came up with identical translations, presumably inspired by the text itself. We might say that the Platonic text acted on us in a more modest ex post facto mode in a similar way—one version would suddenly, after some trial and error, click for all three of us.

Our advice to collaborators: Cotranslating is a form of intimacy, best entered into by those who have the same object firmly in their sights while viewing each other with affectionate respect.

Readership

We thought it essential to keep in mind for whom we meant this translation of the *Sophist*. We meant it for the people that we imagine as standing around in this as in so many other dialogues as spectators and auditors. They are presumably tacitly engaged, like the silently present young Socrates, Theaetetus's friend, who shares our Socrates' name, as Theaetetus shares his looks. Another way to put it is that we thought of our students as they prepare for a seminar by silent reading. Some are quite innocent of the issues, some have, or think they have, insider knowledge, some read casually and disengagedly, and some are intensely serious.

Consideration of audience brought up the delicate question of colloquialism. One device that would keep the conversation casually speechlike was contraction, and we used it a lot, but not in places that we thought were meant to be stuffy, high flown, or solemn. We looked for idiomatic equivalents, but avoided slang (though we had a great time devising some raucous interim translations, such as "wise guy" or

EVA T. H. BRANN

"weisenheimer" for the Sophist himself). While we were well aware that every idiomatic translation will, in time, betray its date, nothing dates more quickly than slang, which even in its day fails, like all truckling under to fashion, to have real appeal for students.

In the course of thinking about drawing readers into the dialogue, we often had occasion to consider what is probably a real difference between the ear of a young contemporary Greek and that of one of our students. The well-brought-up Greek (and not only an Athenian), being nourished on Homer and the tragedians, whose language was no one's spoken Greek, could savor artificialities and archaisms that our students would find simply off-putting. A couple of generations ago, some English-speaking students would have absorbed enough of Shakespeare and Milton to be appreciative of such echoes, but we couldn't count on that. So we put everything into plain current English, sometimes allowing ourselves the merest whiff of high poetry or archaism.

Above all, we tried, in our students' behalf, to put ourselves into the interlocutors' sandals: What is being said, what is being heard, what is being felt, what is being thought? We called on our experience as teachers to guess at the dialogic backdrop of anxious agreement, triumphant dissent, and shamed realization that young Theaetetus contributes. But, above all, we clung to our main hypothesis as trusting readers of the dialogues: that each speech uttered has a discernible meaning contributing to the drift of the conversation and that the translation should preserve that motion.

Our advice here is: In translating, fill out imaginatively not only the conversation within the text, but draw in the external participant, the reading student.

Predecessors

Of course, we took all the help we could get from earlier translations. We used Robin for his intelligently chosen readings, Campbell for his linguistic annotations, Cornford for informational help.

The two translations we had always at our sides were the Loeb Fowler and Benardete. Fowler, though old-fashioned in diction and uninspired in terminology, was almost unfailing in making sense of puzzling passages and turns of phrase.

We consulted Benardete whenever we ran into trouble because of his meticulous attention to every word and because of his linguistic ingenuity. His version is a crib for the better sort of folk; it becomes intelligible if you read it as essentially in Greek and accidentally in English.

Since, however, we were determined to translate not only *from* Greek but also *into* English, we only rarely borrowed phrases from him, though we took many hints as to meaning.

Heidegger translates numerous passages of the *Sophist* in the lecture notes published in 1992 under the title *Platon: Sophistes*. These versions are a reminder that in certain respects the translator into German is to be envied. Some of the forms that have to do with Being go more directly into German than into English. *To einai,* for example, becomes in German "das Sein," while in English the infinitive cannot normally be nominalized; also *to on* readily goes into "Seiendes," and *ta onta* is rendered as "das Seiende," which functions, like the Greek neuter plural, as a collective noun. Probably most provocative and least helpful to translators who intend to be as naively true to the text and as agendaless as possible are Heidegger's terms for *ousia,* which he renders in an uninterpreted and an interpreted version, as it were. In the former, *ousia* is plain "Sein." In the interpreted version, *ousia* is rendered as if it were *parousia:* "das Anwesende" or "das Vorhandene," that is, "the present" or "the at-hand," in accord with his idea that Greek thought suffers from the aboriginal flaw of thinking of Being as if it were a thing.

We puzzled a good deal over the proper translation of *ousia,* being loath on principle, namely the principle that translation should be as far as feasible into an existent language, to invent noncurrent abstract substantives. But we finally decided on "beinghood." We chose it over "beingness" not only because it sounded better to us, but because it had more concreteness, as in neighborhood or manhood; we were mindful that *ousia* means something like "real estate" in ordinary Greek. And we decided to make up a word to begin with because we had an unresolved sense that *ousia,* which in the *Sophist* is usually contrasted with *genesis,* had a peculiar weight, and we wanted the reader to be in a position to attend to that interpretational problem.

I was relieved to see that even German could not deal with the crucial little adverb *ontos,* which for our private amusement only we translated as "beingly," but more soberly, for public consumption, as "in its very being." Thus the phrase that concludes the ultimate collection of differentiating terms reveals *ton ontos sophisten,* "the Sophist in his very being."

Let me return to the advantages of translating into German with two examples.

First, we had long discussions about the translation of *stasis,* the specific other of motion. We settled on "rest," knowing full well that "rest" is wrong insofar as it means lack of, or cessation from, motion. "Standstill" or "stationariness," as designating a condition coequal with

EVA T. H. BRANN

motion, seemed too strained, and we consigned them to the glossary. German is lucky in being able to form "Ständigkeit" quite naturally, as Heidegger does (579).

Second, in 244c4, when the Stranger begins his critique of Parmenides' *hypothesis* of the One, we were pretty much forced to use the English word "hypothesis" with all of its scientific baggage. Schleiermacher uses the Germanized version of "presupposition," that is "Voraussetzung," but Heidegger eschews both and brilliantly writes "Ansatz," with the observation that Parmenides's One is not a supposition to be consequently confirmed but a beginning, an *arche*, an "onset"—which is exactly what "Ansatz" may mean.

Nonetheless, with all the felicities to be gotten especially from the German propensity for easy prepositional compounding, I was continually grateful that it was our lot to be putting Plato into English, particularly American English. In our idiom, we could achieve a plainness and a playfulness that must be, when all is said and done, more pleasing to Socrates, as he listens in, than a lot of linguistic incense.

I think our general advice to fellow translators would be unabashedly to cannibalize and unabashedly to set aside previous translations.

Apparatus

Since we were left very free by our press to decide on supplementary materials, we thought long and hard about our obligation to the text and to the reader.

We come from a school—meaning both a way of thinking and an institution—that has the greatest misgivings about standing between a reader and the book. The extratextual stuff in a volume is, of course, meant to facilitate the approach to the translated text; but really, how can it? Take an introduction. If it says the same thing as the work, it will, assuming that the work is of the highest quality, say it worse. If it says something else, it will keep the reader from the work by that much time. We have a strong faith, based on our common teaching experience, that good books don't need approaching; they need facing, immediately and directly, at least at the first reading.

We compromised that faith, partly because, by the end of our labor, we were simply so full of thoughts that we couldn't contain ourselves, and partly because we know perfectly well that well-instructed students skip introductions and come back to them much later, if at all.

So we decided to keep it short, simple, and straightforward. We avoided historical backgrounding on the principle that Plato would have felt about our doing it much as a landscape painter might if we took his painting and provided it with a broad frame extending the scenery, so as to give the viewer an enlarged setting. We didn't want to deface the dialogue or distract or prejudice our student readers in this way; I should say that at St. John's, evidence of familiarity with introductions is a suspect virtue. But we did set the dialogue briefly in its sequence—*Theaetetus, Sophist, Statesman,* and the mysteriously missing *Philosopher.* We gave a succinct plot outline of the hunt for the Sophist, geared to a new and, we think, quite spiffy diagram of the infamous divisions that play so large a role in the *Sophist.* We pointed out some aspects of the dialogue that had become particularly pregnant for us, such as the generic nature of the Sophist here pursued (as opposed to the named individual sophists Socrates politely persecutes in dialogues like the *Gorgias* and the *Protagoras*). We had a little section on Father Parmenides and the strange and wonderful fact that he, the Stranger's own teacher, attracts the main attack of the dialogue. Then we told briefly what we understood about such deep matters as the relation of Image to Non-being and of Non-being to Otherness. And we left it at that.

Since we made use of the printer's full typographical menu, we had a little note on that. We were very sparing with footnotes, using them mostly to supply what we thought an ancient contemporary reader might have known, or where we thought we detected a joke or an allusion obscure to a current reader.

Our energy went into the glossary, which we put in back, to be used or not. We arranged the Greek terms and our reasoned translations in meaning-clusters. (You will find something similar in the Hope translation of Aristotle's *Physics* and *Metaphysics,* except that we transliterated all our Greek in the hope that students might learn to accent and pronounce words like *phrónesis* and *poíesis* and *mímesis* correctly.) We avoided the alphabetic order so as to prevent the impression that we—or the partners of a dialogue—are ever looking for dictionarylike definitions. We also hoped to provide students with what we thought of as the prototerminology of a coming ontology—or perhaps better a me-ontology, an account of Non-being; the *Sophist* is a spawning ground of metaphysical terms-to-be.

Our advice to translators is to go easy on the paraphernalia of translation.

Editing

The translator's final reading, of course, tries for absolute correctness. But we have to warn the trustful that having a perfect disk is no protection.

Something will get screwed up, there will be unexpected glitches, and, as we learned to our sorrow, it will be in the most carefully construed first sentence.

No matter how good and accommodating the editor—and we have good reason to thank Ron Pullins, the editor-publisher of Focus Press—there will be howlers.

Our advice: Trust no one but yourselves and demand to see final proofs.

Replies

Theaetetus plays to the Stranger by regularly uttering a budget of stock replies signifying slight hesitation, passive assent, positive agreement, or requests for clarification.

After a while, we began to suspect that the rotating litany of responses might not be entirely mechanical. This apprehension made it incumbent upon us to keep a list of our considered renditions of *nai, pos, pos d'ou, pos gar ou, ti de, houtos, anangke, pan, panu ge, pantapasi men oun,* and a dozen others, so that in later readings we could make all the replies consistent. In that way, we would give readers of the translation a chance to discover patterns we only suspected. *Pantapasi men oun,* for example, for which we borrowed Benardete's phrase "that's altogether so," occurs in the dialogue as a strong assent to a summary claim and concludes the dialogue as Theaetetus's last response to the final collection of divisions that catch the true and ultimate Sophist as the expert of the non-genuine. Theaetetus is clearly assenting not only to the definitive, but also to the global character of this final determination of a human type and profession.

Particles

We were similarly anxious to render particles fairly consistently. The dialogic life is in them—*they* indicate inflections of the voice, gestures of the body, and even motions of the soul.

The dictionary, or even Denniston's *Greek Particles,* though they must be consulted to give the limits of usage, cannot do it all. The translators must savor the speech in its context and judge whether it is marked as an inference or a new departure, whether eagerness is being displayed, smiles are suppressed, eyebrows raised, or hands thrown up. We were mindful of typographic and punctuational devices not available to a Greek composer of living speech, and we used italics, dashes, colons, semicolons, and exclamation points liberally to render the force of particles or of emphases indicated by sentential order. I might mention here that capitalization helped us a great deal in translating a dialogue full of terms for forms and kinds designated in Greek by the definite article and a verbal or adjectival substantive such as *to on* (Being), *to me on* (Non-being), *tauton* (the Same), and *thateron* (the Other).

Our advice to translators is to be—within the limits of natural English—consistent, careful, and ingenious in rendering apparently little and apparently automatic elements of the dialogues; they may be more revealing than one realizes at the time.

Techno-Humor

At the end of Bacon's *New Organon,* there is to be found a prescient catalogue of one hundred and thirty "histories" of special investigations that are one day to constitute the sphere of human expertise. It is a strange and wonderful fact that the first such comprehensive ordering of extant technical know-how (that I know of) is found in the *Sophist*—and that it is a send-up. The Stranger, who is not an overtly funny person, engages in what might be called techno-humor at the expense of experts.

As readers of the dialogue, of course, we thought a good deal about the reason why a comprehensive classification of human know-how or technique—we translated *technē* as "expertise," but sometimes as "art," as in "arts and crafts"—should be the approach of choice to the delineation of the Sophist. We were, of course, alert to the startling conjunction of apparently disjunct themes that governs a number of the great dialogues, as the *Phaedrus,* for instance, seems to yoke the unlikely pair of love and rhetoric.

Moreover, it does not take much reflection to see that the Sophist, whose nature is presented here as that of a faker and a know-it-all, should be tracked into the branches of human activity and that, in that great decision-tree, he should reappear in seven places, sometimes among the lowly but genuine crafts and sometimes among the high-sounding but dubious ones. It also made sense that the hunt for this elusive creature should be the occasion for presenting to the world the new dialectic art of division and collection and all its problems—chief among them what might be called the problem of heuristic direction: At what moment in this dialectic enterprise, at the beginning, end, or in between, does new insight arise?

But for us as translators, it was not so much our business to have theories about the inevitable implication of expertise and shamming or about the problems of classification as to render the divisions faithfully into English. And there we were in a pretty good position. As I have said, all three of us come from a college that has distanced itself from specialization, and we were alive to the tragicomedy of defining human beings as the professors of a profession. (Our English version of *sophistes* was, incidentally, "professor of wisdom.") Not that all of us aren't ourselves certified members of the world of expertise. I myself, for instance, began my working life in a profession that the Stranger might have ranged, looking to the three great branches of human expertise called "getting," "separating," and "making," under getting, specifying it as a hunt beneath the soil for fragmented old artifacts carried on by means of pickaxes. We call it archaeology. Recall that the Sophist is first found in the right-hand branch of animal hunting on land, specified as the sham-teaching hunt of wealthy youths.

We tried to preserve the neologic high jinks of some of the divisions. Thus the Sophist is found a second, third, and fourth time in the getting part of expertise as a psycho-trading virtue-seller, and in the manipulating part both as a seller of self-made learnables and as a peddler of other-made learnables: "psycho-trading" renders *psychemporike* and "learnable-selling" *mathematopolikon.*

We had not long worked on our new current project for the Focus Philosophical Library, a translation of the *Phaedo,* before we became aware of the varieties of Platonic humor. In fact, one of us, Peter Kalkavage, began retrospectively to refer to the *Sophist* as a one-joke dialogue, dominated by the techno-humor of the otherwise ponderous Stranger that I've just described. The *Phaedo,* because in it Socrates not only speaks but even makes speeches, is, we discovered, infused with a very different, far more subtle humor, which we are doing our best to preserve. It is the sort of hilarity or jocundity in the original Latin sense, the subdued joyousness and even merriment of the ultimate moment, that belongs to a man going blithely to his death without having lost his firm, even hard grip on the earthly condition. We have come to think of it as the tone of the lightness of Being. It keeps his companions in an ambivalent state of sorrowful exhilaration, suspended between tears and laughter.

The secondary partners, too, of course, are very different in the two dialogues. Theaetetus is, at least vis-à-vis the Stranger, a somewhat stuffy boy, while that comradely pair, Simmias and Cebes, are each in their way pretty lively.

Does bringing out the humor of the dialogues in translations need a justification? I should not imagine so, but I might mention once more that all three of us are receiving our real education in a place to which a way of reading Plato was introduced by Jacob Klein, who in his interpretations was especially alert to the mimetic character of the dialogues. As imitations of Socrates and the conversations he conducted or attended, they were bound to be playful, as Socrates was playful, with a playfulness that is the kindly counterpart of his notorious dissembling, his irony. But not all humor is comedic in Aristotle's understanding of comedy as the imitation of what is laughable, that is, as low or ugly but relatively harmless. The techno-humor of the *Sophist* comes far closer to comedy than does that of the other dialogues, with the proviso that the laughableness of the sophistic craft is not so harmless.

In any case, our advice to colleagues who plan to translate Platonic dialogues is to be prepared not only to laugh themselves but also to be the cause of laughter in others.

Faithfulness

It was clear to us from the beginning that looseness, paraphrase, and interpretative adumbration were intolerable in the translation of any Platonic writing, but especially in a dialogue like the *Sophist,* which is so close to the brink of technical metaphysics and yet so carefully refrains from letting philosophy become a *technē,* an expertise. It does so by going at what Aristotle will later codify as "problems" of Being in an oblique and human way. It is oblique in concentrating, as was said, less on ontology than on me-ontology, the account of Non-being as the ground of imitation or pretense, and it is human in pursuing the Sophist as a human type as much as it does sophistry as a profession. In this morning-twilight of philosophy, meticulous accuracy is especially necessary. So we spent, as I have said, much time on words, determining for ourselves whether they were terms of a trade or not—yet. *Aporia* and *methodos* are examples. Both come to be fixed as terms of philosophy: "perplexity" and "method." But we aimed to preserve, at least in some places, the unfixed original meaning: "impasse," that is, lack of passage, and "way," both of which preserve the playful spatial analogy that is so prominent in the Stranger's reflections on the motion of thought.

We aimed at faithfulness, however, not only in words and terms but also in sentences. The obvious problem is always subliteralness—the risk of producing a contortedly accurate pony. We thought that it was a part of faithfulness to render the various levels of elegance, clarity, and emphasis of the speeches—and the Stranger surely has his obscure and clunky moments, at least as we heard them.

The faith of translators who mean to be faithful must be that, meaning-element for meaning-element, it is possible to turn Greek into English and that this must imply that *usually*—it never pays to be too rigid—one Greek word goes into one English word or typographical symbol, one phrase into one phrase, one clause into one clause, and one sentence into one sentence—in other words, that it is possible to get equivalence without sublinearity. It also implies that one can find an English word order that renders the emphasis of the Greek sentence and English connectives that maintain the Greek flow. One of our last readings was addressed, as I have mentioned, to the attempted eradication of all signs of translaterese. Our trust was that if we stuck faithfully to the Greek, barring simple mistakes and omissions, we would get English that said exactly what the Greek said and with something like the original naturalness and deviations from naturalness. In other words, we had the faith that we might overcome the charge expressed in the Italian pairing *traduttore/traditore:* We hoped that a translator need not be a traitor to the text.

Our best advice to others is not to give in to current hermeneutic theories concerning the essential untranslatability of one language into another, but to suppose, as a starting hypothesis, that even if not *all* human speech can say the same thing, then at least we can think and say practically the same thing as our ancient intellectual progenitors— from which it is evident that the translator's hypothesis is no negligible commentary on contemporary philosophy.

Requirements

The last item on my list of observations concerns the crucial question "What do translators need to know and be good at?"

The three of us did not think that we were required to have a full-fledged interpretation to have a go at a translation. What we needed, instead, was a lively sense of intimations, a sense born of a belief in the unfailing significance of the text. In other words, we came to Plato's philosophic plays with the trust that every word (or nearly every word) was deliberately placed, but that some terms and turns were special signposts to implied meanings. We tried to be alert to oddities of language and emphasis as well as to *hapax legomena* (linguistic singularities which we treated as occasions for literalness, even if it proved awkward). On another level, we listened for high points and crucial junctures, which Plato's most responsible speakers, and, of course, Socrates himself, often signal by a throwaway reference to that one more "little" addition.

None of us are, this is the moment to say, great believers in esoteric readings. We are much too possessed by a sense of the pedagogic generosity of the dialogues, a sense that here a discreetly fierce energy is devoted to carrying interlocutors, bystanders, and readers beyond themselves into realms reachable only by circuitous and indirect means. To put it another way: In the dialogues, we are told as much, but no more, than we need to make us want to think onward. That is why the dialogues are fairly easy to read the first time and get harder to understand as, with each reading, more signals are picked up.

There certainly exist occasionally esoteric writers like Newton who, "to avoid being baited by little smatterers in mathematics . . . designedly made his *Principia* abstruse" (Portsmouth Collection), and authors who touch guardedly on theological or political issues in intolerant times (though they never do seem to escape persecution). Socrates' dissembling and Plato's subtlety, however, are not of this self-protective sort but are pedagogical devices for drawing the learner in—at least, that is our experience. The dialogues work on the principle that "a cat may look at a king" or, rather, "a boy may look at Being." And in any case, they display hardly any attempt to mask the fact that not everything that goes on in these conversations will be of comfort to respectable parents.

So the first translator's requirement is a belief in the many-layered accessibility of the text and an alertness to those signs and signals which the English version should preserve for readers to puzzle over.

A second requirement we put on ourselves was to attempt consistency but to shun method. An intelligent consistency is, we thought, the guardian spirit of open minds. So as far as possible we tried, as I said, to choose the right word and to stick with it even in fairly routine phrases. Thus *phainetai* is almost always "it appears," and *dokei* "it seems." At the same time, we tried to remain open to significant nuances and strange turns within each dialogue, though our avoidance of methodical translating bound to a particular interpretation of Platonic philosophy applied mainly across the dialogues: In taking up the *Phaedo*, we saw once again the truth of the teaching that each dialogue is a fresh world of discourse and is to be faced without preconceptions regarding "Platonic thought." That observation is particularly true as between dialogues in which Socrates guides the conversation and those in which he only listens in or is, finally, even absent.

As far as preparation is concerned, since none of us can really read Greek as a living language, we were glad to see that we could do pretty well on a lot of Greek reading experience to give us a feel for the intention and on enough grammatical expertise to tell us when we needed to do careful parsing. We found that besides Liddell-Scott we needed to have at hand Roget's *Thesaurus* to help us to the word we were looking for.

But we think that, all in all, the main requirement for translators of Plato, and our advice to them, is to believe in the semantic plenitude of the Platonic texts, and to produce an English version that, like the Greek, says more than the translators know.

Notes on Contributors

Claudia Baracchi is an assistant professor of philosophy at the New School for Social Research in New York City. Her most recent book deals with the intertwined questions of *genesis* and war in the Platonic texts.

Eva T. H. Brann is a tutor and a former dean at St. John's College, Anapolis, Maryland. She is the author of "The Music of the *Republic*," *The World of the Imagination,* and *What, Then, Is Time?* She is also a cotranslator of Plato's *Sophist.*

Walter Brogan is a professor of philosophy at Villanova University. He is the cotranslator of Martin Heidegger's book *Aristotle's Metaphysics Theta, 1–3: On the Essence and Actuality of Force* and the coeditor of *American Continental Philosophy: A Reader.* He has written many articles on the interface between ancient Greek and contemporary continental philosophy.

James Crooks is an associate professor and the chair of the Department of Philosophy at Bishop's University in Lennoxville, Quebec. His interests are ancient philosophy and contemporary continental philosophy, and his recent publications include "Dialectic as Counterpoint: On Philosophical Self-Measure in Plato and Hegel," in *Hegel and the Tradition: Essays in Honour of H. S. Harris,* and "Socrates' Last Words: Another Look at an Ancient Riddle," in *Classical Quarterly.* His current project is a book on ethics.

Günter Figal is a professor of philosophy at the University of Tübingen. He is the author of several books, including *Martin Heidegger: Phänomenologie der Freiheit; Das Untier und die Lieve: Sieben platonische Essays; Sokrates; Der Sinn des Verstehens; For a Philosophy of Freedom and Strife: Politics, Aesthetics, Metaphysics;* and *Nietzsche.*

Bernard Freydberg, a professor of philosophy at Slippery Rock University, is the author of *The Play of the Platonic Dialogues* and *Imagination and Depth in Kant's Critique of Pure Reason.* His most recent book is *Provocative Form in Plato, Kant, Nietzsche (and Others).* His books and other published works direct themselves toward untapped imaginative resources in the history of philosophy.

Francisco J. Gonzalez is an associate professor of philosophy at Skidmore College. He is the editor of *The Third Way: New Directions in Platonic Studies* and the author of *Dialectic and Dialogue: Plato's Practice of Philosophical Inquiry*. He has published articles on Plato, Aristotle, and Heidegger in journals such as *Phronesis, Ancient Philosophy, Apeiron,* and *Research in Phenomenology* and has contributed to collections devoted to Plato, most recently *Who Speaks for Plato? Studies in Platonic Anonymity*.

Graeme Nicholson is a professor of philosophy at Trinity College, University of Toronto. He is the author of *Plato's Phaedrus: The Philosophy of Love,* which expands upon many of the points made in his contribution to this volume. His other published works include *Seeing and Reading* and *Illustrations of Being,* and his articles have appeared in numerous journals and collections. In addition to having edited several other books, he serves as a coeditor of the Humanities Press series Contemporary Studies in Philosophy and the Human Sciences. He is a past coordinator of the North American Heidegger Conference and has served on the executive board of the Society for Phenomenology and Existential Philosophy.

John Russon is an associate professor of philosophy at Pennsylvania State University, specializing in ancient philosophy and post-Kantian continental philosophy. His published works include various articles on Plato, Aristotle, and continental philosophy and the book *The Self and Its Body in Hegel's Phenomenology of Spirit*. He is the coeditor (with Michael Bauer) of *Hegel and the Tradition: Essays in Honour of H. S. Harris*.

John Sallis is the Liberal Arts Professor of Philosophy at Pennsylvania State University. He is the author of numerous books, including *Chorology: On Beginning in Plato's "Timaeus"; Shades—of Painting at the Limit; Being and Logos: Reading the Platonic Dialogues* (third edition); *Double Truth;* and *Stone*.

Abraham Schoener is a tutor on leave from St. John's College in Anapolis, Maryland. He is currently studying viticulture in Napa Valley.